C000283254

ARMSTRONG

The Life and Mind of an Armaments Maker

Kenneth Warren

First published in Great Britain by Author House in 2010

Reprinted by Northern Heritage Services Limited 2011, 2013, 2014, 2018 and 2022.

ISBN: 9780955540691

Cover design, Ian Scott Design

Published by:
Northern Heritage
Unit 7 New Kennels, Blagdon Estate, Seaton Burn
Tyne & Wear NE13 6DB
Tel: 01670 789940

See our full online catalogue at: www.northern-heritage.co.uk

Printed by Martins the Printers,
Berwick upon Tweed, UK.

To the people of the North East.

CONTENTS

LIST OF ILLUSTRATIONS

PREFACE

William George Armstrong was a modest man, simple in many habits of life, rather reserved, but by no means aloof. Although he had no children, he was direct and unaffected in his relationships with the young. Over a long and active life, he became an extremely wealthy man, lived in a grand house and enjoyed the space and beauty of a great estate, but he also allowed the public some access to his grounds. Generous, if not particularly imaginative in his attitudes to the poor, he supplied them with coals in winter, built almshouses and few local charities, public or private, appealed to him in vain. His religious faith was not at all publicly displayed, but he seems to have had one. Over many years, he served his parish as churchwarden, and he endowed a site for a new Congregational church. After a close association, which had lasted 40 years, a senior business colleague described him as "the most charming of companions…an excellent host, and in congenial society a striking conversationalist."(1) In short, in many ways Armstrong was one of the better sort of self-made men of the nineteenth century. Like many others who succeeded, he was driving in business and careful to accumulate but he was neither grasping nor too narrow in his conception of the responsibilities that came with wealth. Even so, a serious question remains. It stems from the fact that a large part of his large fortune depended on designing, manufacturing and selling the means of mass destruction and death. How could a man possessing so many commendable qualities devote his considerable talents to such ends? Can a careful study of his career throw light on this anomaly?

There may be three explanations for the mismatch between Armstrong`s apparent character and lifestyle on the one hand and their business foundations on the other. They are not mutually exclusive. He may have been unaware of the implications of his work, believed that the benefits outweighed the costs, or was capable of holding the nature of his everyday work and his ethical standards in separate mental compartments. Each of these possibilities presents a problem. The first seems to indicate a remarkable lack of imagination. The second suggests callous calculation. The third is an extreme case of something all too common in the Victorian age. Inevitably present day assessments of the morality of the armaments business have been coloured by the experiences of the huge and uniquely bloody conflicts of the 20th century, but there can be no doubt that Armstrong was aware of the powers of destruction of the weapons his firm made. Indeed, he devoted his best efforts over many years to increasing those powers. Most of the weapons made by his firm were not used in his lifetime in fighting between "civilised" nations so that the evidence about their destructiveness largely came from far away theatres of war. Perhaps this provided some excuse for a person who in any case seems to have been neither particularly imaginative nor sensitive. He was more concerned with the business of solving technical problems than in sitting quietly to reflect about what the weapons he designed and produced could and would do to human flesh and bones, to families and homes, public buildings and fields. Although in many ways a good man, he had one major defect, a preoccupation with and economic dependence on what later generations came to recognise as tools of the devil.

The wealth accumulated by this quiet, sane man, busily perfecting the means of mass killing, was spent by him or by his successors in quiet environments, in building fine houses and shaping beautiful estates. But his labours also brought together a large workforce to produce what he and others devised. Hundreds, and eventually many thousands, of men toiled amidst apparently endless noise, heat and dirt in huge, black factories, and with their dependents lived out their lives nearby in street after street of closely packed, drab houses. Here again, as so commonly in Victorian Britain, manufacturing abilities were out of step with human values.

In these various respects, the long career of William George Armstrong, lauded by so many of his contemporaries, may now be seen as not only marred but in essence a tragedy. It was an extreme case of the failings of what in his time was labelled as the "progress" of civilisation but some of whose bountiful harvest the century succeeding his own would reap on the killing fields of the Western Front, or later in Stalingrad, Hiroshima and countless other places, and down to our own times. Inevitably, in his long career, issues such as these were obscured by events, the challenges and complexities of everyday life, and the inscrutability of the future.

Kenneth Warren
Ledbury, Herefordshire
Spring 2010

Further information or additional insights about Armstrong and his company would be welcome: warren31_99@yahoo.com.

ANCESTRY, CHILDHOOD AND YOUTH

There is little hard knowledge of either Armstrong`s childhood or his early adult years. Where facts are lacking, snippets of information, if they fit the character of the full-grown man, are remembered, repeated and passed from one account to another. Such elements of "myth" are represented by a number of events or characteristics from his early years. More is known of the context of his home area and family, than of details.

The small Cumbrian village of Wreay, which stands above the little Petteril stream in low hills a few miles south of Carlisle, is now by-passed by a broad sweep of the M.6 motorway. In 1778 a son born to the wife of a local shoemaker, was baptised William Armstrong. Sometime in his `teens William moved to Newcastle upon Tyne, where he found work as a clerk to a firm of corn merchants in Cowgate, a street in the old central district between the Quayside and the present City Road. At that time, Tyneside was in a ferment of economic development. For centuries, it had been renowned for its coal trade, but it was now industrialising. Only a few years before a French visitor was impressed by: "This beautiful river ... rendered highly interesting by the number and variety of manufactures carried on upon its banks."(1) By the 1801 census, a few years after young Armstrong arrived, over 28,000 people lived within the boundaries of the city. It had already spilled out beyond these limits and, in addition, manufacturing and the populations which depended on it, were growing at numerous smaller centres on both banks of the Tyne down to the North Sea. Activating the wholesale process of economic growth were a large number of enterprising men, seizing opportunities to invest in new businesses, advancing the interests of their own families, interrelating and often intermarrying with other entrepreneurs. The rest, the great mass of the inhabitants, were swept up either into jobs created by these leaders or employment in the wider society to which they gave rise. Young Armstrong had arrived at an opportune time.

The retirement of the proprietor eventually left William in control of the corn business for which he had worked, and its name was changed to Armstrong and Company. The new capitalist married well, meeting and winning Ann, daughter of William Potter of Walbottle Hall, whose family was important in the coal trade and in various business enterprises. William and Ann settled in Pleasant Row, Shield Field, a terrace of newly built houses with gardens running down to the eastern edge of Pandon Dene, a winding, partly wooded hollow beyond the town walls, one of the most pleasant "country" walks near the city. Later the dene would be transformed after becoming the route of the Newcastle branch line of the Blyth and Tyne Railway. In 6 Pleasant Row Ann and William reared a family of two children. A daughter, also named Ann, was born in 1802; eight years later, on 26 November 1810, Ann Armstrong gave birth to a son. He was baptised William George. The Armstrong household, small by the standards of the time, was one whose values were shaped by a degree of wealth and comfort, ambition, and a range of leisure interests. William played a part in founding the Newcastle Chamber of Commerce, gained something of a reputation as a keen and accomplished amateur mathematician, and was an early member of the fledgling Newcastle Literary and Philosophical Society. Later in life, he was prominent in local politics. The reforms in local government associated with the Municipal Corporations Act 1835 were made when he was in his mid fifties. He became a councillor, later an alderman, and in 1850 was chosen as mayor of the City of Newcastle upon Tyne. All in all, his life story provided a good example of a rounded concern for business, culture and public service. When he died in 1857, his only son was in his mid forties and already well advanced in each of these fields.

As a young child, William George spent a good deal of time alone. One obvious reason was that he was the only boy in the family and his sister was eight years older. Another consideration was his "delicate" state of health. This meant he was confined to the house for months at a time in order to escape exposure to cold weather. In such circumstances, he learned to amuse himself. Report suggested he showed an early interest in the workings of mechanical things, though it may well be that, in the improving tone of the Victorian age, those who were concerned with the mature man exaggerated the achievements of the child. Indeed, when a leading colleague looked back on a long acquaintance with him, he acknowledged that some of the stories about young William might be apocryphal for "...there is not much evidence that he showed these characteristics in a more marked degree than many boys before or since." On the other hand, it is reported that when five, he was taken by his nurse to see a windmill. As she was distracted, he wandered off to investigate the machinery, and was "...saved from being mangled only a few minutes before the mill was set in motion." A year later, he was making models of machines that he worked with weights hanging over the staircase. In addition to imaginative play, he had various opportunities to see men working with machinery, for among the businesses owned by grandfather Potter was a joiner`s shop. (2)

The boy`s occasional illnesses-it has been surmised they were probably respiratory-had another consequence of great significance for his later life. He was sent for holidays into the countryside, and especially to the little Northumberland town of Rothbury. At that time, it was little more than a village of about 1,000 inhabitants, was neither paved nor lighted and obtained its water from several springs. It possessed few amenities, though a small subscription library was opened in 1815. The physical setting more than made up for any deficiencies. As contemporary accounts recognised, its situation was "... very beautiful, being in a sequestered and romantic glen ... screened by lofty hills from the north and east winds ... [and] considered favourable for invalids". They mentioned that "... many persons in a delicate state of health resort there for the benefit of the air, and to drink goat`s milk, many of these animals being pastured on the hills in the neighbourhood ... anglers in passing up and down the dale, sometimes take up their quarters for a day or two at the Three Moons, the principal inn in the place."(3) Presumably the Three Moons was of no especial interest to young William George, but he delighted in the town and in the River Coquet. Almost eighty years later, he could recall these early visits: "... his genial smile and animated expression showing how congenial a subject it was."(4) "My connection with Rothbury dates beyond my very earliest recollection. The first thing I can remember is living in one of those old cottages which used to stand on the site of the new Congregational Chapel." On these holiday visits, he lodged there with the widow of Dr Storey. The great event of the week seems to have been the gathering of an excited crowd to await the arrival of a courier bringing letters and newspapers from Newcastle. He came by way of Longframlington, for the road from Rothbury to Brinkburn and Weldon Bridge had not then been made. Armstrong even remembered that Wilson, the courier, lived in a thatched cottage on the site occupied in the 1890s by the shop of Dixons Brothers. On these childhood holidays, he learned to fish and, as it seemed to him in retrospect, he had done so from morning to night; as he laughingly added; "They used to call me the Kingfisher". Following the Coquet downstream, he had even been guilty of what he now acknowledged had been a little "poaching" on the Brinkburn estate, many a time creeping under the bushes near the house in order to fill his creel. (5)

Of William`s formal education there is even less detail. He attended schools in Newcastle and at Wickham, west of Gateshead, before being sent in 1826 to finish his general education at the Grammar School in Bishop Auckland. The latter was an area abounding in coal and limestone, but to a boy already keenly interested in engineering one of its chief attractions must have been the Stockton and Darlington Railway, which lay only a few miles away and had only been open to traffic since the previous September. The town itself was pleasantly situated and contained the country seat of the Prince Bishop of Durham. The new boy-or rather youth, for when he arrived he was only a few months short of his 16th birthday-boarded with the master, the Rev. R. Thompson, in his home on the market place. It seems that William was not an enthusiastic student, at least if one can trust a comment he made many years later to a much younger friend, a man who had told him how impatiently he was waiting for his marriage: "I wish I could suggest for your benefit an efficient method of quickening time, but I have generally found recipes for this purpose result in a contrary effect. At school before the holy days I used to try a stick notched to correspond with the number of remaining days-one notch was eliminated every morning until the happy day of release arrived."(6)

In the year William joined the Grammar School his 24-year-old sister Ann married a lawyer, William Henry Watson. Two years later, at about the same time as William left school, she gave birth to a son. Very soon afterwards she died. Whatever his attainments in formal education, William`s short stay in Bishop Auckland had by no means been wasted. By this time, he had much more definitely shown a keen interest in engineering, spending some of his spare time in a local engineering works, owned by William Ramshaw. The visits there proved productive in another respect, for young Armstrong fell in love with the engineer`s daughter, Margaret. She was six years older than he was, and therefore already a young woman. At this time the eighteen year-old Armstrong was unable either to begin work as an engineer or to go further in their relationship. For almost 20 years, he would work in a very different profession, but he never lost his keenness for engineering, and he retained his affection for Margaret.

LAW, EXPERIMENTS AND SCIENTIFIC RECOGNITION 1830 TO 1846

When William Armstrong left his Bishop Auckland school, he and his father had to consider questions of employment and career. His keen interest and aptitude in mechanical things was one consideration. Another was the position his family occupied in Newcastle society: his father had made his way from humble beginnings, but there seemed no reason why the only son should necessarily have to start at the bottom. A way of advance was found through the help of a family friend. Son of a South Shields timber merchant, Armorer Donkin had been articled, and then trained in London before returning to Tyneside, where he began to practice as a solicitor in 1806. A man of character as well as a vigorous and energetic worker, Donkin had gradually built up a fine legal business, made a considerable amount of money, and by the late 1820s occupied a prominent place in municipal and public affairs, and in the cultural life of Newcastle upon Tyne. At his Jesmond home, he provided a weekly open house luncheon for friends, including William Armstrong senior. Donkin was a bachelor, who from their early years had held William`s children in great affection. The solution for the son`s need for useful employment became clearer; he would become a lawyer, and go through the same sequence of apprenticeship, training and daily application which Donkin followed a generation earlier.

Accordingly, in or shortly before 1830, young William Armstrong was articled to Armorer Donkin. Later he was sent to complete his legal education at Lincolns Inn, where William Harry Watson, Ann`s widower husband, a Special Pleader, was a useful contact. One of his fellow law students was Richard Lambert, three years his senior.

Afterwards a wine merchant as well as a lawyer, Lambert remained a friend to the end of his life. Otherwise there seems to be no record of Armstrong`s life in London, though this may have amounted to three or four years. Certainly, in the very extensive correspondence of his later life he never referred to it. What public lectures did he attend-perhaps at the Royal Institution? Was he an enthusiast for the theatre or concerts or art, or was his leisure time used in less commendable ways? There is no known answer to any of these questions, but clearly, his years in the capital helped to mature him. A portrait survives from this period. It was painted in 1831 by Donkin`s friend, James Ramsay, and depicts an assured, handsome young man, by now in his early 20s. In 1833, he returned to the Newcastle office of Donkin and his partner Stable, and after two years was admitted to the partnership, the firm being renamed Donkin, Stable and Armstrong. The practice of law would be his daily occupation for almost 12 more years. Though not his ideal profession, it provided him with considerable advantages.

Near the end of his life, Armstrong recalled his early working years: "The law was not, of course, of my own choosing; my vocation was chosen for me and for a good many years I stuck to the law while all my leisure was given to mechanics. But the circumstances were peculiar ... When I entered his [Donkin`s] office, I was practically adopted by him; I was to be his heir. Such an opening in life was, of course, most attractive; here it seemed was a career readymade for me. As it turned out, of course, it meant the waste of some ten or eleven of the best years of my life-and yet not entire waste, perhaps, for my legal training and knowledge have been of help to me in many ways in business. And all the time, although I had no idea of abandoning the law and regularly attended to my professional duties, I was an amateur scientist, constantly experimenting and studying in my leisure time."(1)Two of his later colleagues were even more positive about the benefits of the long years of his partnership with Donkin and Stable. One pointed out that work as a solicitor disciplined him to handle complicated questions with great thoroughness. He was always a clear thinker and had a gift for lucid expression, qualities which may have initially fitted him for law, but were further developed in its practice, and would later be invaluable. His other colleague stressed that his work in law in central Newcastle established connections with many individuals who

William George Armstrong in 1831 by William Ramsay.
(Courtesy BAE Systems)

would later provide him with valuable support. Meanwhile Donkin was an understanding and tolerant senior colleague, allowing the junior partner "every possible liberty...to follow his own scientific researches."(2) His financial share in the partnership enabled him to put aside some money; more immediately it made it possible for him to marry Margaret Ramshaw. At the time of their wedding on Friday 1 May 1835, he was in the middle of his 25th year; she was already 31.

Of William`s wider life on Tyneside at this time, beyond the daily round of the law office and leisure hours of amateur science, there seems to be no accessible record. In the nation and the wider world, this was a time of great events. Britain`s economy and society were both changing with great rapidity. These were the years of the stormy steps towards and the aftermath of the great Reform Act, of the abolition of slavery, the passing of the Municipal Corporations Act, and the rise of Chartism. These momentous social changes took shape against a backdrop of industrial expansion, agricultural progress and the accelerating spread of the railways. In 1830, another revolution in France ended the Bourbon restoration, and a revolt brought about the creation of an independent kingdom of Belgium. New republics were being established in Latin America. There were important cultural changes too. The Catholic Emancipation Bill was passed in 1829, and in July 1833 John Keble preached the university sermon that launched the Oxford Movement. Tennyson`s first two volumes of poems were published in 1830 and 1833 and in 1837 Pickwick Papers appeared. Armstrong was an intelligent young man who read the newspapers, and moved in intellectually lively circles, but we know nothing of his attitude to any of these things.

In marked contrast to ignorance about such matters, the scientific work in which he spent so many leisure hours-after, as well as before he married Margaret Ramshaw-is well documented. At this early stage, his researches led to no practical outcomes. There was none of that progression essential in the building of major businesses-science, leading on to technological invention, industrial innovation and routine production. For him successful pursuit of that vital sequence of steps would have to wait another decade. Meantime his experiments were largely confined to two fields of research, hydraulic and electrical, and to the relationship between them. A boyhood inclination towards the first of these had been summed up by a remark attributed to one of his aunts: "William had water on the brain." More purposeful work is said to have stemmed from an experience he had in 1835, the year of his partnership and marriage. When fishing in Dentdale, in the far north west of Yorkshire, his attention was attracted to an iron water wheel used to drive machinery at a marble quarry not far from the far bank of the river. In old age, he recalled the occasion in words that described his initial attitude in uncharacteristic terms. The follow up was fully in tune with his usual logical processes: "I was lounging idly about ... when it occurred to me what a small part of the power of the water was used in driving the wheel and then I thought how great would be the force of even a small quantity of water if its energy was only concentrated in one column." He calculated that only about a twentieth of the potential energy of the falling water was converted into usable power. Afterwards, in line with his maxim that "perseverance usually pays", he spent many leisure hours over a period of three years developing a water power engine. Called a "rotatory hydraulic machine", it was described by him in an article in the Mechanics Magazine at the end of 1838. (3)

In the year of this "hydraulic machine", he made fruitful contact with an established Tyneside engineering works, one whose products were of a specialised and rather refined kind. The High Bridge Works of Henry Watson was noted for turret clocks, theodolites, telescopes etc. but its owner later helped Armstrong with much more substantial pieces of work. For six years or so, he made almost daily visits to this works, where he met, consulted and became a friend of Watson, and of his leading assistant John Hutchinson and his two sons. As little notice was taken of his hydraulic machine, Armstrong asked Watson to make a working model of it, and late in 1839, this was tried out. Driven by the pressure in the Newcastle water pipes it produced five horsepower. Again, there was no wide interest, and he decided to try another approach. He designed and made a working model of a crane, in which the "rotatory" system of the hydraulic engine was replaced by the lifting stroke of a piston. It too was tested using the pressure in the town water pipes. As there was still no progress towards any adoption of his system, he gave up this line of work for the next five years or so and turned in another direction. (4)

In the early 1840s, Armstrong achieved greater success than he had enjoyed before by his researches into electricity, specifically static electricity. This work resulted in a misleading early use of the term "hydro-electricity". It was as much a result of an unexpected incident as his earlier research into falling water. In autumn 1840, a worker in a coalmine at Cramlington, Northumberland, experienced a "... curious prickling sensation" when he touched a safety valve which lay in a jet of steam from a leaking boiler. Armstrong heard of this puzzling event and decided to examine the phenomenon using steam from locomotives. Very soon, he was in correspondence with Michael Faraday about his discoveries of the "electrifying" of the steam. An account of his researches was published in the Philosophical Magazine. Next year he read a paper on "The Electricity of Effluent Steam" to the Newcastle Literary and Philosophical Society. As with his hydraulic engine and prototype crane, he turned to Watson to produce a working model to demonstrate what he had discovered. By 1842, he had made a "hydro-electric" machine, which consisted of a boiler of wrought iron, bizarrely mounted on four glass legs to ensure that it was insulated. Steam was allowed to escape from the boiler through nozzles controlled by valves, the friction caused as it did so producing sparks. Nearly 40 years later an authoritative reviewer of the whole field of electricity recalled this "famous hydroelectric machine" which "far surpassed any ordinary electrical machine in the quantity of electricity produced in a given time." It was left to Faraday to take up and trace the exact source of the electromagnetic force involved., but Armstrong at last received scientific and public recognition.(5) During 1843 he made a larger hydro-electric machine, which he helped to install at the Royal Institution in London. Another of his machines was sent to America. Next year, he twice demonstrated the machine at Newcastle Literary and Philosophical Society meetings. On the second occasion, the audience he had attracted was so large that he could not pass through the auditorium to the stage and had to be let in through a rear window. A future industrial leader, John Wigham Richardson, then only a child, was taken to one of these Armstrong demonstrations, and was so deeply impressed that he recalled it in old age: "It was a weird scene; the sparks or flashes of electricity from the machine were, I should say, from four to five feet long and the figure of Armstrong in a frock coat (since then so familiar) looked almost demoniacal."(6). More important for the lawyer-inventor, in 1846, aged 36, he was elected a Fellow of the Royal Society. Two of his sponsors were men of international renown in electrical research, Michael Faraday and Charles Wheatstone.

As researches and production of articles and lectures continued, Armstrong`s daily employment remained that of a practicing solicitor. Understandably he was conscious of his senior partner`s unusually forbearing and generous attitude to his enthusiasms which had now spilled out into his working hours. Writing in October 1843, when he was helping to install his machine at the London Polytechnic, he thanked Donkin for his gift of a "noble pineapple" and then in a rather stilted fashion apologised for his lengthy non-attendance at the office: "My Dear Sir, I hope that my protracted absence from business has not occasioned you much inconvenience." On the plus side, he reckoned that his health had benefited from his time in London, "... and I have received so much notice and attention that the temptation to stay has been exceedingly great."(7) Not long afterwards, he was spending time on a project that would mark his entry to the business world. It was connected to changes in local conditions.

Since Armstrong`s birth, the economy and population of Tyneside had continued to grow by leaps and bounds. Between the censuses of 1811 and 1831-the latter the year in which he came of age-the population of the city of Newcastle upon Tyne almost doubled, to nearly 54 thousand. At about the same time as he came back to the North from his studies in Lincolns Inn, the area was visited by William Cobbett, who recorded his appreciation of Newcastle upon Tyne "... this fine, opulent, solid, beautiful and important town." A few days after he wrote those words, and by now in North Shields, Cobbett wrote an account of his journey from Hexham to Tyneside: "As I approached Newcastle, the collieries, the rail-roads, the citizens` country boxes, the smoke, the bustle, and all the London-like appearance, again met my eye..." The new chain bridge at Scotswood reminded him of Hammersmith bridge "... with everything as much like the WEN as a young ape is like an old one!" He concluded that: "This Newcastle is really and truly the London of the north; it has all the solidity of the city of London; in all appearances of industry and

Armorer Donkin
(Courtesy BAE Systems)

real wealth; all of its prospects of permanency ..." (A few years later, another author almost outdid Cobbett in enthusiasm for Newcastle. For him it was, "...where nothing retrogrades, and few things are stagnant, [and] the very SPIRIT OF STEAM may be said to take up its permanent abode.")(8) Under the provisions of the Municipal Corporations Act in 1835, five townships-Westgate, Elswick, Jesmond, Heaton and Byker-were added to the old town, and by 1841, the extended city contained 70 thousand people. New services were urgently required to meet their pressing needs, and, given the spirit of the times, they were gradually provided. The first gas street lighting dated from 1818. During the thirties, there was a major programme of demolition and rebuilding in the central area, resulting in the splendid new Grainger Street, Clayton Street and Grey Street. One vital service was particularly over-stretched by the growth in population. An unreliable water supply could lead to disaster; and its inadequacy did in fact cause suffering and death to some. For example, during summer

1831, when delivery of water of acceptable quality failed to meet demand, supplies had to be carted from the river. Before the end of that year, cholera was rampant; 306 deaths were recorded in Newcastle, 234 in Gateshead. Enterprise responded to the challenge. From 1832 a Newcastle Subscription Water Company planned to improve the provision of water by taking water from the Tyne at Elswick, filtering it on a large scale and then storing it in a reservoir at Arthur`s Hill. In 1840, another scheme was proposed by the Union Water Company, in this instance involving extraction of water from the River Pont and the nearby marshy area of Prestwick Carr. Yet by 1844, the Union company had not built any of the authorised works, and the Subscription company had been absorbed by a new firm. In this new, much more successful company, Armstrong played a leading part. (9)

The Whittle Dene Water Company was formed in autumn 1844 to build a reservoir 11 miles away from Newcastle along the Whittle Burn just west of Harlow Hill on the Military Road. Its promotion brought together a group of local men. The chairman was Addison Langhorn Potter, Mayor of Newcastle, and Armstrong`s uncle. Two of the other nine directors were medical men; one was a merchant and the remaining six were engaged in a variety of businesses. Three of them would be important to Armstrong in other ventures - Potter, Richard Lambert, his fellow student in London and now a close friend, and George Cruddas, a linen draper, ship owner and railway shareholder and director. Armstrong was the company secretary, not a director, but his leading importance was shown by the fact that when Potter died after nine years Armstrong took his place as chairman. By 1848, the water company had completed five reservoirs along Whittle Dene.

The next stage in Armstrong`s career took him from research and invention and the provision of a public utility into a venture which led directly on into manufacturing. Having failed in his first attempt to produce an hydraulic crane on anything other than a working model scale, he took up research and development work again, recognising that the flow of water from the Whittle Dene works down to the Tyne could provide the power needed to work cranes along the riverside. Over the next few years, he made two more important technical advances in hydromechanics. The first was a response to the fact that in some situations there was no adequate water pressure. In such circumstances, pressure could be artificially created by using a steam engine to pump water into a tank placed in a high elevation, in a water tower. Sometimes however, there was not even a suitable site for such a tower, and his hydraulic "accumulator", introduced in 1850, was developed to solve this problem. This "beautiful arrangement", as a much later authority on hydromechanics called it, used a tall vertical cylinder in place of a large water tower. Into the top of the cylinder was fitted a solid ram which moved up or down through cup leathers or hemp packing and was loaded by fixed weights, so as to produce a pressure in the cylinder of perhaps 700 to 800 lbs per square inch. Engines were used to pump water into the cylinder so as to raise the ram to the top of its stroke. Then, through a catch arrangement, the engines were stopped until water was taken from the high-pressure column in the cylinder through pipes of narrow bore to work machinery, at which point the engines automatically resumed their work, replacing the water. (10)

To promote the commercial use of his hydraulic crane, Armstrong decided to relate its advantages to an activity vital to the success of the local economy. On 24 November 1845, he wrote to the Finance Committee of Newcastle Town Council to draw the attention of its members to a plan he had "matured" for applying water pressure in the pipes in the streets of the lower parts of Newcastle to the working of cranes on the Quay "...with the view of increasing the rapidity and lessening the expense of the operation of delivering ships." He proposed that, along with a few friends, he should prove the principle by modifying one of the existing cranes at their own expense, with the provision that, if successful, they should be leased all the cranes on the Quay. Proof that he was not only an inventor with an eye to commercial applications, but also had a good capacity for what has been recognised as "public relations" was provided by a lecture about the crane which he gave to the Literary and Philosophical Society only nine days after writing to the Finance Committee. In it, he additionally showed a capacity to think imaginatively about the changes in manufacturing which were now underway. After referring to the use of hydraulic power in Greenock, he pointed out that a place like Whittle Dene would also suit admirably but for the fact that it was too far from a situation where the power could be used. But water might be conveyed to a suitable place by a canal and "... besides, the railway system was rapidly diminishing the importance of localities, and would render every hamlet available for manufacturing purposes." He exhibited a model of one of the cranes on the Newcastle Quay, demonstrating the "efficiency, rapidity and ease" with which its work could be done by using pressure from street pipes to drive the machinery. His technical argument was given persuasive force by an appeal to commercial gain and a vague humanitarian concern. The price of the water would be only one third that for wages: "Human labour was the most costly, and for want of a suitable substitute, men were placed in the position of beasts of burden." Early in his lecture he became almost lyrical about the effects of human exploitation of steam: "It is carrying civilisation to the remotest parts of the earth;-it is bringing nations into friendly communication with each other-and it is dispensing all those articles of manufacture which are essential to refined and cultivated life to millions of the human race who would otherwise be without them." Towards the end of this lecture he did recognise that there were losses as well as gains from mechanisation, but, perhaps rather simplistically, claimed that the whole process was in accordance with the nature of man: "The substitution of inanimate power for human labour must unfortunately always be attended in the first instance with the evil of depriving individuals of employment, but the general welfare of the community is unquestionably promoted in every instance in which we succeed in coercing insensible agents into our service, for the purpose of moving machinery. Man was designed to work by his head rather than by the mere strength of his arm, and as he continues to extend his dominion over the powers of nature, his occupations will gradually assume less of the physical, and more of the intellectual character."(11)Not only did this address reveal Armstrong`s interest in wider issues, but also the fact that, at this time, he considered the implications of scientific and technical advances fell within the arts of peace.

Almost two months later, a modification of the proposal made by Armstrong and his friends was unanimously approved by the full council. Together with Donkin, Potter, Cruddas and Lambert, he formed the Newcastle Cranage Company. Having proved his claim to improve operations in the existing cranes, the new company installed

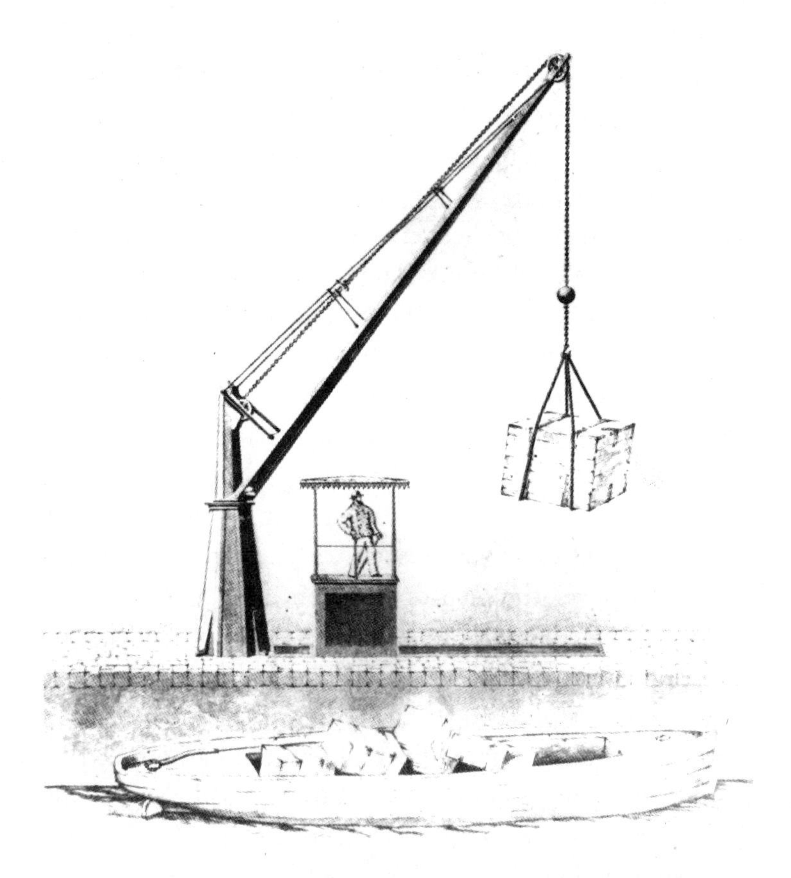

An early Armstrong hydraulic crane
(Courtesy BAE Systems)

three more. Soon construction of cranes according to the same principles would lead him much further. An important factor in persuading him to take the vital next step was the friendship and influence of an older and well-established engineer, a man involved in the early stages of improvements in the condition of the lower Tyne.

Before the first improvement works were begun in 1843, the river Tyne in its lower reaches was very different from the fine, wide, deep stream known today or in the later Victorian era. At that time it was "... by nature a small winding irregular river, with little tidal capacity and no estuary, its depth was small and variable, and a bar existed at its mouth ..." In parts its course was broken by shoals and small islands, in others there were swift currents, high standing obstructions to navigation and in some places dangerous rocks. To improve navigation it would be necessary to undertake major works on the river, deepening the channel and widening and straightening its course. Various schemes were considered for training it and for constructing docks along it, though little progress was made until after 1850 when the Tyne Improvement Commission was established by Act of Parliament. (12) One of the distinguished civil engineers consulted about the condition of the lower Tyne was James Meadows Rendel. He had a long and successful career in his home region, the West of England, before he moved to London to open a new office in 1838. There he quickly widened the range and area of his work. In 1843, he was elected a Fellow of the Royal Society. He may have first met Armstrong at the Society`s meetings, but Lane suggests that they became acquainted in 1845 when Rendel was called on by the Conservators of the Tyne for consultation in connection with a proposed quay at North Shields.(13) Whatever the date or occasion, he and Armstrong soon became close friends. [Armstrong remained loyal to Rendel`s memory long after the latter`s early death. In 1872 when travelling home from his only journey out of Europe, he read a report in The Times that John Coode had been knighted for building the harbour at Portland. He immediately wrote to inform the editor it had been his "intimate friend" the late Mr Rendel who had planned it. (14)] Rendel`s increasing engineering commissions included harbour works and railways both of which involved a demand for crane power, and he naturally took a keen interest in Armstrong`s hydraulic operations. As with earlier working models, the new cranes for the Newcastle Quay were built at Watson`s works, but Rendel succeeded in persuading his younger friend that his invention would not receive the attention it deserved from the practical engineers who were so rapidly transforming Britain, and reaching out to major contracts overseas, unless he also took over its production. He made clear that he could not help in financing such a venture, but assured Armstrong that he could provide, or help procure, orders sufficient to keep a moderate sized factory employed. (15) As Rendel was in close contact with other leading engineers such as Isambard Kingdom Brunel and Robert Stephenson, the market prospects seemed assured. Consequently, before the end of 1846 a new company to produce the hydraulic powered crane was in

James Meadows Rendel
(Courtesy BAE Systems)

course of formation. In January 1847, Armstrong resigned as secretary of the Whittle Dene Water Company; and a month later, he at last gave up his partnership in Donkin, Stable and Armstrong. He was already 36 when he set out as a manufacturer, and it seems doubtful that he envisaged that by the end of his life the small engineering works he now built would be perhaps the largest of all the industrial plants in Britain.

EARLY ELSWICK: MECHANICAL AND CIVIL ENGINEERING 1847 TO 1855

On New Year`s Day 1847 a new Tyneside manufacturing company was formed as a partnership of five men. Each was already associated with the Whittle Dene Water Company, but, in contrast with the situation there, the leading place of one of them was recognised in the name chosen for their enterprise; W.G. Armstrong and Company. Capital was a modest £22,500, of which Armstrong`s share was £5,000-£2,000 contributed in cash and £3,000 representing the value of his patents in the hydraulic wheel and the crane. Addison Potter, Armorer Donkin and George Cruddas each invested £5,000. Cruddas also provided £2,500 to purchase an interest for Richard Lambert, who had no spare capital. A head office was established at 10 Hood Street, east of Dobson and Grainger`s magnificent new Grey Street. The critical next steps were to find a suitable situation and site for a factory, and then to build, equip and staff it.

The location chosen for the engineering works marked an important new departure for large-scale Tyneside manufacturing, for it was up river from Newcastle in contrast with the predominance of riverside sites between that city and the sea. Into the 1840s, the western edge of the built up area lay roughly at Rye Hill. Further out, and stretching down the slope from the West Road to the Tyne, was a fertile area that also contained some excellent seams of coal. There were a few farms, one or two collieries, and a scatter of small-scale industrial operations, including lead and copperas works. In 1800 John Hodgson had erected Elswick Hall, and his son built Scotswood Road through to the new suspension bridge which was opened in spring 1831, providing a crossing over the Tyne. In the area beyond Scotswood

Bridge, there were a few larger scale industries, as at Lemington and Newburn. Five years after this road bridge was opened, the Newcastle and Carlisle Railway was completed from its western terminus to Blaydon. In 1839 a railway bridge was constructed over the river a little way above the road bridge and work began on a short stretch of track running above the riverside haughs along the north bank. This completed the cross-country rail link into central Newcastle. Recognising the potential for development provided by these new transport facilities, in 1839 Richard Grainger paid £114,000 to John Hodgson Hind for the manor of Elswick and the land between the Westgate Road and the river.

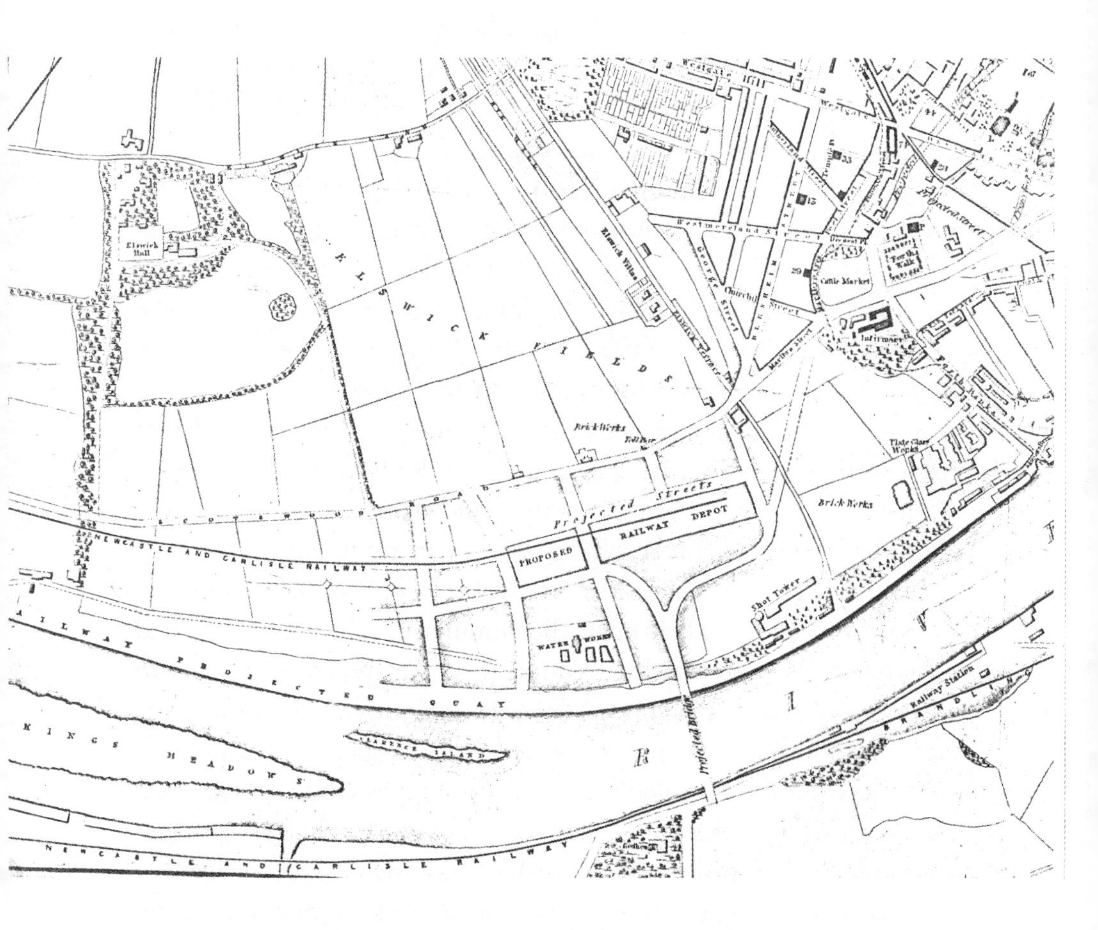

The Tyne valley at Elswick, 1838 (MA Richardson. Plan of the Towns of Newcastle upon Tyne and Gateshead.)

About seven years after Grainger`s purchase of this land, William Armstrong walked over the two western fields of the Elswick estate to assess their suitability for the works he and his partners planned. This preliminary evaluation was followed by a survey. Fifty years later, the Elswick drawing office still contained a copy of the plan that resulted. Dated 29 January 1847 it was entitled "Plan of the two Western Fields on the Elswick Estate, between the railway and the High Water Mark of the River Tyne." By April 10th the company had paid John Hodgson Hind and Richard Grainger between £4,000 and £6,000 for six acres of land, and before that month ended construction began.(1)

Armstrong resigned his law practice in February 1847 and opened his correspondence for the new company on 29 March. From then onwards his letter books, and the cash books of WG Armstrong and Company, record payments for buildings and equipment. Important items were purchased from the major machine tool and engineering centres of the country; among the early orders there was one for a large lathe from Whitworth and Company of Manchester. There was also good business for local firms and service providers. In January and February 1848 for instance, payment was made to Locke, Blackett and Company for white lead, to Elswick Colliery for small coals, and to the Scotswood Tile Company. Timber was bought from Strakers and Love, Benwell Colliery was paid for straw, and the Newcastle and Carlisle Railway for carriage of iron rails from Wylam. (2) On 17 April in a letter to Mr Bourne of the Leeds and Thirsk Railway-a new company produced by the recent railway mania, and whose secretary was the later-to-be famous Samuel Smiles-WG Armstrong and Company expressed hope that their works would be in operation by autumn. Construction continued through the summer and by September had reached a stage at which the accounts began to record payments to millwrights for fixing machinery. Six apprentices were indentured that month, work in the pattern shop began on 1 October and the first bill for wages under the manufacturing accounts appeared on 15 October. Attempting to trace the progress in this first year, Cochrane estimated that by early December 1847 roughly 100 men were engaged in construction or fixing machinery, and only 20 or so in manufacturing. A year later the workforce reached 180; by December 1850, it was about 250. (3)

Before Elswick works was built, five Armstrong hydraulic cranes had been made by Watsons. Now the new company began to take orders for its own products. The first was for four 12-ton cranes for the Edinburgh and Northern Railway. The tender for these was dated 11 August 1847, when construction of the factory was still underway and production would not begin for many weeks. A more colourful episode in building up the order book involved a contract for Liverpool Docks. The engineer of the massive works underway there at this time was Jesse Hartley. By 1845, he had completed his greatest project, the Albert Docks, and now, apparently advised by a fellow civil engineer, William Cubitt, he decided to consider the installation of Armstrong cranes. Unannounced, he turned up on Newcastle Quay to see the crane in operation, and then, as Armstrong recalled in old age, after receiving this unplanned demonstration, he came to his office, only to say little more than: "I am Jesse Hartley of Liverpool and I have seen your crane. It is the very thing I want, and I shall recommend its adoption at the Albert Dock." The estimate for two hydraulic warehouse lifts was sent on 28 August 1847, orders were placed and the first payment of £1,000 seems to have been made by the Liverpool Dock Trustees on 15 May 1848. There were early orders from a number of railway, canal and dock companies, including valuable contracts from Brunel, for cranes for Paddington station. As he had promised, Rendel provided his friend with orders, including, in 1850, ones for hydraulic machinery to operate the gates at the Great Grimsby dock. Cochrane listed some of the orders for cranes for the five years to the end of 1852. For only five railway companies and two dock or canal companies they amounted to 142, ranging in size from 1.5 to 12 tons. It was when faced with the difficulties involved in providing a head of water sufficient to operate the cranes he was installing for the Manchester, Sheffield and Lincolnshire Railway at New Holland, Humberside, that Armstrong invented his accumulator. As well as cranes and lifts, the company made hydraulic machinery for use in mining, and in the case of the South Hetton Coal Company for winding engines. (4)

Elswick engineering works and Elswick Fields, 1849.
(Courtesy BAE Systems)

An early aim was to make Elswick into a general engineering works rather than depend wholly on applications of the Armstrong hydraulic patents. The list of products, given above, suggests that the company largely succeeded, but it lacked expertise in some fields to match that of other, established firms. This brought its first failures. In 1848, it designed and built a locomotive, but failed to find a buyer, and the loss on this cancelled out the first two years of profit in other operations. Even so, by 1852/1853, the works was fairly well engaged, and turnover was increasing. Business in July in 1850 amounted to £3,869; two years later for the same month of the year, it was £10,825. (5) When bridge building began, Armstrongs again had to learn the hard way. On the contract for the Inverness Bridge, completed in 1855, the firm made a heavy loss, but in 1857, it was successful in obtaining a major project that brought the capabilities of the firm to the notice of a wider public and was also profitable. It brought together individuals who would be important in the long-term future of the company.

As engineer for the East Indian Railway Company, James Meadows Rendel had undertaken to build a bridge across the river Soane near Patna. At the time, this would be the second longest bridge in the world. In February 1856, WG Armstrong and Company tendered for construction of the bridge. Almost a year later, and after Rendel`s death, it was learned that this bid had been successful. Reaction to the news was recorded both by Rendel`s son, George, and by Armstrong. The first, in a letter to his younger brother Stuart, made clear both his own close relationship with Armstrong, in whose home he had lived while learning his engineering trade at Elswick, and his satisfaction that the work would be undertaken by such a reliable company: "We have let the large bridge for the Soane to contract. Uncle William has got it. I am very glad of this as it will take a great deal of anxiety from my mind and I shall have many pleasant trips to Newcastle for inspection. If this big work had got into bad hands as it might have done, I cannot tell you what trouble we should have had." Four days before this Armstrong had written enthusiastically to his wife about their success in winning the work: "You will be glad to hear we have got the contract for the entire Soane Bridge-the amount is nearly £68,000. George is delighted at this result and I am glad for his sake as well as ours. It will be a job to bring him often down to Newcastle. Percy [Westmacott] is in great triumph. He has taken enormous pains in getting out the tender and is arranging the method to be followed in the construction." He felt it desirable to add a P.S:"Sixty eight thousand pounds is a large sum for the bridge."(6)

Over its first 16 years the Elswick works made almost 1,800 hydraulic cranes, hoists etc, locomotive, stationary, pumping and winding engines, boilers, and caissons, dock gates, pontoons, coffer dams, barges and wrought iron dredgers. It built 25 moveable and 44 fixed bridges, the latter including the Soane Bridge. In supplying some of its orders, the company provided a comprehensive service. The Allenheads lead mines, managed by Thomas Sopwith, were an example. They placed considerable orders in 1849, so that a few years later Armstrong "...hydraulic machinery is....employed in raising the minerals from the mines, in giving motion to machines for washing, separating and crushing ore; in pumping water and driving saw mills and the machinery of a workshop."(7)

None of the partners had any every day technical competence in engineering. The company was however fortunate to obtain this in George Hutchinson, son of Watson`s manager, who was persuaded to transfer his expertise from the High Bridge Works to Elswick. Hutchinson was made assistant manager and head of the drawing offices. The works manager, Henry Thompson, also came from Watsons. However, the great weight of responsibility for construction and successful operation of the works was borne by Armstrong. As his was the central technical expertise, he was constantly on call; indeed in old age he claimed that for the first 15 years he did not take a single week`s holiday. On many evenings, he worked until 10 or 11 pm and then lay down to sleep on a couch. Such an arrangement seems to have been recognised as inadequate and an interesting sidelight on his recollections is provided by an item on office furniture for 1 March 1850: "Paid Mrs Cummings for feather bed £3. 5s. 0d."(8).

The early operations were not highly profitable. The partners received their first dividend on 1853 operations, but it amounted to 5%, a mere £1,075. Annually they re-invested some of the earnings to expand the business. As a result, in 15 years the capital of WG Armstrong and Company increased from £20,000 to almost £100,000. As most of his partners were unable to, or chose not, to play a prominent part in the business, Armstrong gained greater control. When Donkin died in 1851, he left his interest in the company to Armstrong. Three years later Potter died and his share was bought from his trustees by the three remaining partners. Though valued as a colleague, Richard Lambert was not active. In contrast, George Cruddas, who was already a mature businessman, took over and conscientiously managed their finances. Even so, the responsibility for raising more money seems to have fallen on Armstrong. Cochrane heard him recall in old age an occasion in the early years when he paced up and down Grey Street, turning over in his mind how he might find the capital to keep the engine works afloat. He claimed he had given up walking when the soles of his boots became so hot that it was too painful to carry on. (9)

The task of ensuring that the Elswick engineering works were firmly established involved calls on Armstrong`s attention and time in two other fields. He had to develop contacts with men of commercial power and influence. Business from within the major industrial area of the North East was vital at the beginning and important later, but it was essential to make London connections. He responded purposefully, spending long periods working and living in the capital. Together his unremitting commitment to making a success of Elswick and his extended visits to London inevitably meant that another, vital sector of his life received less attention than it deserved. He had long ago married Margaret, his childhood sweetheart. The evidence seems to indicate that as he dedicated his best efforts to making his way as an industrialist their lives drifted apart.

View of the Elswick and Dunston districts of Tyneside. c. 1850.
(Courtesy BAE Systems)

In the early days of the new works, its surroundings were still green, and a belt of trees in Elswick Dene separated the new industry from the city. The lane known as the Curds and Cream Road ran along the riverside, and on the island just off shore from the new engineering works, there was a public house, the Countess of Coventry. Partridges and pheasants were occasionally seen within the boundary walls, and an apprentice from that time remembered as a veteran in the 1890s that on at least one occasion a hare was chased across what had become the bridge yard. (10)

THE ART AND SCIENCE OF MASS DESTRUCTION; THE EARLY HISTORY OF THE ARMSTRONG GUN

Before the mid 1850s Armstrong`s engineering products were highly regarded but his name was probably completely unknown to the average, ordinary citizen, except on Tyneside. The situation changed dramatically over the next few years, as he became a national figure, and for some a hero. This alteration in status was caused by his involvement in the manufacture of ordnance. A useful starting point for examining the transformation is the Great Exhibition of 1851.

A few weeks before the Exhibition opened, Armstrong wrote to Margaret about his minor role in its successful launch: "There is a precious commotion at the Great Exhibition. It will be Devil take the hindmost. Our work is well forward, but old Cubitt [the builder and contractor Sir William Cubitt, 1785-1861] who is a dreadful fidget to get things done, has thrown some additional work upon us and I found him in dreadful way about the supply of water from the water works, which was so variable in its pressure as to render it inapplicable to the Fountains. It was chiefly on this subject that he wanted to consult me and I have schemed him an apparatus to remove the difficulty and he is now in a great fuss to have it made and set to work. The Building is beginning to look extremely well and there is some magnificent machinery erected."(1) While he was one of those busy with the mundane pressures involved in getting this project of unprecedented magnitude underway, others were thinking about its significance and purpose.

A few months before the opening of "The Great Exhibition of the

Works of Industry of all Nations", Prince Albert addressed dignitaries at the Mansion House. He told them of his belief that the world was for the first time in history on the point of "....the realization of the unity of mankind" and the Exhibition itself would be devoted to a celebration of progress in the arts of peace. When the products of the world were gathered together, this was indeed the overwhelming theme, but there was a discordant note. Alfred Krupp of Essen exhibited a huge block of fine cast steel, but he also displayed a six-pounder gun made from his steel. The gun was admired, but it clearly represented ambitions not in accordance with the aims of the promoters. Within less than three years, Armstrong too became deeply involved in major improvements in field artillery, and before the decade ended, his "system" was pre-eminent in ordnance manufacture in Britain, and only matched worldwide by guns made by Krupp. In short, over these few years a man who had been a partner in a regional law firm, whose scientific experiments and designs for electrical and hydraulic machines were worked out in his spare time, reached the extraordinary position of being chosen in preference to a considerable number of other important British inventors of new heavy guns. His involvement in this field was caused by war with Russia, the conflict which, because of its prime focus, would be known as the Crimean War.

For forty years, neither the British army nor the Royal Navy had fought in a major war. Apart from avoiding loss of life, destruction of property and unproductive expenditure of money, this unusual situation meant that national energies had been more fruitfully engaged in other directions. However, such a generally enviable situation had not helped along the arts of war. When in 1852 Braithwaite Poole, a Fellow of the Statistical Society, published his valuable compendium of <u>Statistics of British Commerce</u> he duly listed both "ordnance" and "cannon," but his accounts of these products made clear how neglected their manufacture had been. Ordnance was "a general name for large guns, which in this country are manufactured chiefly of iron, at the various foundries." "Cannon" for merchant service - in which they served as a defence against pirates - as well as being used in government service were "....manufactured of cast-iron, in the foundries at Carron, Gospel Oak, Warrington, Low Moor, etc., for the purposes of war." In 1851, about 2,000 tons of cannon were produced. Smaller field guns for government service were generally of brass; most "Carronades" of smaller dimensions were made of cast iron for merchant service and export. (2) Despite a general lack of incentive in this age of peace, there had in fact been a certain amount of "progress." The stronger metal now available allowed a gun of a certain weight to fire a heavier shot than had been the case a generation before. Generally, design and production of war materiel lagged behind in an economy that in so many other respects had surged ahead as never before.

Declaration of war on Russia in March 1854 transformed this situation. The industrial revolution had largely by passed weaponry; now design and methods of making armaments rapidly began to catch up with and exploit the general progress of technology. There were major advances in small arms, in vessels of war and in various other lines, but the most striking developments were in ordnance. Here indeed there seemed to occur something like a release of a pent-up capacity for innovation in mechanised warfare. Years later, looking back, a Superintendent of the Royal Gun Factory summarised and looked kindly on these changes: "The long peace which succeeded the Napoleonic wars was highly unfavourable to the progress of gunnery, but a great development took place in the arts and sciences, so that, on the breaking out of the Crimean War, the latest discoveries in metallurgy and the excellence attained in machinery at once enabled inventors to make a great advance in artillery."(3)

Fighting in the Crimea centred on the fortress of Sebastopol. As a result, an important emphasis in procurement of weapons was the supply of heavy guns for siege purposes. From the start, there was innovation. In the early days of the war, James Nasmyth produced a huge wrought iron gun, made up of slabs of iron welded together under the power of the four-ton steam hammer at Patricroft Ironworks, near Manchester. The Mersey Steel and Iron Company had a wrought iron gun weighing 24 tons and with a 13 inch bore and in 1855, Forrester of Liverpool built a 14.5-ton mortar capable of throwing an 18-inch shell. At the Paragon Works, Dundas welded wrought iron bars edge to edge to form a cylinder, which was then bound on the outside by shrinking iron rings onto it. As well as the intrinsic merits or defects of particular systems of ordnance, the supporting manufacturing resources and "connections" of those advocating them helped determine which designs survived to be adopted by the army or navy. Accounts of the time are full of partisanship and advocacy, which confused assessment. A great deal depended on careful choice; in terms of the effectiveness of the armed forces, the safety of men, as well as in relation to the commercial prospects of those manufacturing the ordnance.

Although the urgent needs of war caused a sudden outbreak of inventiveness, some who became involved had other, often pressing, preoccupations, which sooner or later again diverted their attention. Brunel was a leading example. He designed a floating gun carriage for the 1854 attack on Cronstadt, and invented a polygonal system of rifling small arms, which he also applied to large guns. He considered building up the strength of a heavy gun by encasing its barrel in wound wire, but did not succeed in working out a correct method for doing this. Many other things demanded his attention. From 1853, he was busy with the Saltash Bridge, and above all, he was engaged in designing and building the Great Eastern. Another who tried to enter the field was Henry Bessemer. Over sixteen years to mid 1854, he had been granted 32 patents, not one of which was for a military invention, but in August that year, he registered his first patent for naval and military guns. Through to June the following year he lodged three more.(4) In his concern to make a suitable material for guns he set up a laboratory in St Pancras, where he carried on experiments for two years before developing the steel process which would make his name and fortune and transform the metallurgical world. Improvement of the Bessemer process soon took his attention away from ordnance, but as will be seen later, other factors were also involved in his failure to make his mark in this field.

Important ordnance systems were designed at this time by Captain Blakeley, by Lancaster and by Longridge. Lancaster achieved much, but his success was qualified by the fact that he employed a cast iron gun and an imperfectly made shell. As a result, when an apparently better weapon appeared, his design was "summarily dismissed." According to one authority, if the same pains had been spent on it in the laboratory and money had been available such as that "lavished" on more favoured systems, Lancaster might have succeeded. Even so, this expert believed the last had not been heard of his design with its oval bored barrel. (5) James Atkinson Longridge was a compatriot and near contemporary of William Armstrong. Born in Bishopwearmouth in 1817 he was apprenticed to George Stephenson, worked in the Stephenson Newcastle works, and by the early 1840s was employed in continental railway contracts on behalf of the Bedlington Iron Company. In 1845, he constructed the Whitehaven and Furness Junction Railway, before moving back to Newcastle and from there to London. Early in 1855, the frequent failures in the cast iron guns used in the secondary Baltic theatre of operations in the war with Russia induced him to turn his attention to ordnance. He decided that a process involving shrinking iron hoops onto a barrel was inadvisable because it was impossible to ensure correct contraction to cope with the inevitable strains in the gun, and because at that time large masses of metal were of unpredictable soundness. Instead, he recommended use of a central tube with wire laid over it to definitely calculated tensions. Having worked out the necessary formula, he submitted his plans to the Ordnance Select Committee. When one experiment went badly the Committee refused to go further with trials of his system. By 1860, Longridge had produced a sound gun, but after that, he was away working in Mauritius, which meant he was unable to take up the matter again for 7 years. By that time others, who had remained active in the contest, were well established. Longridge continued to advocate his ordnance system for the remainder of his life, but it was never adopted. Technically this failure seems to have been due to questions that were never answered because the necessary tests were not carried out. But as a Superintendent of the Royal Gun Factory at Woolwich put it years later, one view was that "... the ideal gun would be constructed of a vast number of excessively thin rings so shrunk over each other that, on discharge, each should be equally strained." Longridge attempted to approximate this by winding steel wire under tension around a steel tube, a system which "though possessing much ingenuity, has never made way, and might possibly be found wanting in longitudinal strength." (6)

Like a great number of other engineering, metal or shipbuilding firms, WG Armstrong and Company was asked to contribute expertise and manufacturing capacity in the conflict against the Russian Empire. One of its roles was a simple extension from civil engineering, the installation of coaling equipment, notably at Grimsby, which was expected to serve the fleet that was sent to the Baltic. In the early part of the war the company was also invited to produce underwater mines to destroy the ships the Russians had sunk to block the approaches to Sebastopol. The drawings were produced by October 1854, and the mines were made, tested and proved satisfactory both in Newcastle and at Woolwich, but when they were used in the Crimea the electrical detonation apparatus failed to work properly. Apparently, this was because of deficiencies in the way in which the apparatus was handled by the military there rather than due to any inherent fault. Meantime the general defects of British artillery and naval guns were being exposed. A vivid illustration of this was provided more than 30 years later by Admiral Sir John Hay when he recalled that at one time he had been asked by Lord Lyons, commander of the naval forces in the Black Sea, to suspend a 5 ton gun by cable from the foremast at an angle of 33 degrees in order to enable it to throw shot and shell a greater distance. In the light of the problems experienced with guns in the field, at some time during the war William Armstrong began to take a keener interest in ordnance. As a history of his company put it: "More as an amusement for his leisure than for any other reason, he began to consider the possibility of improving the heavy artillery of the British service ... [and] ... with the curious faculty which always distinguished him, of transferring his entire energy and attention to various subjects in turn, he gradually became completely absorbed in the study of guns, carriages and projectiles."(7) In autumn 1854, his involvement became much more direct.

On 5 November, one of the three great battles of the Crimean War was fought at Inkerman. It was a bloody, close-run affair, largely a contest between masses of infantry, in which the French and British were almost overwhelmed by a much bigger Russian force. A decisive factor in saving the day for the Allies was the work of two long 18-pounder guns from the British siege train. Each gun weighed 42 hundredweights, and had to be drawn up to the necessary dominating position by the labours of a team of 150 or so men over a period of three hours. Long afterwards Stuart Rendel remembered how immediately news of this battle stimulated Armstrong`s inventive powers-though he wrongly attributed the effect to the battle of Balaclava, fought 11 days earlier. His own father had angrily denounced "... the absurd ponderousness of the cannon so critically employed" when they learned of the battle as they breakfasted one day. Why had the improvements made in small arms not also been applied to heavy guns? That same morning, Armstrong, visiting the Rendel home, sketched out on a piece of blotting paper his scheme for enlargement to field gun size of the wrought iron rifle. James Meadows Rendel encouraged him with "You are the man to do it."

Whatever the precise circumstances, Armstrong`s response was prompt, positive and effective. In marked contrast, evaluation of his design and prototypes by the armed services was strung out over years. It may be that this leisurely process indicated that great care was taken to ensure the army and navy obtained the best system, but undoubtedly, it also reflected the caution and prejudice of deeply conservative men and organisations. An excellent illustration of the general inertia was provided by the career of the Duke of Cambridge, cousin of the Queen. He took part in the main battles of the Crimean War-indeed at Inkerman his horse was shot from under him. Appointed general commanding-in-chief in 1856, he headed the army for the next 39 years. Shortly after he at long last resigned, an obviously well informed account included the following scarcely encouraging sentences: "Belonging to the pre-scientific period of the British army, he could not easily adapt himself to the new conditions, and in dispensing patronage he was somewhat distrustful of originality, while his position as a member of the royal family tended to narrow his scope for selection. He was thus inclined to be influenced by considerations of pure seniority, and to underrate the claims of special ability." (8) Although this comment refers especially to selection of military men, such an official cast of mind was also scarcely ideal for evaluation of technical advances.

Armstrong recorded that in December 1854, within a few weeks of Inkerman, Rendel submitted to Sir James Graham, First Lord of the Admiralty, "... a communication he had received from me, suggesting the expediency of enlarging the ordinary rifle to the standard of a field gun and firing elongated projectiles of lead instead of balls of cast iron." Graham duly passed on this report, "Construction of wrought iron rifled guns adapted for elongated projectiles", to the Duke of Newcastle, Secretary of State for War. Soon afterwards, accompanied by Rendel, Armstrong met the Duke. "At this interview I was authorised by his Grace to carry my views into effect, by constructing upon the plan I had suggested one or more guns, not exceeding six in number, so as to make the necessary experiments in connection with the subject." A month later Newcastle was forced to resign, for he was regarded as largely responsible for the hardships British troops had borne that winter in their siege of Sebastopol, but in January 1855 Armstrong wrote to tell his wife he had been in touch with Lord Panmure, head of the War Department in the new Palmerston administration: "He is quite impressed with the importance of the subject and wants the experiments to be repeated and more fully carried out in April. In the meantime he will sanction the making of a large gun." Armstrong continued to work away at the commission he had received, concentrating on designing one gun, and by July he had submitted for consideration a 3-pounder breech-loader weighing only 5 hundredweights. Its barrel was turned in the Elswick engine works on a lathe bought in 1847. The early guns made at Elswick seem to have been tried out on the flats at Dunston, across the river, but very soon, Armstrong was also testing them at Allenheads, well away from concentrations of people. In July 1855, he wrote to tell Margaret of his success, at the same time revealing the pressure under which he was operating: "...the gun is at length what it should be. In fact its firing is now becoming really extraordinary and I think it cannot fail to make a great impression when it is again exhibited to the authorities." It was now as good at 1500 yards as it had previously been at 400. He was coming home from Allenheads but might be diverted on the way: "I shall return by the mail fly to Haydon Bridge tomorrow and reach the station at Newcastle (I believe) one quarter before 6 when the carriage may be in waiting. Do not be uneasy if I should not come, although I am fairly sure. The alternative will be an early train on Friday morning in which case I will go to the works." (9)

When submitted, the first gun performed satisfactorily. Even so the Ordnance Committee objected that it was unable to fire either common or shrapnel shells. In response, Armstrong had the gun re-bored, converting it into a 5 pounder able to fire a cast iron shell, and he devised for it time, percussion and direct action fuses. The bore of his first gun was of only 1.75 inches and it was rifled with eight spiral grooves, with an inclination equal to one turn in 12 feet. In contrast to guns previously used, it was light enough to be lifted, without its carriage, by two or three men. As Armstrong had claimed, its performance was even more exceptional. Fired at a timber butt measuring 7x5 feet and 1,500 yards distant, the projectile hit the target nearly every time, the average deviation from the centre of the butt being only a little over a foot. In contrast, ordinary brass cannon of comparable weight were "perfectly" useless at such a distance. (10) In January 1857, by which time his first design had at length been evaluated, Armstrong was invited to make a gun to compete with the service 9 pounder, which weighed 13.5 hundredweights. Inside this weight limit, by July he had produced an 18 pounder. As recalled by

Number 1 gun.
(Courtesy BAE Systems)

Andrew Noble, who was well placed to know, this gun when "... tried in competition with the Service guns at Shoeburyness, utterly defeated them in every detail."

Armstrong`s lead in introducing key elements in the design for a successful field gun did not go undisputed. His provisional specifications and petition for a patent were dated 11 February 1857. A very similar specification had been deposited with the patent office almost two years before by Captain Blakeley. The major difference between them was that Blakeley provided for a tube of steel enclosed in a case or covering of wrought iron or steel, shrunk on to the tube, whereas Armstrong at first substituted a central tube of wrought iron for one made of steel. Bessemer concluded that Blakely and not Armstrong should "... stand before the world as the originator and father of modern built-up artillery." He was by no means a dispassionate observer, for he was convinced that his own plans for ordnance had been conclusively but unreasonably condemned by Armstrong. (11) Certainly, the next few years proved that success depended less on being first with a design and more on capacity to produce it, on contacts in the right places and in the quality of the advocacy commanded by the inventor. In all these respects, Armstrong was better favoured than his rivals. There was however one new system of ordnance which, despite being beaten in the first round of the contest, proved able to call on all of these supporting factors on more or less an equal footing.

Joseph Whitworth was seven years older than William Armstrong, and unlike him had been very thoroughly trained as a practical engineer. After an apprenticeship with Henry Maudslay and working briefly with another leading engineer of the time, Joseph Clement, he set up his own business in Manchester, under a simple but startling sign that revealed something of his quality and spirit "Joseph Whitworth, toolmaker, from London." Soon he acquired a reputation for work of the highest precision, as early as 1834 making a machine that could measure to one millionth of an inch. By the time of the Great Exhibition, he was a world leader in machine tools. In 1854, the government asked him to try to improve the service rifle. The experiments he conducted resulted in a design "... not stumbled upon by accident, but [was] accurately thought out from the first."(12) His rifle far excelled the Enfield, then the standard weapon. From success with light arms he moved on to heavier rifled guns, and it soon became clear that the quality of his product, his standing as a first rate engineer, and the support of influential individuals and organisations, meant that his system of ordnance would be far the most formidable competitor for the Armstrong gun. When most other inventors had retired, or been forced to withdraw from the field as effective rivals, Whitworth remained, accomplished, respected and above all aggressive. A series of major trials and enquiries into the qualities and defects of the two systems would be required before one of them was recognised as superior. Even after that, the runner up retained strong support and a substantial trade in guns.

In July 1858, work began to erect a new factory at Elswick especially to make the Armstrong gun. Less than a year later, it was nearly complete, and a 70 pounder was cast in the first week of June. At that time, it was planned that at full work the Elswick Ordnance Works should turn out four guns weekly. Its main building was 312 feet in length and divided into five distinct "shops" - a blacksmith`s shop which contained the forges and forge hammers for welding the coils, two shops for making the mechanical parts of the gun, a shot and shell making section and a fitting out shop. Operations would be conducted in great secrecy, each worker being confined to his own position in the chain of production. (13) Notwithstanding this secrecy, early in 1860 The Times printed a vivid, colourful description of the operations. They began in the forge shop "... in which at first, the visitor stands aghast to find himself involved in such a raging little world of furnaces and steam hammers, where the glare is blinding and the noise, smoke, dust and clatter tremendous and uncanny ... On every side, in clouds of steam and choking dust, through the thick gloom of smoke, or labouring faintly in the white glare from ardent furnaces, men are seen busy, while every now and then these furnace doors fly open and the crane drags forth a seething mass of metal, hissing and sparkling like a fire king, lighting up the factory with its brilliant whiteness, and leaving a train of glowing particles behind. Careful must the visitor be to give these dreadful masses a wide berth, as the workmen, protected by leather and their faces shielded by crape masks, drag them past to where the steam hammer thumps the reluctant pile of metal into a semblance of its future form, when, after roaring and sputtering under a stream of cold water, it is wheeled off to undergo another of the many stages by which it advances slowly towards completion." A gun was bored twice, each operation taking six hours. (14) Between the date at which construction of this new Elswick works began and the start of operations, the situation for the Armstrong gun had changed.

In January 1858 the Armstrong 18 pounder gun was tried at Shoeburyness against the existing army 32 pounder and three other guns, two of them 18 pounders, the other a 12 pounder. Next month, the Superintendent of Experiments at Shoeburyness praised the "... very extraordinary powers of range and precision of fire..." of the Armstrong gun. The Secretary of State for War shared his enthusiasm. But the processes of evaluation continued to follow a leisurely timetable, and not until August was a Special Committee on Rifled Cannon appointed to assess the respective merits of guns submitted by seven inventors. The secretary of this committee was a 26-year-old captain from the Royal Artillery, Andrew Noble. The committee reported to the War Office that five of the guns - those submitted by Baron Wahrendorf, Laurence, Lynall Thomas, Irving and Vandaleur - had performed scarcely better than smooth bored guns. Accordingly, it recommended no further expense should be incurred in respect of them, but that instead attention should be focussed on the comparative merits of the Armstrong and Whitworth guns. By this time, Armstrong had already made about half a dozen guns in the Elswick engine works, but Whitworth had no finished guns available and could only offer the committee designs or existing government guns re-bored according to his principle. It soon became clear to Armstrong that things were moving strongly in his favour. Having long bombarded her with details about fuses and other matters, he communicated his rising satisfaction to Margaret Armstrong. On his return to London from Shoeburyness on 6 August, he described the fuses as "perfect", told her they had gained "a great triumph with the gun and the shells", and that he felt he had "made converts of all the officers." By mid October, there were more tangible reasons for confidence. The experiments were proving satisfactory, "... and there cannot be a doubt of the Committee being all with me-the more so as Whitworth`s 60 pounder burst the other day at Portsmouth. In fact I now think I have the field to myself." Later that month the Duke of Cambridge visited Shoeburyness, and was so pleased with the Armstrong guns, that when he saw General Jonathan Peel, the new Secretary of State for War, he was "in raptures about them". On 16 November 1858, three months of trials, enquiries and deliberations were at last over. Of the guns submitted by Armstrong and Whitworth, the Ordnance Committee unanimously agreed that the former should be adopted by the services, on grounds of its accuracy, range, perfection of workmanship and the completeness with which projectiles, fuses and other details had been worked out. Reporting to the House of Commons, the Secretary of State for War summed up the situation in vivid terms: at 3,000 yards the score of the Armstrong gun for accuracy was seven times that which the "common" gun achieved at one third of the distance; at the shorter range, existing guns hit an object once in 57 shots, but the Armstrong gun hit it every time. Peel said that in June 1859 when Armstrong`s gun was accepted for service, Cambridge had remarked it could do anything but speak, and General Brereton had told him "... there was nothing in the Arabian Nights half so wonderful as the new gun." (15) After years of laborious effort, designing and building bigger guns, and dealing with trials and enquiries, a series of related arrangements were now rapidly put in place to provide the ordnance for a wholesale re-equipment of both the army and the navy. For the inventor of the system it was a triumph. He had declined to patent his ordnance inventions, but, by act of parliament, the government now took out patents on his behalf and in his name - but withheld their publication.

Armstrong was celebrated and feted. Late in November, he was entertained by the officers of the Royal Artillery at Woolwich. In colourful terms, he reported the occasion next day to Margaret: "... a very magnificent affair it was. Above a hundred officers, all in uniform were present, and we had a most sumptuous dinner. The Mess room is an extremely handsome one and at the upper end, sunk in a deep niche lined with crimson cloth stands a beautiful statue in white marble, the subject being "armed science" ....the light is skilfully directed upon it from glass burners out of view in the ceiling. After dinner, the full band of the Royal Artillery (of which you saw a picture at Bishop Auckland) attended and performed most admirably all evening. In fact, it was a regular concert, mostly of stringed instruments, but accompanied by some singing. I got off with very little speechyfying and altogether had a very gratifying entertainment. Nearly all the officers from Shoeburyness came up for the occasion and I was politely offered a bed by Colonel Henry, one of the staff officers, which I accepted and returned to town this morning, whence I am about to start for Shoeburyness." (16)

It was decided that the gun, until this time built in the Elswick engine works, and soon to be made in the ordnance works being erected by its side, should also be produced by the Royal Gun Factory at Woolwich. In order to carry out the latter, Armstrong was appointed Chief Engineer of Rifled Ordnance in government service, provisionally for a period of seven years. The agreement was dated 22 February 1859 but in fact, the intention to appoint him had been taken by the time Thomas Sopwith dined with the Armstrongs at Jesmond on Sunday 30th January. (17) Two days after the public announcement, Armstrong, accompanied by Sir Benjamin Hawes, Under Secretary of State for War, visited Woolwich Arsenal, where they were received by Colonel Eardley Wilmot, Superintendent of the Royal Gun Factory. At that time, the reputation of this department was poor. A number of Woolwich-built guns had burst. Attempts to obtain suitable materials had failed, and the Factory had not known how to cast the iron mixture used in gun making at Low Moor works in West Yorkshire. Now gun manufacture there had been closed down. As a close associate of Armstrong`s recalled more than half a century later: "Woolwich at this time was little more than a metal foundry, and was about as capable of building an Armstrong gun as a village blacksmith`s shop is capable of turning out a modern motor car."(18) In fact, there were signs of fire in the ashes before this. In 1855-56, when it was decided that the government should supply at least part of the ordnance required by the services, extensive new workshops had been installed. A year or two later another important development was planned. It was one, which, if carried through, would have excluded Armstrong and his ordnance system. On a visit to Sheffield, Wilmot had become convinced of the value of Bessemer`s invention. At the very time at which Armstrong`s gun was accepted, he and Bessemer were planning to build a steel works at Woolwich to supply the metal for a new generation of guns; a forward-looking scheme at odds with the current outmoded methods there. To Bessemer`s dismay this plan now lapsed, as the factory took up the Armstrong gun. By November, Armstrong had succeeded Wilmot as Superintendent. Given the generally conservative nature of top military personnel, and the particular circumstances of the case, the ousting of the existing management in favour of control by a civilian naturally prejudiced some powerful men against the new superintendent.

Though Armstrong was now chief engineer at Woolwich, it was obvious that a considerable time must elapse before operations there could be put in shape to make Armstrong guns. For some time after that, it would not be able to supply all the guns needed to re-equip both army and navy. It was decided that the answer was to continue to draw on Elswick expertise, and that a new, "independent" company should be formed to run the ordnance works there. Accordingly, on 15 January 1859 the Secretary of State for War signed an indenture with William George Armstrong, and next day with the three other partners of the Elswick Ordnance Company, George Cruddas, Richard Lambert and George Rendel. Cruddas was financial head of WG Armstrong and Company, Lambert a sleeping partner. The key man was George Rendel, who had worked through the last few years with Armstrong in developing the gun, and now managed its production in the new works. Under this arrangement, Armstrong would have no direct financial involvement in the Elswick Ordnance Company, though it would make guns of his design for the British armed services. Government guaranteed the £50,000 capital of Elswick Ordnance and agreed to keep it in full work. In one important respect, the arrangement was one-sided. The new company undertook not to supply guns to foreign governments-as a later Director General of Ordnance put it, the Elswick company could not trade with any party other than the British government, but the British government remained free to trade with whichever company it chose. (19) In April 1859, the capital of the Elswick Ordnance Company was raised to £60,000; by October, it had been increased by another £25,000.

In early 1859, with his system accepted, having been knighted and appointed to a key position in government armament production, Armstrong was at a peak of success and popularity. Nationally a prominent figure, on Tyneside he was a hero. Six days after his

George Wightwick Rendel c.1865
(Courtesy Miss R Rendel)

appointment as Chief Engineer of Rifled Ordnance, he returned to Elswick. In that quarter of Newcastle, shops and offices were decorated with flags and "streamers", and workers, their wives and families came out in what was described as "holiday attire." Highlighting the reason for the celebration, a row of cannon was placed in position facing the Tyne. At 3 pm, a carriage containing William and Margaret Armstrong arrived at the gates of the works to "loud and prolonged acclamations." George Hutchinson, manager of the engine works, read a "highly congratulatory address," for which Armstrong thanked him. One rather long sentence in the address referred to the qualities he had displayed in carrying the long work to success: "We who have occasionally been permitted to witness your indomitable perseverance in pursuing your experiments under the most perplexing circumstances, with the most extraordinary zeal and energy, and have observed how frequently your disappointments and failures have been made the key to the successful attainment of your purposes, have become involuntarily interested in your most triumphant success, and do most sincerely rejoice that, to some extent, the value of your invention and service is recognised by the government of our country." Responding, Armstrong expressed a hope that harmony between the firm and its men might be preserved, assuring them that "....it would be his study, as their employer, to add as far as he could to their comforts."(20) The occasion was given the stamp of a true Geordie celebration when a workman sang out a rhyme he had composed in honour of "The Armstrong Gun." Its five verses ended by looking ahead to continuing achievement for him and his workers, and at the wider effects of his invention: "So success to Sir William, and long may it thrive! May his days be as glad as the bees in his hive, Wi` his greatness of mind, he`s the patience of Job, He`s now made a gun that can conquer the Globe.!."(21)

That same afternoon, Armstrong was also congratulated on his honours at a meeting of the Whittle Dene Water Company of which he would remain both a director and chairman for another six years. In reply, he remarked that: "Perhaps the chief ground of congratulation was to be found not so much in the form of any personal aggrandisement of himself as in the additional employment which would be given to the skilled artisans of the district." At about the same time, he was presented with a "memorial" signed by the president, vice-president and secretary of the Law Society of Newcastle upon Tyne and Gateshead, a professional body of which he had once been a member. This gave some sense of how reasonable people could regard his invention as a real public benefit. Again, there was sentiment, but the tone was predictably measured as compared with the enthusiasms of the anonymous Elswick worker: "Your fame in the practical appliances of science to the peaceful purposes of commerce has scarcely been transcended by the Invention which adds power to the Arm of England and ten-fold strength to the national defences. Yet in this your last achievement every home and hearth finds additional safety, and for this every heart owes you and feels corresponding gratitude-a deep personal sentiment is thus added to a national acknowledgement. We venture merely to allude to your Patriotism and disinterestedness in placing your invention at the disposal of the Government."(22)

On 10 May 1859, Armstrong was guest of honour at a banquet held in the Assembly Rooms, Newcastle, and presided over by Sir George Grey, M.P. The vice chairmen for the evening included another local industrialist then near the zenith of a meteoric rise, Charles Mark Palmer. Among the 200 or so-some accounts say as many as 300-of Armstrong`s "friends and admirers" present that evening were other "notabilities" including Robert Stephenson. Various toasts to "Sir William" extended over three hours. Margaret Armstrong was once more present to share in her husband`s glory. (23)

Further large expenditure was needed at the Royal Gun Factory for new shops and equipment, and over the next three years Armstrong machinery was installed and his methods introduced under supervision by him and his assistant, John Anderson. By 1862, when they were at full work, a popular account told its readers that: "....the Armstrong factories [Woolwich and Elswick] may be counted among the most remarkable sights in the kingdom. In each department, whatever the process, it is repeated over and over again, till long parallel lines of similar mills are seen, each busily fashioning a separate gun. Iron at red-heat is first wound round a solid core (representing the bore of the future gun), as tape might be wound around a pencil; then by the action of successive blows from a steam hammer, the strips are welded into a compact cylinder of wrought iron of extreme density. This cylinder, after undergoing several heatings and poundings with the steam hammer, is encompassed with wrought-iron rings of immense strength, and then transmitted to the boring mill. Here the proper calibre is imparted to it; in another department the bore is rifled; in another the outside of the gun is carefully turned; and in yet another, the whole is polished and browned. A gun is several weeks in its passage through these many processes." At almost the same time, processes of manufacture at Elswick were also being described. (24)

THE COURSE OF A MARRIAGE

That a young man of 18 or so should pay court to a woman approaching her mid 20s raises interesting questions about his experience and motivations. Of the contact between William Armstrong and Margaret Ramshaw during his studies in London, or after he returned to join Donkin and Stable in their law practice, there seems to be no record, but in 1835 when he became a partner in that firm, William and Margaret at last felt financially secure enough to marry. Much later, he remarked that at that time it was considered that his choice of wife was a little ambitious. As one who was in a position to know-though admittedly many years later-rather ambiguously put it, Margaret Armstrong was "a woman of strong individuality." (1)

The Armstrongs moved into a house in Jesmond Dene, reasonably well located for access to William`s office in central Newcastle. Except for one charming description from a few years later there seems to be no record of how Margaret spent her time there. However this account does indicate something of the strong individuality which another recollected, and the way in which it was applied to a field in which, years later, she would make her impact on Cragside-gardening. During early spring one year in the mid 1850s, young Fanny Rendel, daughter of James Meadows Rendel, was recuperating from illness by staying with the Armstrongs at Jesmond Dene. She wrote to report her experiences. The conservatory was "quite gay" with flowers and beds filled with snowdrops and crocuses. It was a day of high wind and every half hour or so there was a sharp fall of hail and snow, before the sun once more shone brilliantly between the showers. Although she was in the library, comfortably sheltered from all these variations, she could see that outside: "Mrs Armstrong is walking about with the gardener quite regardless of the weather, her hat tied down over her ears, her dress turned up, and a large plaid round her."(2)

The early years of their marriage are a blank as far as a record of the relationship between William and Margaret is concerned. Then, from a few years later, there survive numerous letters that he wrote home when away on business, and these do throw light on its course. However, it must be stressed that even for this period the evidence is one-sided, for no letters from Margaret to William seem to have survived. Now and later, he not only travelled and worked away from Newcastle, but also took his leisure independently of Margaret. She too might be away when he was at home, working and even entertaining alone. One letter from Jesmond demonstrates the pattern and tone of one of the latter occasions: "I have just received your note, and am glad you are enjoying yourself. As for heat, we have had fires yesterday and today for the wind is in the north east and we have frequent rain. I am sitting puzzling my brain over various perplexities about guns ... I expect George`s party to dine with me today..." (3)

William often told Margaret about his programme, sometimes at great length, and often with technical details. Now and then, he asked her to carry out some task or other, and these might be complicated or even bizarre. In a letter as early as May 1843, when he was enjoying a few days in Rothbury, apparently in the company of Addison Potter, he stressed that "... nothing does me so much good" [as fishing] and gave a brief account of their sport before writing at much greater length about a "little commission" he had for her. It concerned arrangements for his hydro-electric machine As compared with the usual image of a Victorian woman, weak, cosseted and liable to faint, this letter makes clear that at that time at least he saw her as a true helpmate, even in very practical matters. Perhaps he adopted this approach because she was a daughter of the owner of an engineering works; perhaps in part it reflected experiences she had already had during their marriage. The instructions were complicated and his requirements demanding: "I always feared that the boiler would shake when discharging the steam and I think that in order to obviate the probability of accident it will be necessary to apply diagonal props and stays between the legs. The props must be made of wood which must undergo a certain process in order to render it an insulator or non-conductor of electricity similar to the glass. The first stage of this process is to have the wood cut into thin lathes which must be covered up for some days in quick lime in order to extract or dry up the juices of the wood. The wood must afterwards be baked in an oven or before the fire, and then the thin pieces or lathes in which it is cut will have to be cemented together with shellac to form the props of the requisite strength and thickness ... I have also written to Joseph to tell him to get my mother`s pony on Saturday or Sunday at the latest and take out to our house as much quick lime as can be conveniently put into their cart, which will be amply sufficient for the purpose required ... And now comes your slice of the business-when the lime is received it must be laid down under cover (say in the coach house) and a little water must then be sprinkled upon each clod so as to reduce the greater part of the whole into a shelly state. A small watering pan will be the best thing you can use for this purpose and the lime should be allowed to lie about a day to afford time for the water to produce the full effect before the wood is put amongst it. The lathes must then be covered up in the lime, placing them in the centre and not at the bottom of the heap so that they may be surrounded on all sides by the lime, and there they must remain until I get home." After this, it seemed almost incongruous that he should end: "Believe me, most affectionately yours..." (4)

Over the years, on visits or extended periods of work away from the North East, his letters home were often long and usually interesting. They provide detailed insights into his increasing, and increasingly complicated business interests, and whatever their subject, they make clear that he had the capacity to become completely preoccupied with the matter in hand. There was always a danger, perhaps even a likelihood, that business needing his highly focussed attention, as well as often requiring long absences, might bit-by-bit distance each from the other. By the late 1840s, as Elswick works got into production, he often had to visit projects that would use his hydraulic machinery, dock works, railway operations and coaling machines. Through the early 1850s these interests continued, and added to them was his passing role in the Great Exhibition. In January 1852, he was again under pressure: "Since I wrote you last, I have been very busy with the Admiralty and think that now that I have...contact with headquarters I shall get a beginning made." He had seen the First Lord, Francis Baring, and on Wednesday had been with the Surveyor of the Navy to

Blackwall to see the coaling machines. But this was only a part of his workload. "We have got a stiffish order from the St Helens Railway Company ... I have got heavy estimates to prepare here for the London and North Western Railway Company and I fully expect that on Tuesday the London Dock matter will be settled. I am a fixture here with all these and other things until Wednesday next, on which day George Rendel and I expect to return. I am sorry to be so long absent but the present you see is an important crisis in our affairs and I have no alternative but to stay." As he recognised a few days later in a letter to an unknown correspondent: "I have been in London this time so long that Margaret must be despairing of seeing me again..." (5) Soon to all this was added his growing involvement in providing for the conduct of the war in the Crimea. Time and again, he reported on appointments, travel plans and timings, mentioned the people he had met, and sent details of tests of fuses, of experiments with guns and accounts of numerous visits to Shoeburyness. Fortunately, the letters were also relieved by little personal details, including reports on health. An instance came in a letter written on 12 January 1853, when he was working in Kensington on part of Rendel`s scheme for a great new dock complex on the Wirral bank of the Mersey estuary-"these endless Birkenhead plans" as he described them. It was a dreadfully wet day and "I am not in a hurry to go into town today." Then he turned to health: "George has got a bad cold. Mine I think is coming upwards and into my nose. I have got a very good appetite and am getting rapidly stronger although I still use a large pocket handkerchief per day."(6) Despite the one-sidedness of the perspective, it is possible to piece together something of various aspects of their developing relationship from these letters.

First, he regaled her, and must sometimes have risked boring her or making her envious, by reports of the lively times others were having, or details of dinners and parties he had attended. The numerous members of the Rendel family with whom he stayed or was in close contact when in London, seemed always to be travelling somewhere, in connection with work or for weekend breaks or on holidays. In July 1853, Fanny and Stuart were off to Holyhead, and a few days later, they and their parents would form a "Highland Party." He let Margaret know that they proposed to visit Jesmond, either on their way to, or when returning from Scotland. (7) The following February he reported that in celebration of George`s 21st birthday, the Rendel family had taken a "half holiday", even though it was Monday, and had gone off to see the Crystal Palace "... which is now becoming well worth seeing." (8) Though much of his time in London was hard graft, it was relieved by occasional highlights that must have made the regular routines of Jesmond Dene seem rather dull. For example, early in February 1856 he reported he had been to Robert Stephenson`s fine house for a "most sumptuous dinner," and in November 1858 that on the previous evening he had dined with the officers of the Artillery at Woolwich, "and a very magnificent affair it was."(9) Two letters in late February 1859 gave details of his reception by and knighthood from Queen Victoria-which, extraordinarily, he supposed Margaret would have learned about from a report in that morning`s copy of The Times! In the immediate aftermath of this occasion, he thought of taking a short break, but not with his wife: "I feel rather disposed to run down with George to Torquay for a day or two on Saturday and try to pick up my crumbs a little."(10)

More than once he made clear that he not only recognised, but in fact appreciated Margaret`s apparent lack of concern for his every day well being. In adopting such an attitude, she was in marked contrast to Catherine Rendel. On a visit with the Rendels to the Lake District, he reported home: "Today poor Mrs Rendel is in an agony in consequence of two days having passed over without having a letter from Mr Rendel..." In February 1856 he assured Margaret: "I admire your philosophy very much and wish some of it could be instilled into Mrs Rendel, who was in a dreadful way yesterday because Mr Rendel who was at Holyhead had got a stomach ache and was in consequence detained a day longer than was expected. She would certainly have been off by the night train had not a telegraphic message arrived of a satisfactory nature."(11) But on the other hand he eventually also made clear that he resented the fact that whereas, whatever the pressures, he was punctilious in writing to her, she had been by no means a reliable correspondent. Early in 1853, he bluntly told her: "I thought by this time I should have had a letter from you." Six months later things were no better: "I thought this morning was sure to have brought a letter from you, but in this I was disappointed. Perhaps tomorrow will be more propitious." When the next year began, he was with the Rendels at 8 Great George Street, and under heavy pressure from work. He now wrote in obvious exasperation: "It is a week today since I arrived here and, although I have written twice to you, not a syllable have I yet heard from you. Pray when may I expect to receive tidings from you?" Eventually Margaret did respond so that two weeks later he was able to write: "I have received your letter of the 5th for which I thank you."(12)

Gradually his absences and incessant work, and her natural wish to pursue her own interests, seemed to bring a lack of warmth into their relationship. In August 1857 he arrived back in Jesmond one morning when Margaret was at her parent`s home in Bishop Auckland. He wrote to tell her he would attend an "Elswick affair" that evening, but added "… I do not think it at all worth your while to come from Auckland for the sake of attending it. You can however please yourself about it."(13) From early that same year his mode of addressing and signing letters to her changed; a more formal style replacing the earlier, warmer one. Now instead of "My Dearest Margaret" or "My Dearest Maggy" his form of address changed to "My Dear Margaret." He almost invariably ended his letters-written let it be remembered, to his wife-with the signature "WG Armstrong" but from early 1857, instead of "Your affectionate husband, WG Armstrong" changed the form to "Yours affectionately, WG Armstrong." Although, on the occasion of her birthday in 1860, he wrote an unusually full and relaxed letter of good wishes, he never seemed to have, or at least to show, the warm affections of a life partner. In fact, by this time a relationship, which had begun with a boyhood infatuation, had become mundane and sometimes strained.

Some individuals, presumably more sensitive than most, recognised the contribution Margaret made to Armstrong`s success and the strain placed on her by his unremitting dedication to work and frequent and often lengthy absences. George Cruddas, his trusted partner, who was 22 years older, seems to have been one of them. Far from the public gaze, he provided one of the most gracious celebrations of Armstrong`s success at the highpoint of spring 1859, in a simple, and obviously genuine expression of goodwill sent to his wife: "My heartiest wishes are that yourself and Sir William may live in the enjoyment of many years of happiness, may his fame increase with advancing years, and may good health be granted you and God`s blessing be upon you is the ardent desire of, My Dear Lady Armstrong, yours very faithfully, George Cruddas." (14) Another letter of praise for her husband aimed to soften the impact of the disputes caused by his achievements. It was written by the eminent, if controversial, physicist, John Tyndall. In mid February 1864, some six months after the event, he wrote to thank Margaret for the welcome he had received "under your hospitable roof" during the Newcastle meeting of the British Association the previous summer. He continued: "... your husband is a philosopher and I believe a hero. He can therefore bear with indifference the criticisms of both the famous and the ignorant, [* This seems to be the meaning of an unclear passage in Tyndall`s handwriting] but I often thought how you must feel ... and wanted to say to you that among the best men in England your husband might find his supporters and admirers. He is pursuing his own great career - [and] by faithfully doing his work will I doubt not put even his gainsayers to silence. But whether he succeeds in doing this or not, the feelings which manly straightforwardness always elicits in the hearts of honest men will still be his."(15)

It seems reasonable to conclude that the relationship between William and Margaret Armstrong became stale, as they both followed their own interests and commitments. Admittedly, much of the evidence is circumstantial and it would be helpful to have more detailed information. Armstrong seems to have always had an ambivalent attitude to women. On the one hand, given his scientific and business preoccupations and his reserved character, he found many of their concerns trivial; on the other, there are indications, scattered over many years, that at least some of them fascinated him. An early instance of the first of these viewpoints was his 1857 comment on Ellen Hubbard, soon to become Stuart Rendel`s wife. Two months after the death of James Meadows Rendel, in a letter to Margaret, he was outspoken: "At Palace Gardens [the Rendel home] there is nothing new going on except indeed that Stuart and his lady love with her sister are there. She is undoubtedly very pretty and I dare say amiable, but I have not yet succeeded in discerning that she has much in her beyond the very moderate capacity of young ladies in general. I am afraid I

Stuart Rendel c.1864 (Courtesy BAE Systems)

should be sent to Coventry if that remark reached the ears of one of my young lady friends and therefore I trust to your discretion for secrecy."(16) From the same period, there is an example of a very different attitude - and yet it too was expressed in a letter to his wife!

In May 1855, a major banquet was held at the Rendel home. In his account of it, Armstrong referred to two unmarried women who were visiting: "On Monday Miss De Guangos is coming and at present a Miss Jardine, daughter of a Scotch baronet is staying at Kensington." Both names recurred. Early next year Miss Jardine sent him a specimen of her carving in ebony, a paper knife, "...very prettily cut and embellished with painted flowers, initials (WA) in gilt and a fancy portrait of the gun." In 1868, he wrote home from the Athenaeum. After expressing approval for a portrait of Margaret painted by Horsley, he went on: "Miss Guangos as was (now Madame Cavino) has come back to London on a visit. I saw her this morning, as pretty and pleasant as ever - also her husband, a gentlemanly, well-educated young Spaniard....I shall ask them to come to Cragside for a few days, and will try to make their visit hit with the shooting season as they will be nice people for other visitors to meet."(17)

Many years after this, he retained his interest in "pretty" women, and in at least one instance, he attracted regard from an admirer, who expressed herself in effusive, though by no means perfect English. Early in July 1884, Emilia do Riano wrote from Estribo, Granada. She congratulated both him and Margaret on the forthcoming visit by the Prince and Princess of Wales: "Everything will be perfect, directed by your refined and perfect taste, and Lady Armstrong`s supervision." She sent "warmest love," asked him to "Tell dear Lady Armstrong I shall think of her every day and should like to see her gowns." Apparently, Armstrong sent an account of the royal visit and this evoked a warm response: "Dearest Sir William, You are a darling! I cannot say how kind I think it of you to have written me that long letter.....I have always loved and admired you above everybody and nothing goes to my heart as seeing you honoured and cheered."(18)

Armstrong`s own enthusiasms lasted at least until he was about 80. In June 1889, he told George Rendel that at Whitsun they had been visited by Lord and Lady George Hamilton: "She is a very charming woman with lots of go in her." Two years later he sent to Noble an enquiry he had received about a widow`s pension: "I enclose a letter from poor Mrs Thurlow, that pretty woman that everybody liked when she lived in Newcastle."(19) None of these instances suggests any impropriety by Armstrong, but they do seem to indicate that he was by no means as preoccupied, solemn or withdrawn as seems to have been so often supposed. That he told Margaret about them possibly points to a lack of sensitivity. It is far sadder that, as far as can be traced, after the early years he seems not to have thought of her in similar terms.

AN UNSTABLE RELATIONSHIP: ELSWICK AND WOOLWICH 1859 TO 1863

Perhaps it was inevitable that such high points as those reached in 1859 could not continue. As things turned out, three years of success with the Armstrong gun were followed by a crisis. Contributing to the latter were various unfavourable factors. To the public-nationwide, even if not on Tyneside-the "Armstrong factories" of Elswick and Woolwich were "government establishments." Indeed the former was once described as "more in the nature of a contractor`s foundry...an auxiliary and supplement to the gun-factory at the Woolwich arsenal."(1) Armstrong`s own position in relation to the two works was ambiguous. He was head of the Gun Factory and nominally had no part in the Elswick Ordnance Company. Even so, the latter existed only to produce his gun, and in practice, he could not avoid being involved with both establishments. Giving evidence to the Select Committee on Military Organisation on 1 June 1860, he pointed out that his experimental guns had all been made in the Elswick engine works, and that he had no share in the Elswick Ordnance Company. But he also told the committee that he inspected the guns made at Elswick, and "I spend a large portion of my time there."(2) Later that summer it was Armstrong, not the partners of the Elswick Ordnance Company, who invited Captain Andrew Noble of the Royal Artillery to join George Rendel in managing those works. He knew better than anyone the resources of Elswick and continued to draw on them for help in producing his gun. For instance, on New Year`s Eve 1860, from Woolwich, he sent Noble a tracing of a new coil he wanted for use in a 120 pounder: "Be sure that the coil be perfectly sound. It must be hammered on a mandrel as you now make the inside coils."(3)

Implicitly or explicitly, the press too recognised the anomaly of the situation. Discussing activity on the Tyne early in 1861, the Colliery Guardian described Elswick as "Sir William Armstrong`s Ordnance Works."(4) That summer the Newcastle Chronicle in an excellent report, "Elswick as it was and is", mentioned that the ordnance works had in hand a 200 pounder breech loading gun and that "...into this piece the most recent improvements, invented by Sir William Armstrong, will be introduced." A new 15 ton hammer had been installed and would be used for the 300 pounder gun "... ordered for the English (sic) Government at the suggestion of Sir William Armstrong...." Until that summer, when a butt for testing guns was built on the south side of the Tyne, near the west end of the island of King`s Meadows, all guns made at Elswick had to be sent to Woolwich for testing. (5) Giving evidence to an enquiry that year Noble argued that there were advantages in having two sources of supply for the gun: "Rivalry ensures a continuance of a state of activity and efficiency, and of other able minds being employed on the same subject, so that improvements will probably be made in the article manufactured."(6) Next year, before the Select Committee on Ordnance, Brigadier General J St George, Director of Ordnance, maintained that Armstrong had not tried to exercise any undue influence on the workings of the committee. Yet, inevitably, there were situations in which his loyalties might be inclined more to one of the two works than to the other. The existence of such anomalies could be expected to undermine his position if demand for the gun flagged.

From 1859, the Armstrong system of ordnance was adopted by the army and navy, and they began to replace their older types of guns. This programme provided abundant work for both Elswick and Woolwich. At the beginning of 1860, it was anticipated that the reconstructed Gun Factory at Woolwich would make 1,000 Armstrong guns that year and Elswick about 650. (7) At whichever place the guns were made, evidence of their effectiveness was found on the trial ranges at Shoeburyness or Portsmouth. A more eye-catching public demonstration was provided at Eastbourne during that summer, when in the presence of the Duke of Cambridge, the effect of shot and shell from an Armstrong gun, was tried over a distance of 1,000 yards on a Martello tower. Though its walls were nine feet thick, the tower became untenable after the first fifty rounds. (8). More impressive still, a number of relatively minor wars gave opportunity for the merits of the new ordnance system to be proved in the field. The results were by no means uniformly favourable, and indeed showed up a number of problems, registered some failures and caused lively debate about the general success of the Armstrong gun.

There was a brief conflict with China. In summer, 1859 Britain and France failed in an attempt to enforce the ratification of the 1858 Treaty of Tientsin. They followed this up by organising a military expedition to Peking. Its first objective was the forcing of the Taku Forts guarding the entrance to the Peiho River. As Major Hay, Assistant Adjutant General of the Royal Artillery Expeditionary Force, reported, their Armstrong guns were always the first to be ordered up when artillery was required. On 28 March 1861, when he received the freedom of the London Gunmakers` Company "... for the important services he has rendered to the nation by his great improvements in the science of gunnery," Armstrong alluded to "… the satisfactory results obtained with his guns in China." But the inventor of this gun system was inevitably also associated with some of the very unpleasant results of its use-results for which he never seems to have expressed revulsion. Before a parliamentary committee, a British officer described the effects of the gun in the Chinese operations: "Certainly the Armstrong guns, we all thought, were terribly effective, and they saved a great deal of loss on our side. Photographs were taken, showing how the bodies lay about inside. There were an immense number killed by the Armstrong guns ... I saw the segments of the Armstrong shells, lying about just inside the casements, and the wounds you could see, were made by them. Sometimes you found a bit in the wound; you cannot mistake the wound." (9). The general tone of the Chinese venture in which these guns proved themselves was indicated by the fact that after Peking was entered the allies chose to burn the Summer Palace of the Chinese emperors. The invaders even erected a monument bearing an inscription in Chinese, which pointed out that such was the reward of perfidy and cruelty! (10)

In 1863, the Armstrong gun was also employed in a short onslaught on Japan. A British subject had been murdered by followers of Prince Satsuma on an open road which had been "made free to Englishmen by treaty." Admiral Kuper was sent with a fleet from the China Squadron to Satsuma`s capital, Kagoshima, to demand satisfaction. Instead of providing it, the forts there opened fire, and in response Kuper "... then bombarded the town and laid the greater portion of it in ashes." There were conflicting opinions as to the working of the Armstrong guns in the bombardment, but any deficiencies could not be simply blamed on the gun itself; for it was reported later that the men had had little practice with it before the action, and on one of the warships none at all. As a senior British official-himself a naval officer-put it almost fifty years later: "It was not a brilliant exploit in any sense, but its results were invaluable; for the operations of the British ships finally convinced the Satsuma men in the face of Western armaments, and converted them into advocates of liberal progress."!(11)

According to Cochrane, in the course of four years to 1863 the Elswick Ordnance Company received £1,063,000 in orders from the British government. Official figures indicate a sum over £200,000 higher, but this included projectiles and fuses as well as guns. Having peaked in 1860-61, orders fell away sharply in each of the next two financial years. (12) Although for a time Elswick and Woolwich had both been fully employed, there followed sharp variations in activity. At the end of the 1860-61 financial year and before arrangements had been settled for 1861-62, operations in the Rifled Ordnance Department at Woolwich were restricted solely to completion of orders in hand. 250 forge men and others were laid off. However, by midyear the works had resumed its former activity and was turning out a large number of heavy naval guns. Early in 1861 the coal and iron trades of the Tyne were depressed and activity in its then great chemical industry was described as "very so-so", but, though men in some industries were on short time, the Elswick Ordnance Works was fully employed and labour skilled in the manipulation of iron was said to be "tending" there. The tone in parliament and of the country seemed to be such that "... there is little fear that we shall have to record any cessation or diminution in the manufacture of Sir William`s deadly engines of warfare." In fact, a sharp down turn did occur and by May 300 of the men employed on the night shift in the ordnance works had been paid off. Again, there was a revival and by late December, great activity was reported in the ordnance department. It was remarked that no outsider was allowed in unless he had a letter from the Under Secretary of State. (13)

On 1 May 1862, the London International Exhibition opened. The world had changed greatly over the 11 years since the Great Exhibition, not least in relation to the activities in which Armstrong was now involved. As one Victorian historian put it: "... no one felt any longer any of the hopes which floated dreamily and gracefully round the scheme of 1851. There was no thought of a reign of peace any more. The Civil War was raging in America. The Continent of Europe was trembling all over with the spasms of war just done, and the premonitory symptoms of war to come...Poetry and prophecy had nothing to say to it."(14) This time the exhibition had a section devoted to ordnance. There were 15 exhibitors, including CW Lancaster, Captain Blakeley, the Mersey Steel and Iron Company, the Secretary of State for War, the Whitworth Rifle and Ordnance Company and Sir WG Armstrong and Company. The Handbook to the Industrial Department of the Exhibition described the Armstrong gun as a product of "... the triumph of skilled labour directed by science." (Among innumerable other trade displays in South Kensington, on this occasion the Sheffield firm of Naylor Vickers exhibited steel bells!)(15) In fact, circumstances were now moving strongly against both Armstrong and the Elswick Ordnance Company.

By 1862, Woolwich and Elswick together had largely completed the task of reequipping the armed forces. Since 1859, Elswick alone had supplied 3,500 guns, in calibres from 2.5 to 7 inches. It also made a number of large naval guns, which it was better able to produce than Woolwich, because, at least until 1862, it had a heavier hammer than was available there. The new weapon system was unquestionably vastly superior to what had gone before, but it was also much more expensive. Moreover, there was a good deal of evidence that costs of production and the prices paid to the Elswick Ordnance Company were higher than those for Woolwich. The Ordnance Company estimated it cost £426 to make a 110-pounder gun at Woolwich in March 1862 whereas their cost was £500. In material and labour costs, Elswick was the cheaper works-£268 per gun as compared with £289.50-but on the other hand, it had costs that its rival either did not have, or failed to allow for. For example, Elswick provided for depreciation and interest on capital, and also for a profit per gun of £36. 11s. War Office officials reckoned the gap in costs was even wider, the Accountant General at the War Office stating that the price paid to Elswick for a 100-pounder gun was 50% more than for the same article made at Woolwich. The Superintendent of War Office laboratories reckoned £80,000 of the £292,875 paid for projectiles from Elswick had been profit.

Although the costs quoted seemed unfavourable to the Elswick Ordnance Company, it was acknowledged by some of those involved that the evidence might be unreliable. The Accountant General reckoned direct comparisons between the two plants was difficult if not impossible, in part because the government factories neither used a professional accountant nor were their accounts kept by double entry. In any case, even if true, the claims meant that it was under Armstrong control that the Royal Gun Factory had been more efficient and economical than Elswick operations. A statement from the War Office indicated that for certain guns and projectiles supplied by Elswick at a cost of £593,276, as much as £242,174 could have been saved if they had instead been made at Woolwich. But again, there were complicating factors. John Anderson, Armstrong`s assistant at Woolwich, believed that their unit costs might be reduced still further if they had the benefit of the orders at present going to Elswick, and George Rendel attributed his own higher costs partly to the fact that they had made fewer guns than Woolwich. Anderson paid eloquent tribute to the part played by Armstrong in making Woolwich a success, pointing out that he did not know any man who had given "one 20th" of the attention to the appliances for making the gun or putting it together. In relation to Elswick, he was frank enough to admit: "Perhaps I might not work the gun factory so well if I had not a little opposition."(16)

The reliability of often-striking cost contrasts between the two gun plants was twice questioned in the course of an 1863 report from the Select Committee on Ordnance. Firstly, "It is obvious that the value of this comparison rests entirely upon the accuracy of the principle upon which the cost of the articles produced at Woolwich has been arrived at, and the evidence on this subject is conflicting." Secondly, "A uniform system of accounts should be adopted for the manufacturing departments at Woolwich, by which the cost of guns and other produce may be clearly ascertained." (17)

Overall a number of circumstances, many external, but some determined by his own character and temperament, worked against a continuation of Armstrong`s involvement in the Woolwich operation. As Stuart Rendel summed it up long afterwards, there was a natural reaction after the first enthusiasm for the Armstrong gun. It upset those connected with the superseded system and disappointed advocates of alternative new ones. The civilian management which Armstrong introduced at Woolwich "gave serious umbrage" to the artillery people who had formerly run it, made a victim of Eardley Wilmot, the Gun Factory`s previous superintendent, and "deprived the corps not only of prestige, but of highly valued berths for its superior officers." Professional journals and institutions provided opportunities for verbal exchanges between various critics and disputants. "In short, Lord Armstrong found that he was being exposed to publicity in a form peculiarly obnoxious to his reserved and reticent character. He suffered acutely under the sting of heated and personal controversy." (18)

In October 1862 there occurred an event vital to the future of Elswick and the direction of Armstrong`s life. It was decided that output of Armstrong guns should be reduced, and the Secretary of State for War informed the Elswick Ordnance Company that he would send it no more orders. Three months later, it was made clear that Woolwich would undertake the entire manufacture of rifled ordnance, a decision well received there because it raised the prospect of reinstating large numbers of artisans and labourers already laid off. (19) This decision produced a radical response from Armstrong. On 5 February, he wrote from Newcastle to the Under Secretary of State for War. His letter was direct, and clear but also restrained and reasonable- in short, very much a reflection of his character. He pointed out that the ending of the government agreement with the Elswick Ordnance Company had left it with a much larger plant than could be run successfully, and the partners of that company therefore wanted him to join them to help. "After much consideration I have come to the conclusion that under all existing circumstances my proper course is to give up my appointment under Government and I accordingly send you herewith my formal resignation. I am anxious however that as little inconvenience as possible shall be occasioned at the War Office by my taking this step and I beg there may be no hesitation in applying to me for any information or assistance which it might be in my power to afford. I shall remain here until Monday to carry out some experiments and shall be at the War Office on Thursday." A week later Earl De Grey wrote to accept his resignation and to inform him that the Secretary of State "... cannot permit your official connection with this Department to cease without conveying to you, as I am now directed to do, his high sense of the zealous and efficient manner in which you have invariably discharged your public duties, and of the advantages which Her Majesty`s Government have derived from your services while holding the appointments which you have now resigned."(20) The Times recognised Armstrong`s situation had been intrinsically untenable: "So long as he held this official post his position was at best ambiguous, and the less scrupulous of his enemies strove to turn it to his disadvantage."(21) However wise those words were, the changes meant that Woolwich, and still more Elswick and Armstrong, had to find new directions with some urgency.

For a considerable part of 1863, efforts were made either to sell the ordnance works to the government or to secure adequate recompense for termination of its contract. The total capital outlay on the works had been £168,000, but after assessments of the plant and making due allowance for depreciation, by January 1863 the company informed the British government it was willing to sell the whole operation for £137,000. When this offer was rejected, attention turned to compensation. The matter dragged on and was eventually settled by arbitration. £65,000 was to be paid, but, as the company was allowed to keep some depreciated plant, it has been suggested the real value of the compensation received was £85,000. (22) The next step was to merge the ordnance and engine works to form a new company, and the deed for its formation as Sir WG Armstrong and Company was signed on 1 January 1864. Of its seven partners, three were survivors from the original engineering company - Armstrong, Cruddas and Lambert. The other four were George Rendel and Andrew Noble from the ordnance works, Cruddas`s son, William, and Percy Westmacott, head of the engine works. Through the years, Sir WG Armstrong and Company would remain active in commercial engineering, but it also possessed a major, recently built ordnance works for which there seemed little likelihood of obtaining large new orders from either the army or the navy. As consideration began of the problems created by these circumstances, Armstrong also faced a new assault on the quality of his gun.

ARMSTRONG AND NOBLE

William Armstrong first met Andrew Noble at some unknown point during the second half of the 1850s when both men were involved in the evaluation of advances in field guns. Armstrong had been a manufacturer of engineering products for about ten years; Noble was a respected, successful and young army officer. Early in 1860, when busy at Woolwich, Armstrong told Noble: "I look forward to a jolly contest with Whitworth during the ensuing summer and have lots of new guns coming on for trial." On 4 August, he invited him to join George Rendel in managing the Elswick Ordnance works. Initially the engagement was on a trial, short-term basis, but it became permanent, as a result of which Noble was involved with Elswick operations for the next 55 years. In 1860, he was the newcomer in a remarkably young team of leading men. Armstrong was almost 50, but Percy Westmacott was 29, George Rendel 27 and Noble 28. Throughout the last forty years of his life, Armstrong was in close contact with Noble, who from the 1870s was effectively day-to-day head of the company. Of all his colleagues, Armstrong found him the most congenial. Their compatibility was recognised by outsiders: "Those who had the privilege of knowing both the late Lord Armstrong and Sir Andrew Noble will readily understand that when they met, natural attraction induced them to work together. No man ever had a clearer eye for reading character than Lord Armstrong. That was one of the chief elements of his success; combined as it was, with a wise determination to pay true value ungrudgingly for services. In Captain Noble he found a young man ambitious, energetic and full of enthusiasm for scientific study and research."(1)

Early in their relationship, Noble was the one who was learning. He had been a military officer; now he had to master engineering and the economics of business. Armstrong was a careful teacher, though sometimes rather pedantic. Two 1865 letters reveal him in this educational role. The blast furnaces at Elswick were being brought into production, and he had very definite ideas as to how they should be run. On Friday 21 July, he wrote from the quiet of the Athenaeum with detailed guidance about operations in this new division of their business. His comments are more fully considered elsewhere. A few months earlier, writing from Cragside, he provided his new colleague with an elementary lesson in the economics of production. The subjects were the "studs" used in the gun and the materials of which the guns were made: "Nothing very new occurs to me respecting cost of production. The points are: 1st The question of cost depends not only upon value of labour and material but also upon considerations of interest, depreciation and liability to change of process. That it is possible to make machinery to perform all operations without any hand labour at all and yet that articles so manufactured might be more expensive than those made altogether by hand; that turning is cheaper than planing because the tool is always cutting; that the cost of studs may be set against the extreme accuracy which is required in the hexagonal projectile. 2nd That coils are cheaper than steel cylinders both as regards value of material and facility of turning and that they are much more secure against concealed flaws."(2)

To some extent the close working relationship between the two men was due to the fact that Noble seems never to have shown any tendency to question the opinions of his senior colleague, but over the years there developed both mutual respect and affection. Their voluminous correspondence covered many things - technical matters, company issues, family events, Noble`s health and his apparent inability to avoid overwork, their journeys and visits. It also revealed Armstrong`s own intense activity. Three often repeated themes of his letters-a search for scientific recognition, the importance of attention to health and the relative unimportance of the pursuit of money-highlighted Noble`s problems and the concern and generally greater good sense of Armstrong. A continuing if minor issue between them was the legibility of Noble`s handwriting.

In May 1861 writing from 9 Hyde Park Street, Armstrong sent a gentle rebuke: " I have received from you an old telegram which I suppose is such to show that my writing is liable to be misread as well as yours. But this is my conjecture because after calling in the assistance of all the adepts at your writing in this house I am unable to decipher the note by which the telegram is accompanied." Early in 1865 he wrote: "I got your letter of yesterday, the greater part of which Stuart and I between us have managed to read and as to the remainder we fancy we guess your meaning rightly." (3)

With Armstrong`s help, Noble sought scientific recognition, specifically the honour of membership of the Royal Society. It proved a long search. In February 1860, Armstrong informed him: "I return your Royal Society paper signed….." but year after year there seemed to be problems, not all of them caused by Noble. In February 1865 Armstrong wrote: "I was at Lubbock`s yesterday and met Tyndall there. He said he did not know what he had been thinking about to sign your R.S paper in the general knowledge instead of the personal knowledge column, but he will correct the mistake." A few years later it was a failure on Noble`s part which threatened another attempt. Tyndall wrote on 5 March 1870 to "My Dear Armstrong, It is now Saturday, but Noble has not come ... I must know his method and results; it will greatly strengthen me on the Council. You may rely upon my readiness to back so good a man." On Monday, Armstrong asked Noble: "Why did you not see Tyndall….I do trust you will call before leaving London." Three days later, at the end of another letter, he was more optimistic: "I am very glad to hear of your doings at the Royal Society. I feel quite confident of your election this year." Noble was at last elected a Fellow of the Royal Society in the course of the year. (4)

Another leading theme was to urge Noble not to be excessively concerned if, despite their best efforts, they were unsuccessful in any venture. In spring 1862, they were having difficulties in France. Armstrong suggested Noble should visit Rouen to sort out problems with some castings, but he also tried to calm him down: "I fear you will be worrying yourself very much about this French business, but recollect what cannot be ended must be endured. Such things will happen in the best regulated families….Make the best you can of it and pocket the loss. It was not your fault ..." Commitment to work meant that Noble was frequently unwell, and from the start of their association Armstrong pressed him to take better care of his health, for despite the long period during which he too had worked unceasingly, he had at last learned that in the longer run moderation was the better course. When he wrote from the Athenaeum early in 1867 he was outspoken: "Do learn common sense by experience and consider health before money. Think about securing it as much or more than you think about making money. It is absolutely astonishing to me how a man of your understanding can be so infatuated as you are upon this subject. Unless you completely change I would not insure your life till you are 40 at any premium." (5) By that time Noble was already 34.

Shortly before the British Association meetings in Newcastle, Armstrong asked Andrew Noble to look over the draft of his presidential address, but "...don`t give yourself too much trouble about it. You should think of nothing but play till you get well. I am glad to hear continued accounts of your progress...you are not going to be allowed to do any sort of work until you get strong."(6) As ill health became a common topic, Armstrong slipped into the habit of communicating his own problems as well as expressing concern and even recommending possible remedies for those of the other man. Early in 1871, they were both under the weather when he wrote: "Mind you take care of your cold. It is least trouble to attack it at first. My leg is getting nicely well. The place where I felt the crack is now like a big black eye but no swelling and I walk without difficulty if not too fast." Predictably, Noble failed to take caution and was rebuked for his failure: "You are lucky to have escaped the natural effects of travelling at night with a cold on the chest. You might just as well have gone by the 10 train on Saturday morning. You will get caught some day with a bad illness."(7) Similar themes recurred in their correspondence for more than a quarter of a century. A sequence of letters in 1869 provides examples of the rich mixture of the features of their relationship.

Early in 1869, Andrew Noble was away on company business when his wife, Marjorie, gave birth to another addition to their family. Armstrong adopted a playful as well as slightly critical tone in his letter to the absentee father. His remarks also raise interesting speculations about either Marjorie Noble or his own powers of observation in these not very familiar matters: "If our telegram reached you in a more intelligible form than yours reached us you will have been made aware that you are the father of another child which this time is of the feminine gender. The event occurred this morning and when I left Jesmond all was going on well, and I have no doubt is still doing so. I saw Mrs Noble only last night and observed nothing unusual about her." (8)

In mid May, he was in more mundane mood when he informed Noble about his return to the North: "I shall be at the Central Station tomorrow evening by Express, but go direct forward to Morpeth and thence to Cragside where I shall remain until Wednesday evening." Often he mixed company news with family matters, reference to their travels or issued invitations to stay. There were interesting details, often quite unrelated to business. For example on 30 June, he discussed their "segment" shell [a variation on shrapnel] at a time when Noble was at Tavistock for some experiments, before telling him he had seen his family at Cragside on Sunday: "...all well and flourishing." He then mentioned he was having problems with game birds: "The jackdaws are rather persecuting the young pheasants having devoured 4 or 5, but are now suffering the just penalty of their depredations, by traps." (9)

Equally typically, before the end of the year he was once more worrying over Noble`s health, but even then could not avoid including items of business. On Saturday 20 November, he wrote from Cragside; "It is no use your coming here for a night ... Make your arrangements to come here with me on Friday or Saturday and take a couple of days for amusement after all your worry and work." (10) Less than three weeks later from the 8 Great George Street offices he wove self interest into solicitation for his colleague`s well being: "My Dear Noble, please to telegraph me on receipt of this and say whether you got yourself a thick fur rug when in London. If not I will get you one and bring it down. I presume you have mine with you. Please telegraph at once that I may have the benefit of using it on returning. I shall come down on Friday morning or possibly go as far as York tomorrow afternoon."(11)

Armstrong sometimes seemed eager to manage even the details of the search for improvements into which he steered Noble. In summer 1876, he discussed his problems with a distinguished visitor, and more than five years later added as a postscript to a letter concerning the wire used in building up the construction of guns: "I hope you are better and slowly acquiring common sense in the management of your health." When he was ill during summer 1883, Armstrong not only recommended rest and time off work, but this time had a specific remedy: "I would suggest your writing to Messrs Brand and Co. 10 and 11 Stanhope Street, Piccadilly, W. and order them to send you every day for a week by parcels post a small pot of essence of beef. The best kind will not keep after the pot is opened. It is a splendid thing for giving strength in cases under medical treatment."(12)

Year after year the amiable relations between Armstrong and Noble continued. The older man valued the scientific abilities of the younger man, fully recognised his capacity for work and appreciated his devotion to the firm. He realised that, for various reasons, the Rendel brothers were now less wholly bound up in the firm, and Noble`s unwavering commitment was accompanied by an increase of his power within it. It seems that the only important instance in which these good relations were for a time seriously impaired occurred in the 1880s at the time of the merger with Mitchell and the creation of a new limited liability company, Sir WG Armstrong Mitchell and Company Limited. After they were restored, Armstrong explicitly recognised that, whatever the outward appearance, Noble rather than he was now effective head of the firm.

As the plans for the merger and public flotation developed, George Rendel for a time left the company for a senior post at the Admiralty. Though now an MP, Stuart Rendel, who had serious doubts about the amalgamation, was eager to ensure that he and his friends secured large shareholdings. The only Rendel brother now on the spot was Hamilton, a leading factor in the Elswick engineering works. Armstrong`s dispute with Noble stemmed from a disagreement with Stuart and the intervention of Hamilton in the interests of his brother. Armstrong reacted decisively in a letter written to Stuart, but on the same day, he wrote severely to Noble, who had once more revealed his concern about money for which Armstrong had so often chided him in the past. Referring to Stuart`s letter which had reopened the issue of share allocations, he went on: "I cannot doubt that this is the result of the most regrettable step which you took of telling him you did not care what shares he got if you were allowed to increase in proportion. You thus made the question a mere personal one between you and him and implied that the settlement made at the last meeting was not incompatible with an increase on his part. I must also tell you that I was greatly annoyed on Wednesday by Hamilton coming to me fresh from an interview with you and addressing me as if I were your opponent as well as Stuart`s in the matter of requiring new shares. You must excuse my saying that I am and always have been sufficiently alive to your interests to render it unnecessary for Hamilton to contend with me as your advocate either at Board meetings or in private." He had drafted a letter to Stuart "... but upon reflection I think it folly to harass myself any further about these personal contentions for shares and I have therefore to request that you as next in seniority will inform your colleagues that I withdraw from the chairmanship of the company upon the ground of my failure to affect a settlement of the share question upon a satisfactory basis and my inability to stand the worry of contentions on the subject. I did intend to come in this morning and bring Stuart`s letter with me but I am really not equal to any more dissensions so I send this by messenger." Notwithstanding his obvious distress, he ended his letter "Yours affly"; he signed his letter to Stuart "Yours truly." (13)

Immediately, Armstrong began to repair this damaged relationship with Noble. Only a day after sending his letter by messenger, he wrote again. He still thought it unwise for Noble to exceed the limit of £213,000 in shares, but he now set out his thoughts reasonably and at the end was conciliatory: "I would not have taken the course I have done had I felt that I possessed your undivided confidence in the difficult matters we have had to contend with, but you take counsel with Hamilton as well as with me, and in some instances, as in the case of determining the number of shares you were to take, you have been more guided by him than by me." In further action in this field, he wanted to make sure that Noble consulted him alone. He ended: "Forgive my plain speaking in this matter. I dare say it is unpleasant but to understand the action I have taken you must understand the state of my mind." (14) Early next year, when they were considering the development of a new shipyard, Armstrong stressed that he wanted the engine works, the new steel works and the "ship department" to all be answerable to the Managing Committee. Noble would be at the centre of the whole extended structure: "The position which you will henceforth occupy will entitle you to a leadership which I think will have a salutary effect." By summer 1884, Armstrong Mitchell had responded to pressures from Italy by agreeing to build a new works at Pozzuoli on the Bay of Naples. A year later there had been scarcely any progress and Armstrong sent Noble his ideas of what should be done. But he made clear he would not impinge on the latter`s freedom of decision taking-unless it meant a lack of methodical action!: "You will of course consider this letter merely in the nature of advice. If you prefer any other course of proceeding I shall make no opposition provided it be not of a desultory nature and that it does not involve you in any personal labour beyond the giving of general instructions."(15)

NEW COMPETITORS AND NEW GUN TRIALS

Even during the period of the apparent triumph of the Armstrong gun, trials of other systems of ordnance continued. A few were from overseas. As early as December 1859 Armstrong informed his wife: "My little 6 pounder of 3 cwt was tried yesterday against the new French gun of about four times the weight and beat it hollow." At some stage in the trials a 20 pounder was submitted by Krupp and a 12 pounder by the Bochum Company. At the end of July 1861, at the summer meetings of the Institute of Mechanical Engineers in Sheffield, an 18 pounder produced by Bessemer from a single ingot of his own steel was exhibited. He contended that the steel works he and Eardley Wilmot had planned for Woolwich "... would have rendered wholly unnecessary the erection of a second arsenal at Elswick."(1) Armstrong had given the decision against the use of steel in guns which caused the failure of Bessemer`s scheme, but he also claimed to be not only confident in his own gun, but open to any attempt to better it. In October 1861, the Ordnance Select Committee spent two days at Elswick. (2)

Despite adoption of his system two years before, and the progress of replacement of older systems, in both the artillery and navy, a lively and sometimes unpleasant press debate about the Armstrong gun was now underway. In The Times Captain Edward P Halsted was particularly critical. On 25 November, Armstrong wrote a long response, which The Times published two days later. It was reprinted as a pamphlet. He pointed out that notwithstanding the continuing controversy, 1,622 of his guns had been proved, and he adopted a lofty stance in face of opposition: "My time is too limited to permit of my involving myself needlessly in controversial warfare[!], and it is not reasonable to expect that I should continually have to defend my gun in the columns of the press, through all the stages of its progress and development, against incessant attacks by opponents unusually ill-informed as to their facts." He explained why he refused to engage more fully in controversy: "In the long run the best weapon must win the day, whether it be mine or another`s, and I am as sure that my gun cannot be written up into success, as I am that if successful it will never be written down."(3) A few weeks later Halsted again wrote to The Times but this time his letter was not published, and he too chose to publicise his views in a pamphlet, "The Armstrong Gun: A Rejoinder to the Letter of Sir William Armstrong 27 November 1861, published in The Times." It was Halsted`s turn to seek to occupy the high ground of offended dignity. He did so rather less graciously than his opponent, noting that the latter`s Times letter "characterises my alleged misstatements throughout in terms, all of which are personal, incourteous, and more or less offensive up to the point of impugning my veracity."(4) Under such circumstances, discussion was unlikely to yield the truth.

Most important of all rivals, Joseph Whitworth had never given up the struggle to have his gun replace the Armstrong gun. For the 1858 trials he had only submitted designs or government guns which he had re-bored, but since then he had spent much more on experiments than Armstrong, had built his own guns, and he was determined they should be tried against the system which had triumphed earlier.(5) Even whilst Armstrong dominated the Royal Gun Factory, Whitworth kept up the pressure, and he received strong support from influential sources, including the important journals, the Mechanics Magazine and Engineering. Early in 1860, his ordnance was tried against the Armstrong gun in Liverpool, and its strength as a competitor was recognised. In March, the contest between the two systems was brought before experts. Armstrong seems to have tried an Olympian attitude. On 1 March, he wrote to Margaret Armstrong from Southend: "Whitworth and his gun are of course all the talk. Both he and I have strong supporters so I fancy we shall have a fine contest during the ensuing summer. In the meantime, I am content to let him have his flourish. I shall quietly work away trying to improve at all points."(6) Three weeks later, he reported on a confrontation at the

Institute of Civil Engineers. His tone was jaunty, but there was an undertone of uncertainty: "The great gun discussion closed last night at the Civil Engineers. Whitworth had one of his guns there and read in a very clumsy way a very clumsy statement written in a very indifferent spirit-that is to say rather sour and surly. The President summed up and the matter stands just as it was. Had I not opposed and shown fight, Whitworth would I have no doubt extracted an expression of opinion in his favour from the Institute. As it is he has met with a decided check. It is extraordinary how the press has been silenced since my appearance." (7) But Whitworth fought on, and in summer 1861, when activity at Elswick had begun to flag, he visited Woolwich Arsenal and entered into an agreement for official trials of his guns. Immediately afterwards the Arsenal was provided with two 80 pounder Whitworth guns to try against two of the same size made in the Royal Gun Factory, in other words Armstrong guns. (8) In early November 1862, only a few days after Elswick received notice of the end of its business with the armed services, Armstrong felt compelled to write once more to defend his gun in the columns of The Times. This time the immediate cause was an article on ordnance in the Army and Navy Gazette, which seemed, "... not so much what is to be fairly said upon the subject as what can be said upon the subject by the friends of Mr Whitworth." He affected to be disdainful of the controversy into which circumstances had forced him, as well as limited by his official position: "I have neither time nor inclination to follow my anonymous literary assailants round the circle of the daily and weekly press, or to contradict or correct the various pieces of intelligence that appear with significant persistence about my guns. My position exposes me to attacks and one-sided statistics seem to be a favourite weapon with the friends of some inventions. Usually I am compelled from press of business to leave them unanswered. I can only trust that my silence in such cases will be imputed to the right cause." He pointed out that in February 1860 he had suggested a "friendly contest" of his and Whitworth`s guns. "I still hope that our contest may be of an amiable nature, although my friendly dispositions have of late been rather severely tested." Four days later, Whitworth responded, pointing out that although the Ordnance Select Committee had visited Elswick, they had not been to his works. He also said Armstrong had

"... made some statements, the tone of which I regret." (9)

The Armstrong letter to The Times had contained a suggestion: "... it is high time that a proper and systematic comparison should be made between Mr Whitworth`s gun and mine, and that the public should no longer be swayed about by inaccurate statements and by desultory and uncertain trials, which leave such ample room for partisans on either side to put their own constructions on the results obtained." (10) This led on to full and very protracted enquiry into the merits of the two systems.

HEALTH, PRESSURE OF WORK AND NEW VENTURES: EARLY CRAGSIDE AND THE RIDSDALE OPERATIONS

Frequent ill-health had led to numerous trips to the countryside for William George Armstrong in childhood. Later in life his physical exercise seems to have been confined to fishing, shooting and often vigorous walking. His powers of concentration on one objective at a time to the exclusion of other concerns achieved impressive results in invention and technical applications, but seem to have done so at the cost of strains on his physical well-being. During the early years of the engineering plant he worked exceedingly hard, later claiming that during his first 15 years at Elswick he had taken not a single weeks holiday and many nights worked until 10 or 11 pm. (1) There were frequent visits to and long periods of labour in London in an unending search for orders to keep his works fully engaged. Even if business was available it was important to make sure it was profitable; the failure of the Elswick designed locomotive in their earliest years had been a salutary lesson in this respect. When he was in London, his working day followed a heavy and by no means healthy course. Staying with the Rendels in their Westminster home early in 1854, he wrote:: "... since I came I have been daily going through the same process of breakfasting at half past eight, business till 7 and bed at 11, generally playing one game of chess with Mrs Rendel after dinner." The problem of securing remunerative work continued; as he told Margaret early in 1856, "I have been working hard for orders and although there is lots of work coming forward there is great reluctance at present to go to immediate expense."(2)

A few years later, there were new pressures; managing the gun factory at Woolwich, attendance at gun trials in exposed locations, and tensions accompanying committees of enquiry. Meanwhile the everyday labours of the ordinary commercial world continued. Completely different, but another call on his time and energies, he now moved in circles in which grand dinners and parties took up some of his evenings. In a spring 1859 letter to Margaret`s mother, he referred to such commitments. As rare occasions, they might be enjoyable but they easily became burdensome. He had been at a party at General Peel`s the previous evening where "Dukes and Duchesses, Ambassadors and Ministers were as thick as blackberries." For various reasons he did not find the party routine congenial: "A little of this sort of thing is very well by way of curiosity but I may easily have too much and I find the late hours do not suit my long day`s work. However I am in better health than usual notwithstanding my hard work."(3) Later that year, reorganisation of the gun factory and the need to equip artillery batteries to be sent out to China required him to be at Woolwich every day "... and very troublesome business it is ..." On Friday evening 9 December, he explained the situation to Margaret: "I have just returned from Woolwich, without lunch or anything to eat since 8 o`clock it now being half past 6, but while dinner is preparing I write a few lines to let you know my doings." He added, "I have been rather threatened with my complaint of last year but think I am now right again." A few weeks later he travelled to Dover to see the blowing up of old fortifications by shells fired from his gun. The weather was "... awfully bad-snow, rain and wind, no shelter and mud ankle deep ... How I escaped taking cold I cannot understand, but I did so."(4) Shoeburyness was a notoriously exposed location and he and his associates now spent many days there. Visits to the test ranges carried on long after he left government service as month after month his gun was tried against Whitworth`s. The parties continued in London but more than ever, he was now feeling the wear and tear of this way of life. In June 1865, he reported on a "tremendous swell party" at the home of the Count de Paris, where the company had included the Prince of Wales, the Duke of Marlborough, Prince Mustapha of Egypt and "a dozen others of the same sort." "The count made himself very agreeable to everyone, but I get tired of these things." Once more, he was under the weather: "I am still not well and am taking hylefools [?] medicine which I dare say is doing me good."(5)

In addition to being very conscious of his state of health, while at the same time conducting his everyday working life in a manner scarcely favourable to it, the experience of many of Armstrong`s leading contemporaries in engineering provided vivid illustrations of how injurious both to good health and long life such a highly pressured work regime might be. Some of these men were good friends. He had known James Meadows Rendel since before Elswick works was built, and for many of his London visits in the 1850s the Rendel Westminster home was his own London base. Rendel now had a wide range of engineering commissions both in Britain and overseas. Although he did not go out himself, his firm designed and constructed the East India and Madras Railway, and the Pernambuco Railway. In 1853-55, the firm reported on the harbour of Rio de Janeiro. He personally visited and advised on harbour works at Genoa and prepared a scheme for a new naval dock and arsenal at Spezia. At more or less the same time, he was consulted about plans for development of Cuxhaven and construction of a naval dockyard on the River Jade near Wihelmshaven, more than once visiting north Germany in connection with these schemes. He planned a canal across the Isthmus of Suez. By summer 1856, though only in his 57th year, he was tired and his health was failing. Late in October he caught a cold and within little more than three weeks died. Armstrong was with him daily during his illness, and realised that Rendel`s almost unexpected passing was caused by "his frame being apparently too exhausted."(6) In a letter to Robert Stephenson two days afterwards he made clear it had been a moving experience to be present: "Our dear friend Rendel died on Friday last and will be interred at Kensal Green on Wednesday. His end was calm, dignified and peaceful and the memory of it has left a soothing influence upon his family which mitigates their grief. I was with him in his last moments and my long intimacy with him terminated with many endearing circumstances."(7) Afterwards he was active in helping to ensure that Rendel`s business passed in good shape to his two senior engineering sons, Alexander and George. The shock demonstration of the deadly effects of incessant work was soon followed by others.

I K Brunel was four years older than Armstrong. Though above all remembered for railway engineering, bridge construction and schemes for great iron ships, he too had been involved in provision of war supplies for the Crimea and had turned his great ability and energy to design of heavy ordnance. In the mid 1850s, he was above all preoccupied with the Great Eastern, the building of which occupied four years before she was at last floated in January 1858. That year he felt compelled to decline the presidency of the Institute of Civil Engineers on grounds of ill health. The Great Eastern began her maiden voyage on 7 September 1859. Two days earlier Brunel had suffered a stroke, and died on the 15th at his Westminster home. He was only 53; the life of his father, the distinguished engineer Mark Brunel, had ended only ten years before, when he was 79. On Saturday, 24 September, Armstrong wrote to tell Margaret that on the previous Tuesday he had attended "poor Brunel`s" funeral; "I grieve very much for his loss." He went on: "Robert Stephenson I am sorry to say is ill. I fear almost dangerously so."(8) George Stephenson, who, in his young working days had lived the hard life of a common labourer, had survived into retirement to die at 67. Robert, raised in relative comfort, had like Brunel and Rendel lived through the stress of the railway mania. Almost at the same time as Brunel died, he returned mortally ill from Norway to which he had travelled on business. Less than three weeks after Armstrong first wrote of his ill health, Stephenson too was dead. He was 56. His passing was marked as a calamity in northern England. On the industrial rivers of the North East, all work ceased, shipping lay silent and flags flew at half-mast. Through the streets of Newcastle 1,500 employees of the locomotive works of Robert Stephenson and Company processed to a memorial service. From London Armstrong wrote to tell Margaret about the funeral service and burial in Westminster Abbey. (9)

The deaths of these three great engineers and friends coincided with heavy pressure on Armstrong from various directions, and he too was visibly under the weather. In a diary entry for Thursday 18 September 1859, his good friend, Thomas Sopwith, noted that he heard of Brunel`s illness only on the day before he died. His illness had been talked about that evening at Armstrong`s dinner table: "... and his death took place at the very hour when my friends and myself were separating after spending the evening at Jesmond." Sopwith went on:

"Constant occupation and anxiety seem at present to be telling on Armstrong`s health, which I fear is far less robust than was Brunel`s a few years ago; and on every side I see examples of premature decay and death, induced by undue pressure of mental exertion."(10) The danger that this sort of intense activity could cause serious health problems other than the physical effects, which cut short the lives of his friends among the great engineers, had been shown even at Elswick. In spring 1851, Armstrong had engaged a 21-year-old engineer to work in the drawing office. By mid 1853, Percy Westmacott was manager of the engine works. When Armstrong went to Woolwich in 1859, he left him in full technical direction of that section of their operations. Early the following year Westmacott had to travel to Dresden in an effort to recover from a nervous breakdown. In this instance recovery and a long life lay ahead, but the warning was clear enough. (11)

Although at the time of the deaths of Brunel and Stephenson Armstrong was fully employed, over the next few years he began to make at least some provision to reduce the pressures under which he worked. In summer 1860, he persuaded Andrew Noble to join George Rendel in running the Elswick Ordnance Works. Over the next three years, for reasons not of his own choosing, he lost both British outlets for his guns and his post at the Royal Gun Factory at Woolwich, and rejoined the Elswick engineering and ordnance operations. By summer 1863, search for alternative, overseas, outlets for Armstrong guns was getting underway but it had not yet yielded practical results. Already he had become involved in arrangements for the Newcastle meetings of the British Association, of which because of a refusal from the Duke of Northumberland, he took the presidency. This meant he had to prepare a major address. When it was all over, he felt a need for relaxation and a change of scene. It was at this time that he thought again of the pleasure which visits to Rothbury had given him in the past. He decided to return there for the first time for many years.

Occasionally, during the early years of married life, he had made return visits to Rothbury, and had once more fished in the Coquet, which had provided so much joy in his boyhood. Early in May 1843, after an illness, he wrote from Rothbury to Margaret. The letter concerned business, but it also conveyed his simple joy in getting back to familiar places and former habits: "I am now getting well as fast as can be. I have been almost continuously in the water this glorious day and there is nothing does me so much good. I heartily wish however that the fishing would get a little better. I can`t imagine what is the matter with the trout that they won`t come and be killed." (12) A few years later, his daily work, duties at the water company and then preoccupations as a newly established manufacturer of hydraulic machinery not only took up his working hours, but also spilled over into his leisure, cutting off all thought of further holidays. In old age, he claimed that after 1848 he did not visit Rothbury again for 15 years. Having never been a pace-maker in the commercial race, in that time the little town of which he was so fond had if anything slipped back.

Rothbury township, extending well beyond the built up area, increased in population in the early nineteenth century, reached 1,014 in 1831 and then fell away; the 1861 census recorded only 798 people. Significantly, a directory of the 1850s referred to it as "the village, formerly a market town."(13) But, though its market had been discontinued, four fairs continued to be held there every year. Visiting at this time, the topographical writer, Walter White, was not generally impressed. It was: "Chiefly one wide street… [and] ...retains sundry rude touches of the past; miserable thatched cots, which set off the ambitious style of the newest houses."(14) Scattered farmhouses and cottages occupied the more fertile areas of the large parish, the rest was "... sterile hills, naked rocks and black heaths." Nearer the town, even as the parish reached its peak population, Debdon Hill and Cragend Hill between the Black Burn and the Debdon Burn, had presented "... a most dreary and desolate aspect of heathy hills and rugged and naked cliffs." Thirty years later, after making sure of his accommodation at the Three Half Moons, White "rambled the time away till after sunset, in pleasurable recognition of half-forgotten scenes; up the hill on the Alnwick road, to get a view of Crag End, a grand range of cliffs, grim and rugged, the edge of a dreary waste bestrewn with rocks and boulders." (15) Four years later Armstrong made his own momentous return to the area.

Happy memories and his own more immediate circumstances were the prime motivating forces for his visit in late summer 1863. There was another, more general and new factor of some importance; a spurt in the construction of, and forward planning for railways in the interior of Northumberland and neighbouring counties. In 1862, the Waverley Line was opened from Carlisle to Edinburgh, and the existing track of the Border Counties Junction Railway was extended from Plashetts to join this new main route at Riccarton Junction. That year the new Wansbeck Railway was opened from Morpeth to Scots Gap, and in October, a meeting was held in Morpeth to promote another line, the Northumberland Central Railway, to run from Coldstream through Wooler and Rothbury to a junction with the Wansbeck Railway at Scots Gap. The promoters of the Northumberland Central were major landowners; it was hoped that much of the necessary capital could be raised in anticipation of an increase in land values caused by the railway. Royal assent was given to the Northumberland Central Railway Act on 28 July 1863. By early the following year its route was staked out, and land had been purchased for the section between Scots Gap and Rothbury,

According to a local historian, the view out on the Alnwick turnpike from Rothbury at the time Armstrong made his return visit to the area in late summer 1863, was far from inspiring-but it must be remembered that representing it so was a means whereby the changes which later occurred could be made to seem all the more miraculous. Apart from the hills "in all their sombre grandeur; the only other objects being the Peth Head farmhouse, the remains of the Peth Foot house, and on the other side of Debdon Burn an old hovel, rejoicing in the name of Tumbleton, while rotten hedgerows and ruinous stone dykes here and there intersecting the moorland gave to the little valley of Debdon a lonely, neglected, and barren aspect."(16) Fortunately, the first edition of the six-inch Ordnance Survey map was published at this time and provides an independent and objective representation of the contemporary landscape, and a baseline for recording later changes.

Reminiscing with a scientific associate on a snowy October day in 1893, Armstrong was in reflective mood. He recalled how, feeling "a need of a little rest" at the end of the British Association meetings thirty years before, "I thought I should like to see the old place once more, and accompanied by two friends, we drove from Morpeth [then the nearest railway station] and stayed over the weekend. The morning after our arrival we walked down by the side of the river beyond Thrum Mill and scrambled along what is now called the Cragside hill, and sat

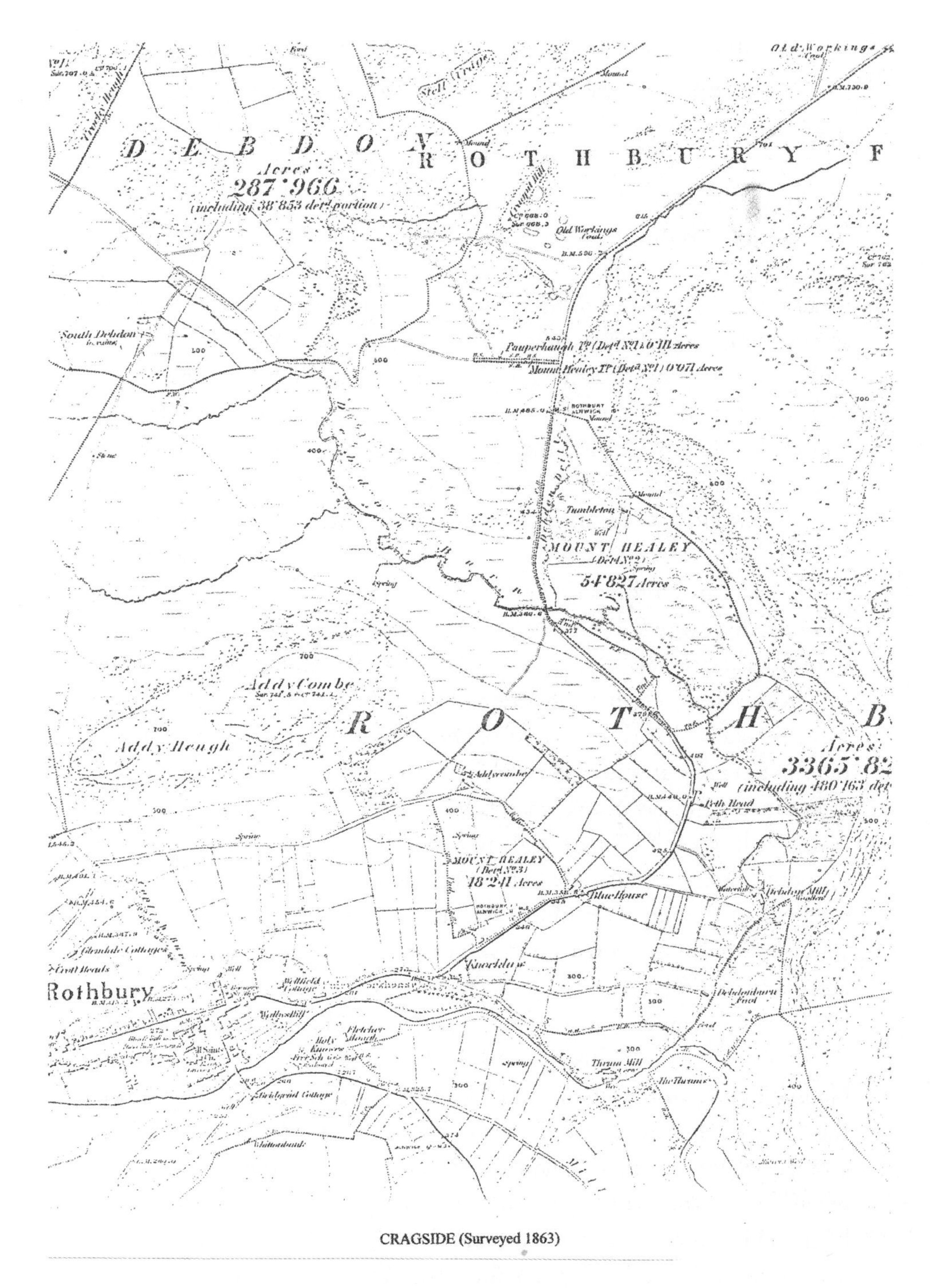

Cragside area 1863
(Ordnance Survey Six inches to a Mile map, surveyed 1863)

on a boulder just above where the house now stands." A lane ran down to the old mill. As they looked up the valley, Armstrong said to his friends: "What a pretty park that would make if all those hedges were taken away." They walked on to Debdon Bridge, before returning on the footpath alongside the burn to rejoin the road near Thrum Mill. Passing the ground on which his electric light house was eventually built, Armstrong remarked that it would provide a pretty site for a small house, the sort of thing he would like to build so as to be able to spend summer weekends there. His 1890s recorder went on to a rather ambiguous account of Armstrong`s memories of what happened next. It seems to have been yet another example of his persistence when he had settled on anything: "I thought nothing more about it, but on my return to Newcastle the house at Rothbury haunted me so much that I made enquiries about the site with the intention of buying it, but, owing to the title deeds being so intricate, the cost was going to be more than I cared to incur, and so I abandoned the idea. Archdeacon Thorp, who owned about 20 acres of land, on part of which Cragside is built, hearing that I wanted to build at Rothbury, instructed his solicitor to offer it to me, and after a little negotiation I bought it."(17) It seems likely that this account of the genesis of Cragside is accurate, but there exists another, somewhat different record. It occurs in the memoirs of Andrew Noble`s wife, Margery.

According to this, on an occasion when Noble was suffering from a bronchial cough, a change of air was prescribed. Armstrong reacted in predictable fashion: "Rothbury is the place; it cured me as a youth when I was almost grown up. I went there, drank goats` milk, fished and I was almost able to walk all the way back to Newcastle when I left." Following such a fulsome recommendation, the whole Noble family went over to Rothbury. While they were there, Armstrong and George Rendel visited them, and with Noble, Armstrong walked down the Coquet to Thrum Mill. He remarked he would like to build a cottage where he could spend a few quiet days in the country, and when they spoke to a man leaning over a gate, the gorge at Thrum Mill lying behind him, he enquired if any fields around there were for sale, and received the reply: "This is for sale." Armstrong bought the field. (18)

Whatever the details, the accounts agree about the next step. After acquiring a small area, Armstrong had to buy extensions to it. By spring, 1864 things were making headway. On Friday 11 March, he wrote to tell Margaret that the previous day at Shoeburyness they had successfully fired a 600-pounder gun against unusually thick plates, and that day he had presided at a council meeting of the British Association. But his most important news was: "I hear from Mr Dees [successor to his old firm of Donkin, Stable and Armstrong] that he has purchased Mr Cree`s fields at Rothbury for me and a small slice of Storey`s will now complete all that is of any importance to possess." He was to leave London on Saturday night "... and the carriage must be at the station on Sunday morning at the usual time."(19) He wanted to start building immediately. For a time, presumably on occasional visits to the project, he and Margaret occupied the two upper rooms of the four-roomed miller`s house at Thrum Mill, and his agent, Bertram and Mrs Bertram lived in the two rooms below. At this time, he planned a house of perhaps eight or ten rooms and a stable for a pair of horses. Variously described as a "country house", a "lodge" or even a "shooting box", it was constructed from fine freestone quarried on the hillside nearby. For a time he seems to have referred to it as "Rothbury" but soon decided to call it "Cragside." By November 1865 that address was used in a letter to Noble. Armstrong played an important part in choosing the furnishings for the new house; Margaret seemingly had very much a secondary role.

On Friday 17 March 1865 from the Athenaeum, he gave Margaret advance warning of his travel plans. It seems she was already at the new house, but he made arrangements to suit himself and seemed off hand in his treatment of her: "I think I may see my way to leaving for Newcastle on Tuesday morning and in that case I shall most probably go forward to Rothbury on Wednesday afternoon. This however need not at all affect your movements. If you feel disposed to remain at Rothbury until about the end of the week I will come back with you in the carriage, but as I am still a little uncertain in my goings and comings, you had better do what is most convenient and agreeable to yourself ... I will bring down the clock I have got for the upper sitting room at Rothbury. It can stand in the sitting room of the old house [the miller`s house?] until the new one is ready. I hope you find your quarters comfortable and that you like the appearance of the new building and the grounds."(20) By midsummer, there had been a good deal of progress but the house was still unfinished. On 14 June, a busy Armstrong again wrote from the Athenaeum: "I was glad to have your letter this morning giving so cheerful an account of the prospects of more rapid progress at Rothbury. It will be an immense comfort to go into the house the next time I am there, though at present I do not see much chance of being able to leave London early enough to get to Rothbury for the Race Week. I met Mr Dodds, the plasterer, at the Newcastle station as I was coming away and he urged that the floors should be laid down in order that he might get on with the ceilings which would otherwise be much shaken by nailing down the boards. If this were done, he might be prepared to send more plasterers."(21) Early next summer, he was at Cragside and Margaret in Newcastle, when he wrote what seems to be the first surviving letter to her bearing the heading "Cragside, Morpeth" and carrying his crest. He reported: "... the painters have gone and the dining room is now clear for the furniture. Everything is looking very pretty here but rain is wanted." (22)

From an early date, Cragside, like their home in Jesmond Dene, was pressed into service as a place of hospitality for friends, colleagues and possible customers. Early in September 1867, Armstrong wrote home from Dudhope House, Dundee where he was staying during the meetings of the British Association. As he put it they had been "... most hospitably entertained here," and he wanted to extend the same sort of welcome in his new home. As usual, his plans were clear and his instructions precise.: "My present intention is to get away tomorrow before the Scotch Sunday sets in and I am pretty sure to be at home by the night train which arrives at the Central Station I think about 1 o`clock in the morning, but you will see the exact hour by referring to the Bradshaw. You can therefore send the carriage to meet me at that hour. Sir John Lubbock and Tyndall will come to Cragside on the 20th." (23)

By the late 1860s Cragside house stood, solid, square, and stark against the still bare and boulder-strewn hillside. Its site was unquestionably impressive, but the house was scarcely a grand country home for one of Tyneside`s rapidly rising leaders of industry. Meanwhile Rothbury was about to become more accessible as a result

Cragside house 1870.
(Source, Dixon 1903)

of the delayed completion of part of its railway. Realising they lacked capital to build the whole line as planned, in 1865 the directors of the Northumberland Central Railway took a puzzling decision. They would first build the southern section across the moor from the Wansbeck to the Coquet rather than the northern, agriculturally more important section in the Till basin. In spring 1866, the failure of the major banking house of Overend and Gurney brought on a major financial crisis, but that October a large meeting was held in Rothbury at which several new members were added to the committee to negotiate with local landowners. One of the new members was William Armstrong. Plans for the line north of Rothbury were dropped, but in summer 1870 trains began to run between Scots Gap and Rothbury. The line formally opened for traffic on Tuesday 1 November. The event was celebrated by a dinner at the Rothbury Hotel, presided over by Earl Percy, and followed by a ball. On the same day, Armstrong threw open the grounds of his Cragside estate to the public. (24) Even more important for the future, he had already met an imaginative architect with a rapidly advancing national reputation. It would be under his direction that the small house was transformed into something more suited to be the home of a successful capitalist. Long before this was done Armstrong had begun a second, more prosaic and less successful project in rural Northumberland.

While Armstrong, George and Stuart Rendel and Andrew Noble were distracted either by the ongoing business of the Armstrong and Whitworth Committee, or in efforts to find alternative markets for the capacity of the Elswick ordnance works, the engine works continued in its established commercial lines. For instance, in summer 1868, when Noble was engaged on gun business with the Belgians and Prussians and also visited Paris, Armstrong sent news that the Engine works balance sheet was closed and, "after the usual treatment," showed a divisible profit of £28,600. Unfinished contracts seemed to promise an equally good result for next year. A few days later, he set off for Cardiff where dock extensions promised considerable orders. (25) By no means all their commercial enterprises were financial successes. This was the case with their investment in the iron trade in the mid 1860s.

The modern A 68 through Northumberland follows an impressive route. For much of its length it is straight, but in one short stretch, it diverges sharply from the line of its Roman ancestor, Dere Street, to rejoin it again a few miles further on at West Woodburn. In the angle between the two sections of the road is the little settlement of Ridsdale. It is now little more than an isolated, and-except for through traffic-somnolent ribbon development, bleakly exposed by elevation and aspect to the elements. However, it contains two features, which are clues to a more active past. The ruins of a stone built blast furnace and a public house called <u>The Gun</u> are relics of its association with Elswick, almost 25 miles away to the south east. They are also reminders of some of Armstrong`s own admirable qualities. Throughout his business career, he usually succeeded by virtue of an exceptional capacity to concentrate on the objective in hand and to pursue his aim relentlessly. Ridsdale was one of his less successful projects but experiences there brought out not only these qualities but also his ability to put things in their true perspective and not to be depressed by shortfalls, which dismayed some of his apparently less well-balanced colleagues.

In the late 1830s, just before the establishment of the Consett Iron Works, two blast furnace plants were built in the interior of Northumberland, at Hareshaw and Ridsdale. They used coal and iron ore found in the Scremeston Measures of the Limestone Series of Carboniferous rocks. Both works suffered from difficulty of access to their outlets, and failed in 1857 at the time of the collapse of the Northumberland and Durham District Bank. Ironically, at this very time the general accessibility of the area-though not directly to Ridsdale-was greatly improved by the opening of the Border Counties Railway from Hexham, up the North Tyne valley to the Plashetts coalfield. By 1859, a link from Morpeth to Reedsmouth was authorised as the Wansbeck Railway, and the line was completed in 1865, passing less than a mile north of Ridsdale. Early in July 1862, the Ridsdale Ironworks was offered for sale in Newcastle. It was remarked at the time that there was abundant iron ore on the estate, but only two or three bids were made and they did not reach the moderate figure expected. The ironworks were eventually sold for only £3,500, with the estate passing to Armstrongs. There were two ends in view, use of the iron ore in new blast furnaces, and trials of Elswick guns on the high moors. (26)

It was decided to build the new blast furnaces at Elswick. There the company also installed puddling furnaces to supply the wrought iron used in the manufacture of Armstrong guns. The expanding engineering works offered other outlets for cast and wrought iron and it was possible to sell pig iron to the multitude of various metal using trades on Tyneside. By summer 1864, the blast furnaces were under construction. In the first instance, there were two furnaces, but later another was added. Even in the early days iron making caused a good deal of trouble as the management, lacking any previous experience, felt its way into the new trade. As operations started in summer 1865, a sequence of letters from Armstrong to Noble illustrates how close an observer of their operations the former was and how he worried away at problems until he came up with a solution. They also made clear that it was not always a comfortable thing to be his close, but subordinate associate.

On Friday 21 July, Armstrong wrote from the Athenaeum: "I think you might very safely and properly diminish the cut off point on the blast engine to six tenths instead of two thirds at which it was yesterday working. It will make very little difference in boiler pressure to make this alteration and will save a lot of steam. The engine should be painted and finished bright before starting for good. All leakages, of which I observed several yesterday about the cylinders and valve chests and steam pipes, must be stopped. All noises also must be silenced, for remember, wherever there is noise there is wear to say nothing of nuisance. The air valve fans ought to be made thoroughly good so that you may be independent of the leathers having to accommodate themselves to chinks or irregularities in the iron. Be sure not to set away before all these matters are made perfectly right." On Saturday he returned to the subject, for obviously Noble had suggested a step with which he disagreed, and on Monday, he wrote again: "I have made some alterations in your specifications. Please examine same and if all right make fair copy and send it to me by return." By Wednesday, things were better but there were still reasons for criticism: "I am glad the engine is now doing well. I was surprised to hear that you had been using mineral oil, which is quite unfit for heavy bearings unless it be for cleansing. With what boiler pressure did you get 4.5 lbs air pressure? If it was not more than 50 lbs I think you might safely cut off at half stroke before you go to work. What think you as to this…? I hope all your noises are rectified and smoke avoided." (27)

By spring 1867, the iron department was in deficit, and this seemed to depress Noble. In contrast, Armstrong remained cool, balanced and ready to give careful consideration to ways of improving the situation. On 21 March, when he sent statements from the ordnance, foundry and blast furnace departments, the last had made a loss, the size of which had been aggravated by depreciation in their stock of iron as prices fell quite sharply that year. He recognised the loss was "... very serious, but pray do not make it more serious by worrying yourself about it. You are no more identified with that undertaking than I am and I should consider myself very foolish if I gave way to doleful dumps about it. I assure you it will vex me more to see you fretting yourself than it does to lose the money and your partners will feel as I do. Considering the splendid position of the Firm in regard to aggregate profits it would be a shame to grumble at a loss which we can so easily bear." Over the last 12 months, after allowing £15,500 for depreciation in the ordnance works and £4,500 on the foundry, they had earned a dividend of £34,000 and received another £18,000 as interest-so that in total their earnings for the year had been £72,000. Without the loss at the iron works it would have been £92,000. Yet this was not a cause for panic "Now as to the Iron Concern we must lay our heads together like <u>men of business</u> and <u>cooly</u> decide what steps should be taken, at all events to <u>diminish</u> the loss. Burn this note as soon as you have read it, and believe me, ever truly yours WG Armstrong."(28) Three days later, and now writing from Cragside, he took up the question of; "...what steps should be taken." As always, he was rational, and showed concern for the well-being of a senior colleague, but he was yet again guilty of trying to micro-manage what was rapidly becoming a major industrial complex: "I want to have a talk with you on Iron Concerns and think it best to write to you with a few points for your consideration. Firstly, I would suggest the expediency of blowing out the local iron Furnace [probably he meant the one working on local, that is, Ridsdale ore]. You will say this will increase the charges, but the question is, shall we suffer as much loss on this head as we shall on the other. This must be reduced to calculation and the decision based on actual figures. Secondly, I think we should cease baring at Ridsdale for the present and try mining especially as we already have a considerable tract already bared. Thirdly, we must make a great effort to get a reduction in rates of carriage. Fourthly, I am of opinion that the mines are not visited sufficiently often by partners and it is palpable to me that your important duties in regard to artillery matters are incompatible with your exercising the required amount of personal supervision at Ridsdale. I would therefore propose that you and W. Cruddas be a Committee of management acting chiefly at Elswick and visiting the mines periodically. But in order to obtain the necessary current supervision and personal superintendence both at Ridsdale and the Furnaces and to maintain a proper harmony of action between the two places, I think the <u>Committee</u> should have a competent man to act under them. I don`t like buying in new men and I think that the duties of T Clarke might be extended so as to supply the want. The committee would of course be an open one so that all or any of the partners could if they pleased take occasional part in the proceedings. I anticipate that this arrangement would be a great comfort to you as it would divide your responsibility and relieve you from the unpleasantness of identifying yourself with this unfortunate department of our otherwise prosperous concern." (29)

Throughout Armstrong`s life the blast furnaces remained a relative black spot in their affairs. In early years, they continued to use Ridsdale iron ore and produced "Ridsdale" iron, largely for sale. The furnaces were operated until the end of the 1890s when they were sold and dismantled to make room for expansion in other departments of the works. In 1900, both Armstrong`s and their own last year, the blast furnace account showed a gross profit of £10,000, a little over 1.5% of the company total. Meanwhile Ridsdale moors became useful to the company as a sparsely populated and remote area suitable for testing heavy guns. In this way, long before the War Office began to use the huge area north of Elsdon and Otterburn, Armstrongs pioneered these occasionally noisy intrusions into the peace of the Northumberland uplands.

THE ARMSTRONG AND WHITWORTH COMMITTEE: WESTMINSTER AND SHOEBURYNESS

Armstrong`s plea for a cool, careful evaluation of his and other ordnance systems received a speedy response, and a few weeks later, only two months after the War Office informed Elswick it would buy from it no more guns, a Special Committee was appointed to explore the relative merits of the Whitworth and Armstrong guns. It would compare them under a number of headings-accuracy, penetration, range, rapidity of fire, ease of working, capability of standing rough usage, simplicity of construction and comparative costs. As Andrew Noble, secretary for the earlier ordnance enquiry was now joint manager of the Elswick Ordnance Works, Henry Dyer, who had practical experience from the trial ranges, was appointed in his place. The enquiries of the Armstrong and Whitworth Committee went on for over three years. They were based on two types of evidence, testimony from manufacturers and military men and the results from a long succession of field trials.

Whitworth demanded a special civilian representative on the committee and nominated Penn the marine engine builder. Although opposed to the principle, Armstrong put forward William Pole, a civil engineer, former assistant to James Meadows Rendel, and now an independent engineer and professor of civil engineering at University College, London. The tone of the hearings was indicated by the fact that after only one or two meetings Penn resigned. He was replaced by MacDonald, manager of The Times newspaper, an obviously valuable ally. Whitworth gave evidence on 6 January 1863, and two days later, the committee heard from Armstrong. The two principal protagonists were followed within the first week by testimony from master gunners, and from the assistant superintendent of experiments at Shoeburyness, Henry J Alderson. Writing home in July 1863 Armstrong reported: "Our committee is going on and we are in the thick of the fight. George Rendel commenced his evidence on Saturday and will proceed with it on Friday. Noble follows. The case of our opponent is already getting damaged and I have no doubt will soon break down entirely." If he really expected an early end, he soon proved to have been far too optimistic, for proceedings dragged on. Eighteen months later, more testimony from Andrew Noble was followed within a few days by another appearance by Whitworth. (1) There were repeated visits to the artillery ranges.

The centre of activity for major gun trials was the ranges laid out at Shoeburyness, three miles south east of Southend, where Thameside mudflats gave way to sand. Sparsely populated, South Shoebury parish had only 202 people and little more than a signal station at the 1831 census. Over the next 20 years its population fell away, but the London, Tilbury and Southend Railway was built to a terminus at what was now called Shoeburyness, and during the 1850s, there was a sharp increase in numbers, in part due to the opening of a brickfield, but also because of the erection of artillery barracks at Shoebury Fort. Here Armstrong and his close associates spent many days, in contact with senior army and navy men, representatives of rival ordnance systems and sometimes experts from foreign powers. As with Noble, in the case of the earlier enquiries, a few of the military men eventually became business colleagues. The days of trial firings provided an exacting and often exhausting experience, and they were occasionally disappointing and sometimes acrimonious. Press accounts, letters and reports to Elswick from Armstrong or his colleagues provide insights into circumstances and progress.

Weather conditions along the Thames estuary varied dramatically. When in mid November 1863 there were preliminary trials of a 13.5 inch (600 pounder) Armstrong gun, they were "... all that could be desired. A slight mist out at sea lifted just before the experiments commenced, and the sea shone out as clear and as warm as on a spring day. The wind too, which in the early morning was somewhat cold and biting, moderated into a gentle breeze, setting across the range, just sufficient to waft away the smoke from the mouth of the gun." Those present on this occasion included generals Tulloch and Dacres, Colonel Lefroy, Armstrong, the engineer William Fairbairn and "... many other notabilities in the military and engineering world." A week or so later, the same gun was tested against a mounted replica of one side of the warship HMS Warrior. This time Noble represented Armstrongs. Though it seems to have had little impact on the accuracy of firing, all day long gusts of wind and rain were driving across the range.(2) The often harsh weather and noise from the guns could be very wearing. When, in February 1865 Pole resigned, it was partly because his strength and nerves could not stand the strains of the experimental ground. (He also felt he was not well qualified to act in opposition to MacDonald-"who is purely an advocate.") Armstrong thought of replacing him with John Percy, metallurgist to the Royal School of Mines, but he would not accept the appointment. Pole then suggested Stuart Rendel, George`s younger brother, and Armstrong informed Noble that he would go along to the War Office to propose him early next week, unless he heard any adverse opinion from Elswick.(3). Stuart already had considerable experience in helping prepare for Ordnance Committee enquiries and on the ranges, and he was appointed. Although only 31, and well-equipped from a legal training, he too felt the strain. Many years later he claimed that the mass of detail and the statistics he accumulated during the field trials and had to have at his finger tips during discussion of their results: "...over-strained either nerves or mind or both, and [I] have suffered from over-sensitiveness of the brain ever since."(4)

There were other problems. On Thursday 9 February 1865, JH Lefroy wrote to tell Noble that a 7-inch gun had been dispatched from Woolwich on Tuesday and they had attended Shoeburyness that day in order to fire it. But it had not arrived: "... the bargee perhaps had friends at Gravesend." Another gun had burst: "No one was hurt but a good many had narrow escapes." They hoped to catch up a few days later: "The tide suits all next week at Shoeburyness and we shall most likely go down on Tuesday and stay over Thursday." (5) Sometimes, intense rivalry between the protagonists gave rise to disputes. In such circumstances, Armstrong generally managed to keep cool. In June 1864, he was annoyed by the actions of Colonel E M Boxer concerning conditions of practice at Shoeburyness, but warned Noble: "We must be firm but at the same time act with temper and avoid vexing the committee."(6) Four months later, there was a more serious problem. F Eardley Wilmot, the man Armstrong had replaced as head of the Royal Gun Factory, wrote to him to complain that in the presence of officers on 10 October, Rendel had stated that gunners were being bribed to greater exertions in favour of Whitworth`s guns, and that representatives of the latter were always hanging around the place which gave them opportunities to offer incentives. Wilmot pointed out that the only men allowed into the area had permits: "If Mr Rendel has any grounds for his statement it will be necessary for me to request that I may be furnished with them. If however this statement was merely made during a moment of annoyance I do not care to hear anything more about it. It is not the statement but the truth of it that is of any importance." (7)

As Eardley Wilmot`s letter indicated, the effects on participants of the uncertainty, tension and wear and tear were considerable. For a long time the issue seemed in doubt. In June 1864, Noble received a report from Armstrong on the state of things at Shoeburyness: "Things go on pretty well here, but there is some little reason to feel anxious. Whitworth`s 12 pounders have not broken down in any single way, and of course this strengthens the hands of his friends very much." He then considered the inclinations to one or other of the two systems by the various members of the committee, ending with "Pole is indolent and gives us no hearty enthusiastic support. You know that I am far from being doleful over the trial. I would not write as I do above except that you should know the real truth." (8) Early in 1865 when he saw the proposed preamble to the report, Armstrong told Noble: "It must be resisted tooth and nail. It takes up all the old stories against the guns with a view of establishing a strong prima facie case against them." He was planning to see General Taylor and the War Office about the "inadmissibility" of this. (9) Later that month, the committee put the Elswick company in an awkward position by asking for their contract prices. Armstrong suggested to Noble that they should reply that these varied according to quantity and other circumstances, and that they quoted a range of prices, and only produced actual contracts confidentially, assuming that Whitworth did the same. He wanted him to let Stuart Rendel have a statement of prices such "... as you think should be furnished."(10) Four months later firing trials were still underway and the hard struggle continued in committee. In mid June, Armstrong let Noble know: "Stuart had a very good day in Committee yesterday and found himself very much better supported than he had previously been. Taylor in particular was very determined and used strong words to the great annoyance of old General Rumley. The War Office has refused to sanction the further experiments proposed by the Committee and ordered them to complete their report as soon as possible. My intervention therefore in the case has been quite successful." The second day of this session was "severe fighting but we came off fairly well...the sitting is again going on." After another six weeks he wrote the "fight goes on." "Tomorrow I think will finish it. The results are generally favourable, at least both Stuart and I both think so, though we don`t get all we are entitled to. I think there is not room now for much damage."(11) By this time, Noble was apparently depressed, and late in June Armstrong wrote to encourage him: "I have also received your lugubrious letter about the A&W. This makes me feel quite unhappy about the state of your digestion. Be satisfied to know that Stuart says, and Dyer says, and Young says, and all our friends say that so far the report on the 70 pounders is decidedly in our favour. I dare say our opponents think themselves just as hardly dealt with as we do. You will find it much more comfortable if you learn to look on the sunny side rather than on the shady side of things. If you cannot do this voluntarily try what blue pills will do. Nothing poisons blue devils so well as blue pills." (12)

At last, the enquiry did end. It vindicated the Armstrong gun, but it was not an altogether convincing victory, and Stuart Rendel felt it necessary to submit a dissent from the majority report. Much later he claimed that he had made all the difference, declaring "... unblushingly the plain fact, that but for me the Whitworth case would have triumphed."(13) The journal Engineer concluded that the "true story of the guns" was not to be learned from the book with that title from Sir Emerson Tennent, for, having been a shareholder in the Whitworth Ordnance Company, he had written "in a spirit outrageously partial to the Whitworth ordnance." But its own, even more sobering conclusion was that, having spent millions on trials "... we really have no gun as yet." Two years later the ordnance expert, General Lefroy outlined the high costs of the enquiries by the Ordnance Select Committee, and a few months afterwards told Noble "The root of the evil is the spirit of rivalry and mutual jealousy between the advocates of the different constructions, and that we can never cure."(14)

Some observers concluded that, whatever the formal outcome, in reality Whitworth not Armstrong had triumphed. Certainly, Whitworth thought so. Shortly after the report was produced, he wrote to Earl de Grey and Ripon in a tone showing that rather than being resolute in defeat, he had convinced himself that he had really won: "Viewed as a whole, and making due allowance for the manner in which the committee was constituted, I am not dissatisfied with the report. Through its carefully worded details there is no difficulty in perceiving that my system of artillery has maintained a decided advantage over the several systems of Sir William Armstrong." He claimed his gun was superior in range, accuracy, penetration, in shrapnel against segment shell, in endurance under strain, in simplicity of construction and in cost and safety of projectiles and fuses-in essence the whole of the criteria adopted by the inquiry. Eight months later he went so far as to republish the committee`s report in a more convenient format than the blue book. Commenting, Engineering wrote: "The report shows, as is well known, a general superiority of the Whitworth over the Armstrong shunt gun and a decided superiority over the Armstrong breech-loader ... The question now is, is the superiority sufficient to justify us in changing all our existing ordnance? Upon this point much difference of opinion would naturally arise, but we may expect to see other nations arming themselves with the best weapon, and this we have to bear in mind in choosing our own." Further compounding the confusion, four months later the same journal reported the trial and rejection by the navy of Whitworth guns and by Woolwich of nine Elswick 64 pounders. Later, the other leading engineering trade journal, Engineer, which in 1864 had reprinted a despairing article from the Mechanics Magazine; "The Future of the Armstrong Gun" concluded that £3 millions of public money had been spent on the trials of the two systems only to leave Great Britain without a satisfactory gun. (15) There was an even clearer illustration of the uncertainty that remained. Despite the "victory" of his system at the conclusion of the enquiries of the Armstrong and Whitworth Committee, Amstrong`s company failed to be allocated any more British government orders. Between 1859 and 1863, the Elswick Ordnance Company had received work from the British government worth £1,063,000; the value of orders received between 1864 and 1878 amounted to about £60,000. (16) This by no means meant the end of the Elswick Ordnance works, but it did require a change of direction.

WIDER THINKING AND CONSERVATION

Energy conservation was a long-term interest for Armstrong. It had begun at least as early as his observation of the waste in the use of falling water, which had set off his researches into hydraulic power. Years later, his letters reveal a concern for efficiency in the operations of his own works. In 1855, although already busy with ordnance experiments, he took part in a committee of the Northumberland Steam Coal Association, which looked into the reduction of smoke produced in burning Hartley coal in marine boilers. A few years later the British Association was asking questions about energy efficiency when it tried to procure details of steam trials from the Admiralty - only to receive the response that "...the ships of the Royal Navy only employed steam occasionally, and only as an auxiliary power."(1) In 1878, as president of the Institute of Mechanical Engineers, he highlighted waste in his claim that in an ordinary engine only one thirtieth of the energy in each ton of coal was applied to useful work. He emphasised the need to make use of water and the potentials of solar power. In research, application and exhortation, he returned time and again to these themes.

Outstanding as was his ability to concentrate his thoughts on practical problems, on a number of public occasions Armstrong also revealed much broader thinking and even striking powers of imagination. Energy featured prominently in these reflections. An early example came in his paper "On the Employment of a Column of Water as a Motive Power for Propelling Machinery", read to the Newcastle Literary and Philosophical Society on Wednesday 3 December 1845. At that time, long before his attention turned to armaments, he shared the infectious optimism of those champions of capitalism who believed it was inevitably accompanied by material progress. This would filter down to more of the population and out to the wider world, improving human well being. Speaking to "... a very crowded audience" he referred to the steam engine as a major agent in this process: "It is carrying civilization to the remotest parts of the earth - it is bringing nations into friendly communication with each other - and it is dispersing all those articles of manufacture which are essential to refined and cultivated life to millions of the human race who would otherwise be without them."(2)

A quarter of a century later his presidential address to the Newcastle meeting of the Institute of Mechanical Engineers gave him the opportunity of the centenary of Watt`s steam engine to bring the ramifications of its central role in modern life to a wider audience. Using words which some who knew him may have found surprising, he stressed one could not contemplate the results produced by the steam engine, "...without feelings of enthusiasm." "To appreciate how much we owe to the steam engine we need only consider for a moment what our position would be if we were deprived of its agency. The factories which clothe all the nations of the earth would be almost extinguished. The deep mines which supply almost all our mineral wealth would be abandoned. The manufacture of iron would sink into comparative insignificance. Horses and sailing ships would again become our only means of transit. All great engineering works would cease and mankind would lapse into that condition of slow and torpid progress which preceded the subjugation of steam". (3)

Such ideas were thought provoking, but by no means profound. In other addresses, he showed a capacity to provide more memorable illustrations or to follow through lines of thought into fields that one would not ordinarily associate with him. Examples of each of these appeared in two addresses given in Newcastle. In August 1863, in his presidential address to the British Association, delivered in the Town Hall, he provided listeners with a simple illustration of the advances made in bulk transport. The precision of his figures may be questionable, but his description was vivid. When packhorses were used to carry coal down to the Tyne a load amounted to only 3 hundredweights. Afterwards, roads were improved, cart transport replaced packhorses, and 17 hundredweights became a standard load. Later still, over wooden rails, a horse pulling a four-wheeled wagon could move 42 hundredweights, and now with haulage by a locomotive - "that crowning achievement of mechanical science"- 200 tons of coal could be moved at a cost in fuel which was scarcely more than the value of the corn and hay which the packhorse had consumed in carrying 3 hundredweights over the same distance.(4) Ten years later, as their president speaking to members of the North of England Institute of Mining and Mechanical Engineers, his thoughts ranged even more widely, into fields from which his interests and competence might have been expected to hold him back, but in which he proved to have important things to say.

His appointment to Woolwich, the extensive use of his gun in overseas conflicts with backward societies and a few years later the long-running tests of his ordnance system against that of Whitworth, made William Armstrong well known nationally and indeed even more widely. During the 1860s, he also achieved prominence in relation to other spheres of business, and particularly in the sudden crisis of confidence about the very basis of British industrial leadership, the continuing supply of coal. His interest in this derived in part from his long term, general concern for efficiency, in part from recent practical experience in examining the heating power and other properties of coal.

Questions of efficiency, waste and cost came up in his correspondence with Andrew Noble over the operation of their blast furnace operations. Practical experience with the use of coal had also been gained in 1857and 1858, when he had served along with a Durham University professor and another engineer in the effort financed by north country coal owners to prove that coal from the North East was not, as the Admiralty had decided, less fitted than Welsh coal for use in warships because it produced more smoke, giving early warning of their approach. He concluded that production of smoke was "... unnecessary and inexcusable". (5) Five years later, he intervened in a debate about the general future of coal in Britain.

At the beginning of the nineteenth century British coal production was about 8 million tons. By the time of Victoria`s accession output was 23 million tons and by 1860 it reached 80 million tons. Although the North East by this time produced less than one quarter of the total, its coal not only supplied the capital but provided the foundation for the great agglomeration of industries which stretched for some 15 miles along both banks of the tidal section of the Tyne, and of which Armstrong`s own operations were a growing part. This wealth in coal had shaped the features which so distinguished this area from the upper reaches of the extensive drainage basin of the Tyne, the very area to which those controlling Tyneside business were now looking for recreation and increasingly for their homes. The contrasts were well summed up in a popular account of the time: the North Tyne from Kielder to Hexham abounded in "picturesque villages and gentlemens` seats"; the South Tyne from Haltwhistle to Hexham ran through "a district crowded with old castles and peel towers". Below Hexham the united streams flowed through southern Northumberland, an area "which presents charming scenery and is studded with castles and country seats," but from Blaydon onwards "…its banks are lined with foundries, furnaces, docks, wharfs and quays."(6) Taking a less parochial perspective, coal provided the very foundation for British economic leadership in the world. Robert Stephenson, Armstrong`s near contemporary and friend, had celebrated the triumph of this coal age in vivid style: "We are living in an age when the pent-up rays of that sun which shone upon the great carboniferous forests of past ages are being liberated [sic] to set in motion our mills and factories, to carry us with great rapidity over the earth`s surface, and to propel our fleets, regardless of wind and tide, with unerring regularity over the ocean." Armstrong shared his recognition of the centrality of coal, but feared it might eventually fail as a reliable foundation for national greatness.

His presidential address to the British Association in Newcastle upon Tyne in 1863 was delivered in the Town Hall to a gathering of some 3,000 people. It was praised for recognising the importance of conveying scientific truths in an intelligible manner to the general public. (7) He surveyed the changes of the last 25 years, turned to railways and then focussed on coal. Drawing on the work of the geologist, Edward Hull, and statistics about the mineral industries collected by Robert Hunt since the mid 1850s, he outlined the vital but, as he saw it, endangered role of fuel in the national economy: "The greatness of England [sic] much depends upon the superiority of her coal in cheapness and quality over that of other nations". But the area of the coalfields of the United States was 37 times that of the British fields. Moreover, while both production and consumption were increasing rapidly much of what was raised to the surface was wasted. Combustion in ordinary furnaces was so poor that "...clouds of powdered carbon, in the form of smoke, envelope our manufacturing districts". Much of the heating power from gas was lost from furnaces; open fireplaces were inefficient. The vital question was: could Britain`s accessible reserves of coal continue to meet mounting demand?. Armstrong was clear in his doubt about this: "Contemplating the rate at which we are expending those seams of coal which yield the best qualities of fuel, and can be worked at the least expense, we shall find much cause for anxiety ... We have already drawn from our choicest mines a far larger quantity of coal than has been raised in all other parts of the world put together; and the time is not remote when we shall have to encounter the disadvantages of increased cost of working, and diminished value of produce." Next year he estimated that the available coal in the United Kingdom-that found in seams of not less than two feet in thickness and within 4,000 feet of the surface-amounted to 80 billion tons. At current rates of consumption, this reserve of coal would be sufficient for 930 years, but if the rate of increase in consumption of recent years went on, it would be gone in 212 years. For the coalfields of the North East-in which he estimated 2.5 million tons or 13% of the yield was currently burned, and therefore completely wasted, at the pit mouth-the expectation of life was scarcely 100 years.

Others took up the theme. Two years later, in The Coal Question, the economist and logician, William Stanley Jevons, recognised that: "As the source especially of steam and iron, the mineral is all-powerful...coal therefore commands this age..." But extrapolating the current rate of increase in consumption - which Jevons claimed was going ahead in a geometrical ratio - he concluded that the supply could not be sustained for more than three or four generations. From this he drew logical and disturbing conclusions: "... a reduction in the ratio of increase in consumption meant a check to the manufactures and prosperity of the country, that this reduction must inevitably come within a very short period, and that, probably within a lifetime, England must be prepared to enter on a future of comparatively diminished prosperity, and to see the manufacturing and commercial pre-eminence she had hitherto enjoyed in the world pass to other nations - probably the United States of America."(8) A year later, the cause was given added weight when John Stuart Mill took it up in the House of Commons. Early that May, in the course of his annual financial statement, Gladstone accepted Mill`s argument, concluding that if things went on at their present rate there would be no coal left by 1970. Two months later a decision was taken to appoint a Royal Commission to enquire into British coal supplies. Among the commissioners were four prominent geologists, Robert Murchison, Joseph Jukes, Joseph Prestwich and the Duke of Argyll. Other members were John Percy from the Royal School of Mines, Robert Hunt and Sir William Armstrong. Both Noble and Armstrong gave evidence. The Commission reported in 1870 and the evidence collected, maps, plans and diagrams were published a year later. The findings more or less confirmed Armstrong`s earlier estimates of the coal which might be accessible to mining, and encouraged progress towards more efficient use.

John Tyndall, physicist, controversialist and friend of Armstrong, added an over-dramatic if thought-provoking commentary to the findings of the Royal Commission: "I see no prospect of a substitute being found for coal as a source of motive power. We have, it is true, our winds and streams and tides, and we have the beams of the sun. But these are common to all the world. We cannot make head against a nation which, in addition to those sources of power, possesses the power of coal. We may enjoy more than their physical and intellectual energy, and still be unable to hold our own against a people which possesses abundance of coal; and we should have in my opinion, no chance whatever in a race with a nation which, in addition to abundant coal, has energy and intelligence approximately equal to our own. It is no new thing for me to affirm in my public lectures that the destiny of this nation is not in the hands of its statesmen but of its coal owners, that while the orators of St Stephen`s are unconscious of the fact, the very life-blood of this country is flowing away."(9)

For his part, Armstrong in the short term would make at least one effort to reduce the dependence of his own firm on an uncertain coal supply. This was associated with a sharp upward movement in prices which immediately followed the Royal Commission in the early 1870s, and which more obviously coincided with an economic boom. Over five years to the end of 1871 the annual average price of the best north eastern coal, "Wallsend Hetton", in London was a shade under 19s a ton. In 1872 it rose to 25s 6d and in 1873 reached 32s 0d. The author of the "Money Market" in The Times was much exercised by this increase: "... all the actuaries in England would find it impossible to apportion the degree in which each of the various influences at work has contributed to the rise in the price of coal". Four factors were identified- increased use in steamships and in iron manufacture, wage rises and high profits. The author stuck to his commitment to capitalist economic wisdom: "No one will fancy that the coal owners are so different from all other traders that they have failed to take advantage as far as possible of all the circumstances of the time, and, indeed, it would be a point for regret, instead of for approval, if they had attempted to introduce philanthropy into business by offering their produce even at a fraction below the highest price they could fairly get."(10) During this boom, Armstrongs seriously considered freeing themselves from the uncertainties of the open market by acquiring their own coal supply. But the boom ended in autumn 1873 and for much of the rest of that decade the economy was depressed. Throughout the rest of the century, coal prices did not even nearly approach the exceptionally high levels of 1873.

Despite relaxation of the commercial pressure, in the longer term Armstrong showed keen interest in alternatives to coal as a source of energy. In pursuit of them, he would become, though only in experiment or domestic scale application, a pioneer of new technologies using electricity. He had researched in this field and would return to electrical experiments at the end of his life. More prosaically, his interest in armaments manufacture helped provide at least one alternative means whereby some of the more obvious threats to Britain`s position in the world might for a time at least be resisted.

GUNS FOR THE WORLD; ELSWICK ORDNANCE AFTER 1863

One of the conditions of the 1859 arrangement between Armstrong and the British government had been that the Elswick Ordnance Works should not sell its products overseas. It was a necessary restriction, for so highly regarded was his new ordnance system that it could have commanded important outlets there. On 1 June 1860, when examined by the Select Committee on Military Organization, he was asked by the chairman of the committee-Sir James Graham, the man with whom the first contacts about guns had been made on his behalf in December 1854: "Is it the fact that most advantageous contracts might have been entered into by the Elswick company with foreign governments.?" He replied: "Most undoubtedly; contracts of an enormously beneficial nature might have been made with them, but the Elswick company waived that entirely".(1) In other words he seemed to imply that choice rather than mutual agreement with government had meant that Elswick had not taken up these opportunities. By 1863, when the links between government, the inventor and the Elswick Ordnance Company were severed, the Armstrong gun had already been tried in Russia, Turkey, Austria and the United States.(2). Now these and all other governments possessing both inclination and money were at last free to make arrangements with Elswick. In turn, the company was able to seek for work abroad to compensate for the effectively complete loss of outlets at home. One or two further impulses were necessary before Sir W G Armstrong and Company was fully launched on a career as one of the leading private suppliers of heavy ordnance to the world`s armies and navies.

When the Armstrong gun was first developed, Britain still seemed the undisputed leader in world industrialization. This fact led to a widespread belief that if other nations wanted ordnance of the highest quality they would have to come to Britain to buy it. Indeed this arrogant claim was spelled out by one of the leading engineering journals in spring 1859 at the time when the arrangements between the Government and Armstrong and Elswick were made: "With Armstrong`s gun there is literally no secret worth preserving at all, save that great one which can neither be sold or divulged - our manufacturing superiority. If an Armstrong gun was presented to each arsenal in Europe, their engineers might, and would undoubtedly try, to make them, but their efforts would only result in long delay, immense expenditure, and in their sending over to have them made here after all. It is a popular, but nevertheless, a very great error, to suppose that the weapons which are made here, if seen, can at once be made to any extent in the arsenals of France, Russia, Austria or Prussia". This extraordinary superiority complex, it must be noted, was qualified by the "at once" of the last sentence, which acknowledged that Britain`s leadership would be a wasting asset. Even so, there was some truth in the claim. For a time, Elswick and other British gun makers could command the markets of the world in the weapons of mass destruction. However, from the start there would be one major exception, Krupp of Essen. At home, Whitworth continued to compete with Elswick for foreign business. Year after year, he continued to criticise Armstrong and his supporters through the press. As late as 1875, he responded in The Times to criticisms from General Sir John Adye about the dangers of using a "brittle" material like steel for guns: "The position that Sir John Adye lately held as adviser to the Secretary of War on artillery subjects must have weight with those who have no opportunity of forming a correct opinion on the subject". (3)

A first, tentative effort to find new ordnance work, within the British sphere if not for the armed services, was made by the Elswick Ordnance Company two months after it was informed that the government would place no more orders. On 21 December 1862, the company wrote to the Under Secretary of State for War asking if he would sanction a modest non-government sale: "Amongst the continual applications we receive for the supply of guns, some are from merchants anxious to secure the production of Armstrong guns for their vessels trading in the eastern or other seas, in which they are liable to the attack of pirates." The War Office hedged on this matter. (4) Already Whitworth`s gun had been evaluated in various foreign countries. In France, it was tried and rejected. In Copenhagen a Whitworth 32 pounder burst. There were trials in St Petersburg during 1862, but there again a 35-pounder burst. Not long before the British government wound up its arrangement with Elswick, the Brazilian government made enquiries about buying some modern rifled ordnance from Britain. As Elswick was ruled out by its arrangement with the War Office, the Brazilians ordered from Whitworth. When the loss of government work occurred, Stuart Rendel attempted to use news of the Brazilian order won by their rivals to persuade Armstrong to recognise that if he no longer made guns others were ready to take his place. Moreover, as the Armstrong and Whitworth Committee was still considering the merits of the two systems, to have given up would have been highly detrimental to Armstrong`s case. Armstrong argued rather differently, pointing out that, after enjoying a well-paid government post and receiving honours, he could not at once turn to supply ordnance to foreign powers. Rendel in turn stressed that foreign orders would enable them to maintain the reputation of their system and to improve on it.

For various reasons Armstrong resisted Rendel`s pressure to seek for orders overseas. He looked at the matter, as the latter recalled, "with much indifference", but eventually he conceded to the extent of telling him: "If these are your opinions you are perfectly at liberty to try to give them effect, and if you can obtain orders for Elswick by all means do so, and to make it worth your while we will give you five per cent commission upon the orders you bring us." If this account by Rendel, written 40 years or so later, can be relied upon, it seems that as far as the firm`s principal was concerned the future great overseas Armstrong armaments business began in a rather half-hearted manner. Some of those involved soon proved that they at least were fully committed to the new course. Fortunately, the times were propitious, for the creation of new states, war, or plans or fears of war were widespread throughout what Victorians-apparently with no sense of incongruity-frequently referred to as the "civilised" world.

The Russian Empire, humbled by defeat in the Crimea, was moving on to re-equip its army with modern weapons. It proved willing to include as possible suppliers even those nations, which had inflicted that defeat. Italy, which was proclaimed a kingdom in 1861, urgently needed to weld together what until then had been separate nations and to tackle huge regional disparities in development and wealth, but it soon began to equip itself with the military trappings of an important power. A year later, Bismarck was appointed First Minister of the Prussian Crown, and set in train the processes, which within nine years created a German Empire following wars of mounting scale, with Denmark, Austria and France. Already, in early spring 1861, when Armstrong seemed firmly installed as superintendent at the Royal Gun Factory, and the Elswick Ordnance Company was an independent operation, the bombardment of Fort Sumter, South Carolina marked the opening of the American Civil War. Over the next few years, there were important orders from both the Union and the Confederacy for overseas suppliers of the means of destruction.

As a result of his participation in the gun trials and the accompanying government hearings, Stuart Rendel, though not trained as an engineer, had acquired a sound grounding in the field of ordnance. He was young, energetic and socially well connected. Such assets enabled him to play a key role in finding overseas orders for Armstrongs to replace lost British army and navy business. Even so, though actively cultivated, the search for foreign work took a good deal of time before yielding results. Rendel wrote to men who were prepared to act as their agents and to the representatives of likely foreign governments. In such letters, he carefully tried to make clear that his company was in a new situation but had already gained an outstanding position. It was important to indicate that other countries-and by implication some nations that his correspondent might not wish to gain a march on his own-were likely to buy Armstrong guns. The whole approach is brought out well in two letters he wrote in summer 1864, the first to an agent, the second to a senior representative of a foreign government.

Rendel`s letter to an agent in contact with the Brazilian government was written in the Royal Hotel, in Southend on 15 June. Its tone was confident: "Now that we are in the field we are cutting every one out. We are making for both sides in America, largely for the North, also for Italy, Denmark and some minor powers. We are in active treaty with

France and Russia, whose agents, specially sent over in the last month, inform us that we shall receive orders immediately". His other letter was written almost two months later, and to M Carvallo, the Chilean Minister. He began by making a virtue of what had been a crisis: "The exclusive contract by which the British Government enjoyed a monopoly of the services of our Firm being now closed we have the honour to inform you that, though we do not cease to manufacture guns for Her Majesty`s Government we are now at liberty to manufacture them for foreign nations as well." He outlined the great resources of his company, mentioned how many guns it had produced, and quoted the Ordnance Committee on their excellence. He ended this letter to the Chilean with a PS which was outstanding as a blatant call to action, an early example of a technique used time and again by arms salesmen: "P.S. Amongst other guns now making at Elswick may be seen those recently ordered by the Peruvian Government."(5)

Although his associates undertook much of the often-lengthy search and laborious negotiations for armament orders, Armstrong played an important part. He often met representatives of foreign governments, either in London or in Newcastle. When they came to the North East, he sometimes provided them with hospitality. His was always the ultimate authority, in relation, for instance, to arrangements for payment. The role he played in the early years of foreign business may be illustrated by two interrelated fields for the company`s ordnance operation, the Ottoman Empire and Egypt. Turkey chose to buy ironclads from various British shipbuilders but decided to arm them with Armstrong guns. At the same time, the Khedive was seeking to acquire modern armaments, partly to gain increased independence from his nominal master in Constantinople. Stuart Rendel made the first contacts with both parties but afterwards Noble and Armstrong became involved in negotiations with Musurus Pasha, Ambassador Extraordinary and Plenipotentiary of Turkey in London and with Efflatoun Pasha, emissary of the Khedive. Reports of these contacts show Armstrong and his senior colleagues feeling their way into an unfamiliar field of work, indicate the uncertainty of the business and that arrangements were then relatively unsophisticated. (6)

In August 1864, at almost the same time as Stuart Rendel was seeking to open up South American outlets, Andrew Noble let him know that he had heard that the Turkish Admiral and some of his staff were to stay near Newcastle. He wondered whether Rendel could do any more in that direction. (7) By October, contacts had been made and arrangements were so far advanced that Musurus had informed Elswick that his country had fixed on 8 inches as the bore for the armaments for their first ship. Three months later, when the Ambassador told Armstrong he had decided to order the type of copper lined powder cases Noble had proposed, the latter wrote to Elswick that when the order was received "... you will have to make stipulations about payments. He has paid the Admiral`s account and instructed Arif Bey to hand me a cheque for the balance on Monday". Apparently this payment was delayed but within another ten days Armstrong reported that he had the "Turkish Admiral`s balance" of £4,586 3s 6d, and Noble could "tell W. Cruddas that I have forwarded the cheque in a registered letter, addressed to the firm and posted with my own hand in time for first post, so if he does not get it don`t let him blame me". (8) Within a few weeks, there was a complication: the Turkish Admiralty had informed Musurus of its unhappiness about a difference in the price quoted for powder cases by Armstrongs and by Woolwich Arsenal. Armstrong believed the Ambassador wanted them to supply the cases, but was looking for an argument to justify his preference. He asked Noble to join him to meet Musurus. There were more problems about "money matters", but by early July it was the turn of the Turks to complain. On the first day of the month Armstrong, called at the embassy and found Musurus "... very dissatisfied at the delay." The Sultan was placing "... a most powerful pressure" on him to get the first ship [being built on the Clyde] sent off complete, and nothing except the want of their guns prevented this. The Ambassador was "... quite willing to pay us £10,000 on account if we can give an undertaking to have everything delivered on the 12th." Armstrong wanted details from Noble, stressed that delivery of the guns should not wait for carriages, and, in a postscript mentioned that: "Arif Bey had told Musurus that he believed that we had plenty of guns but that we had let other governments have them." Three weeks later, he sent Cruddas another cheque from the Turks. Later that summer the Turks wanted more guns, but Armstrong now had difficulties with Musurus, "... however we parted very good friends and I think I have arranged the matter pretty nearly". (9)

On one occasion, when the company sold some guns ordered by Turkey to others, and had failed to give notice of their intention, they were told by their financial advisors that they had no right to do so and had made themselves actionable for damages. (10) Fear of this sort of liability made an ex-lawyer like Armstrong wary in shaping financial arrangements. The Turks continued to order guns and Armstrong, though leaving the managers of the ordnance works a good deal of initiative, oversaw what was happening and continued to play a role. Late in August 1866 Noble was in London negotiating new orders, when Armstrong contacted him about arrangements. He wanted the contract "...so framed as not to prevent our selling in default of payment. I may here observe that there is one advantage in dispensing with a payment in advance, viz that the property remains vested in us and all difficulty about selling is thereby avoided."(11) Next day, Friday 31 August, he wrote another long letter to Noble from Newcastle. It exemplified his relaxed relations - lit by an occasional flash of humour - with his partner, but also the continuing uncertainties, technical and financial, of the business in which they were now engaged. Noble, yet again, required reassurance: "My dear Noble, I telegraphed to you this morning that you might shorten the time for second delivery of the Turkish guns if necessary and that you should use your own discretion in the matter freely. If we can only get the outstanding claims discharged I would not much care for any risk we might incur on the whole 16 guns and carriages provided only we keep ourselves at liberty to sell if we be not paid. You will observe that we are already committed to 8 guns and carriages so that the additional risk would only be on the second 8.....the whole 16 guns would cost us net £10,000, the price being about £15,000 and suppose that the Turk did not pay and that we had to sell at half price-which is about the worst that could happen-then the actual loss would be about £2,500, but on the other hand we would have gained £7,500 by getting the extras paid (and here I may observe that I am by no means very confident of getting the Egyptian portion if we break with Musurus). Moreover by getting the £3,000 instalment of first contract carried to a different account, we shall extinguish that objectionable contract so that altogether our position would be greatly improved. But then we have a good chance of getting paid for the new armament in which we should have attained everything. However if possible let us limit the risk to the first 8 guns. Rendel is in trouble about the steel barrels and is going to write to you specially on that subject. If Musurus would accept our honest advice he would have coil barrels by preference and get the guns cheaper. It is vexatious that while we and the gun factory authorities [presumably Woolwich] are both in favour of coil barrels as more reliable, and while all experience shows them to be so, yet we cannot get them substituted. I think if he were told that we were making coil barrel guns for Russia, France and Norway, though only on a small scale, he would probably sanction the change. Up to the time of my writing this-viz 2.30 o`clock-we have no telegram from you except about your dinner. I go to Cragside this afternoon at 5 and take Mr Cruddas with me. I hope to hear from you there on Sunday morning." Then he added a P.S. "Your telegram arrived just as I had concluded the preceding letter. I am glad you have got the matter arranged. I think we shall be better without any contract whatever. In fact I would rather it stood as a verbal arrangement though of course I presume he will require a memorandum or letter. In framing that memo: we must take care not to commit ourselves to damages in demurrage of ship if time be accidentally exceeded. I would rather have penalties as in the last contract than this viz £5 per gun per week after the first month. Be careful what you put in writing. Recollect that a letter or memorandum has the same effect as a contract. Take care also not to deprive us of our right to sell in case of default of payment. Freshfield is our solicitor and you can consult him". (12)

In January 1864, a few days after its amalgamation with the Elswick Engine Works the Elswick Ordnance Company informed The Times that no Armstrong gun had yet been shipped to any foreign government and, rather surprisingly, according to his own records, Stuart Rendel received no payment on commission before 1867. (13) However, bit by bit, the foreign contacts widened and the order books were filled. Among the first were orders from both North and South in the American Civil War. John Scott Russell, Brunel`s renowned collaborator in the construction of the Great Eastern, acted as intermediary between Federal representatives and Armstrongs, and Stuart Rendel`s friendships were vital in the initiation of their contacts with Confederate agents searching for supplies in western Europe. In the mid and late 1860s, Rendel paid extensive visits in the interests of the ordnance business both to Vienna-after the war with Prussia-and to St Petersburg. In the latter, he was helped by family connections, and it was partly through the help of friends that he was able to obtain initial contacts for business both in Chile and in Egypt. Such contacts led on to others in the same world regions-with Brazil, Argentina and Peru and, as seen above, with Turkey. Although he later wrote that he could not recall how he became acquainted with him, Rendel`s personal connection with a young Italian captain, living in humble lodgings on "the other side of Blackfriars Bridge" was the origin of what eventually became their biggest overseas venture. It dated from1864, at a time when Captain Albini was engaged in trying to persuade Belgium to adopt a rifle design he had invented, and was also acting as his nation`s naval attaché in London. By late August 1864, Albini had brought them orders for 600 pounder guns. For some years, Rendel claimed he was "the sole channel of communications between Captain Albini and Elswick," but before the end of the 60s, the business there had become too big for that. (14) In fact it was so important that two days after Christmas 1867 at the end of a letter to Noble mainly concerned with weather, health and so on, Armstrong wrote:"I hope the new Italian Ministry will involve no change in artillery policy." On the evening of Friday 18 September 1868, he met up with Rendel and Albini in London, settling arrangements for the Italian to become their agent. Albini was to receive £600 a year plus a 2% commission on business he secured for them, the agency to begin as soon as he could arrange to relinquish his present appointment. (15) While the various negotiations to win foreign orders were underway, William Armstrong remained closely involved in improving his ordnance system, attending trials at Shoeburyness, and at the same time was active in the whole and widening business of Sir WG Armstrong and Company.

ARMSTRONG ORDNANCE AND THE BRITISH ARMED SERVICES 1863 TO 1880

Although Sir WG Armstrong and Company was successful in finding new customers overseas, it also kept up efforts to restore the links with the army and navy so abruptly broken in autumn 1862. It would clearly take time for easy relations to be resumed, and when he wrote a year later to JH Lefroy about the results achieved in tackling difficulties with time fuses for large guns, Armstrong still seemed frosty. He adopted a strong attitude to rights, even if he did not mention the old question about patents. Eventually he had "perfectly satisfactory results" with fuses. "When I say I, I must include Noble who has worked at this perplexing subject as hard as I have done". They would be glad to supply the War Office with a hundred of them for trial, but if they were then judged successful, the question "... will arise who is to manufacture them in quantity. The Elswick Company has gone to a fearful expense in experiments upon these fuses and it is monstrous to suppose that private manufacturers are to devote their money and their energies to such subjects if the fruit of their labour and expenditure is to be quickly appropriated by the War Office and the exclusive manufacture of the articles entrusted to the government establishment. If therefore I place these fuses at the disposal of the Committee it must be upon the understanding that the improvements which have rendered them efficient are not to be adopted by the Government without my sanction. I have no disposition to be exacting, but I must confess I am less disposed to be generous in these matters than formerly". (1)

After Armstrong left the Royal Gun Factory, his successor as manager of the ordnance department there, RS Fraser C.E, developed what was claimed to be an improved version of the Armstrong gun.

Before the end of 1864, Fraser had simplified the manufacture of the breech mechanism, making it from one forging. Not only did the gun have fewer pieces but also it was made from cheaper materials, and major cost savings were claimed. The Engineer reported that whereas an Armstrong 13-ton gun cost, "we believe," about £1,800, the expense of a 12.5-ton Fraser gun would not be over £400 to £500. Having been tried at the Woolwich butt, the Fraser gun was sent for trial at Shoeburyness. There in August 1865 one gun blew out its breech. In the course of that summer arrangements were made for Armstrong to receive payments in cases when Woolwich used his pattern of guns. There were subsequent personal communications on the same subject. (2)

Through the sixties and the seventies, the Woolwich monopoly on supply of guns to the army and Royal Navy seemed, as Stuart Rendel later put it "both fatal and irremovable."(3) Year after year, the firm made numerous approaches to the services, but though occasionally encouraged by interviews, was unsuccessful. After the death of Palmerston in 1865, Earl Russell became Prime Minister. He promoted the Marquis of Hartington, who had been undersecretary, to be Secretary of State for War. Soon after his appointment, Armstrong arranged to meet him. He reported to Noble: "I have seen Lord Hartington today and had a long discussion about the Armstrong and Whitworth report. He showed no adverse feeling and I left with him a carefully prepared memorandum of the points of my case against Whitworth."(4) Another early and more difficult government contact was Hugh C. E. Childers, Liberal MP for Pontefract, Civil Lord of the Admiralty in 1864 and 1865, and between 1868 and 1871 the First Lord in Gladstone`s first cabinet. In the latter post, Childers determined to have a naval building programme even in times of peace, but emphasised the importance of improvement and economy. At the end of 1869, he visited the Manchester gun factory, and, as a rival publication put it, The Times reported the occasion in a manner favourable to Whitworth: "From the first to the last the article is written with a view to force Whitworth ordnance on the attention of the public". (5) On Saturday 19 February 1870, Armstrong too took the initiative, writing to the First Lord from the Athenaeum to ask to be allowed to call on him. Though courteous, his letter managed to convey the idea that the head of the navy would be failing in his duty to provide the best defence for the nation if he did not take account of what his firm could supply: "Sir William may be allowed to observe that the experience of the Elswick Ordnance Works and the extent of operations are such as would render it inexpedient in a public point of view, that its practice should be overlooked in any important decision on artillery..." Though prompt, the reply from Childers made clear that Elswick could expect little. By its very lack of flexibility it amounted to a snub: "Sir, I shall be happy to see you here at 11 o`clock tomorrow morning but the pressure of the public business at the present time must prevent me from giving attention to any question except such as it may be necessary to discuss in reference to the current business of the department." Unfortunately, Childers` letter was wrongly addressed to Hyde Park Gate rather than Hyde Park Street and consequently Armstrong did not receive it until 27 February. As he wrote that day to Stuart Rendel, "... from the content it is plain I have lost nothing by not attending".(6)

The lesson of the attitude adopted by Childers was well learned. Over the first two years of Gladstone`s second administration he was Secretary of State for War. Stuart Rendel, the Liberal MP for Montgomeryshire from 1880, apparently suggested that he should make an approach to the Secretary on behalf of his old company, only to be told by Andrew Noble: "My Dear Stuart, I have your letter re Childers. I cannot forget that Childers was an active enemy of ours, and although politics may make him friendly to you I cannot suppose that he likes us and would go out of his way to injure us."(7) Fortunately, by that time Armstrongs were no longer automatically barred from supplying the British services.

As well as striving to find customers for guns, throughout this period Armstrong and his senior colleagues had been struggling to improve their ordnance system. Both the material and methods of construction were involved. Steel was costly and not always reliable. In 1864 estimates made at the Royal Gun Factory were that the cost of a steel tube was at least 50% more than the cost of a wrought iron tube gun. Since the late 1850s Bessemer had been convinced that steel was the best material, and between 1858 and the opening of the International Exhibition in 1862 had made "to order" at his own

Sheffield works 92 mild steel guns, and was by then building ten more. Over the years, his confidence in his own steel increased, and writing to The Times in spring 1879, he claimed: "At the present time my apparatus could produce 500 tons of mild steel per week ready for pouring into the moulds at Woolwich, at a cost not exceeding £5 10s per ton, if made of English iron, or £8 if made from Swedish pig; thus producing the highest quality of steel at less than half the cost of the iron bars used to make the Armstrong coils." But Bessemer steel often contained gaseous inclusions and under extreme conditions this meant that the quality could not be relied upon. Whitworth introduced a hydraulic system designed to compress the liquid steel, expel the inclusions and thereby produce sounder ingots. During the 1860s, the Siemens brothers developed their open hearth process, which was capable of producing better steel than the Bessemer converter. Open hearth steel was discussed at the British Association meeting in 1868, at which it was praised by both Bessemer and Armstrong, although it was not yet commercially successful. By 1865 as well as making steel, Whitworth was buying it from Krupp and Firth. Armstrongs obtained the steel they used from "all the greatest makers, including Krupp and Firth and Cammell". But commenting on this, Noble added: "I think they are the greatest steel makers we know, and none of their barrels are perfect." Two years later in evidence to yet another of the numerous committees which enquired into the making of ordnance, Armstrong claimed that from the first he had favoured steel for the inner tube of ordnance, but that the reason he had not adopted it was that it was difficult to get material of the right quality. But over the last ten years, the quality of steel available had advanced so much that "... I have no hesitation in saying now, that under the existing circumstances, and with the benefit of the experience which has been had, steel is a preferable material for the barrel to coil." The appendix of a report in 1870 contained evidence from Whitworth on this matter but it also recorded the bursting of steel guns.(8)

A letter of October 1874 showed how much effort Armstrong himself was applying in this field, and, incidentally, highlighted one of the problems of their coil construction as compared with an all-steel barrel. In pursuit of a solution, he was prepared to inconvenience both himself and the man who was now becoming his senior partner. In some exasperation, he contacted Noble from Cragside about their 100-ton gun: "I have been flogging my brains over this design and have come to the conclusion that we are exceeding the limit of beneficial thickness. We can take about 3 inches off the diameter ...without diminution of strength. It is no use laying on additional coil if by so doing we only crush the tube-and if to save the tube we relax the shrinkage we simply undo all that we gain by increase of the thickness. I want to have this matter thoroughly discussed with you and to have the benefit of your calculating powers and I propose that we take Sunday for the purpose. I am satisfied that the material of the gun may be shoved with safety considerably beyond 6 tons per inch provided the contractions be properly adjusted and I can see within small limits what they might be. I shall expect you by last train tomorrow." He added a PS. "The designs had better be laid aside until all Questions be determined." (9) The problem recognised in this letter limited the size and especially the girth of the guns they could make. One way out of the problem was to replace heavy iron coils with wire winding around the inner barrel. This was done over the next few years.

By the 1870s, breech-loading ordnance was firmly accepted in continental services, but from 1864, the British services had reverted to muzzle loaded guns. The latter were difficult to load and even heavy guns had to be fairly short. There was a perennial danger of double loading. On 2 January 1879, this led to the bursting of a gun on HMS Thunderer. (10) Avoidance of such disasters was one factor favouring a re-evaluation of breech loading. Another was associated with advances in propellants. Largely as an outcome of researches carried out by Andrew Noble in close association with Frederick Abel of Woolwich, chemist to the War Office, the old black powder, which released all its energy at the moment of ignition, was replaced by slower burning powders which continued to add velocity to the projectile as it moved along the barrel. The sudden release of energy from the old powders accounted for the bottle shape of the heavy guns of that time. In contrast, slower release in the newer powders enabled the designer to produce slimmer, longer barrels. But muzzle loading was difficult in longer barrelled guns, and it began to be recognised that the reintroduction of breech loading was a necessity. Fortunately, technical progress, pioneered in France, improved the breech loading systems at this time. Anticipating the results of the1879 Committee on Ordnance, which set out to examine the respective merits of contemporary muzzle and breech loading, Armstrongs, built two breech loaders designed to use the Noble/Abel powders. (11) At this point rivalry between the two services also played a part in changing the situation.

The Admiralty had, as Stuart Rendel recorded, "... shown symptoms of declaring for independence of Woolwich", and though the latter attempted to counter this by offering the Navy guns which "seemed better than Elswick guns" they failed at proof, and the Navy therefore turned again to Elswick.(12) A breakthrough occurred early in April 1879. In the end, it seems to have been achieved by George Rendel who reported at once, personally to Sir William in London. Stuart Rendel sent his own account of his brother`s success to Andrew Noble: "He was sent for by the Board of Admiralty this morning and is exceedingly pleased with his interview. I had 20 minutes talk with Key*who had seen Mr WH Smith+ after George`s interview. There can be no doubt that George produced an excellent effect. He delivered in fact a little lecture, not volunteered but extracted. He had private talk with Barnaby++ and Hamilton# I also have seen Barnaby. Altogether, we seem to stand as well as possible with the Admiralty and we do not need to fight our own battles or oppose other people. George indeed was careful to defend Woolwich from too impetuous attack by Admiral Hamilton. Events are going for us seemingly in spite of The Times and Daily News and I am glad to find George in good spirits. I left him just now with Sir Lintorn Simmons** and he is going to see Nugent (?) Admiral Hamilton is to come to Elswick next Monday to see the 40 ton gun as now arranged."(13)

After testing at Shoeburyness, the breech loaders built in anticipation of a change in policy were ordered immediately. By autumn that year, Armstrong could see major prospects opening once more for British orders: "I think one may see a growing preference for BLs even for field guns and I think we should try to take the lead in their introduction into the British service. I believe our experience would now enable us to make a first rate weapon which would beat anything Woolwich could produce at present". (14)

A few years later, at the time of the Queen`s Golden Jubilee, it was claimed that the Royal Navy was within sight of making good the unfavourable effects of its long neglect of breech loading, but that the Army was still lagging. In an 1887 survey of the reign, Lord Brassey, editor of the Naval Annual, wrote: "The decision having now been made in favour of breechloaders, the British Government has taken in hand the difficult and costly work of re-arming the Navy with a vigour which will soon enable them to recover the ground lost during the long and anxious period of deliberation." In the same volume, General Viscount Wolseley was outspoken about the backward state of army guns. Owing to the "fatal mistake" of returning to muzzle loading "our field artillery is so far behind that of Continental nations. In no other army is the horse artillery armed with such an inferior gun as our 9-pounder muzzle-loader. We have at last adopted a 12-pounder breechloader, which is superior to any other gun of the same weight: but England, we are told, is too poor to supply more than a small number of them this year. For some time, perhaps for years to come, we must therefore rest content with our inferior guns". (15) In the light of this it was fortunate that Armstrong`s fortunes were linked above all with the navy. More directly, by the 1880s they had become a major shipbuilder. In this field, too there was great scope for expansion. At the end of the year following the Jubilee, a report was published on the late naval manoeuvres. It contained the sentence: "The main lesson which these Manoeuvres emphasise is that Great Britain, whose maritime supremacy is her life, is very far from being as strong as she should be on the seas, either in "personnel" or "materiel"."(16) The large prospect of naval orders, for warships and for guns, held out by such a conclusion, would lead to immense expansion of his firm during the remainder of Armstrong`s life.

* C Astley Cooper Key (1821 - 1888) had active service experience in the RN. 1878 appointed Admiral and 1879 - 1885 was lord of Admiralty. + WH Smith (1825-1891) after developing station bookstalls, libraries etc, in 1868 became an MP and in 1877 was appointed by Disraeli to the Admiralty. ++Nathaniel Barnaby (1829-1915) from 1870 to 1885 was chief naval architect and director of naval construction .# Admiral Richard Vesey Hamilton (1829-1912)

was in 1880 director of naval ordnance ** Sir John Lintorn Simmons (1821-1903) was inspector general of fortifications 1875 -1880.

LABOUR RELATIONS AND THE STRIKE OF 1871

By the time he reached his fiftieth birthday, Armstrong was renowned as an inventor, firmly established as an important manufacturer and honoured as a leading contributor to the power and world standing of Great Britain. Through his fifties, his business grew, but now he and his partners, having lost their prime position in supplying heavy armaments to the British services, were struggling to find alternative outlets for their ordnance capacity. Increasingly Armstrong spent time at Cragside, and had a number of important outside interests, as in connection with the British Association, the Newcastle Literary and Philosophical Society and the institutes of both Civil Engineers and Mechanical Engineers. Everyday control at Elswick was now exercised by Percy Westmacott, George Rendel and Andrew Noble, but even so, Armstrong remained very actively involved in the affairs of Sir WG Armstrong and Company. In this period, he also revealed his thinking on a number of economic issues, and began to be tested over his willingness to apply the theories about which he spoke. In the engineers strike of 1871 he came once more to national prominence, but this time not as a heroic engineering pioneer, but as an intransigent leader of employers. Over a number of years, his views about labour had been changing and they were gradually brought to the attention of a wider public.

His appointment to Woolwich, the honour of a knighthood, and choice of the Elswick Ordnance Works as a second provider of Armstrong guns to the Army and Royal Navy had made Armstrong into a hero on Tyneside. Within a year or so, the effects of the unpredictable flow of orders for war material, and then the blow of a decision that no more guns would be purchased from Elswick, reduced his popularity in the district. As Dougan has pointed out, by this time his company had become too big, and the control system within it too complicated, for continuation of the old, easier communication between the workforce and their head. (1) The 3,000 or so men and boys employed by summer 1861 were not only a much larger but also more diverse workforce than had existed in those early days. An article in the Newcastle Daily Chronicle in August 1861, on "Elswick As It Was And Is", mainly focussed on growth of population and the spread of streets and houses, but it identified another change, that in the nature of the workers. It no doubt pleased its readers by its eulogy, but this moved on from generous observation to unwarranted conclusion: "No nobler set of workmen than the Elswick artisans are to be found in the country. Industrious, skilful, and independent, they wear their heads as high as the proudest aristocrat in the land. Many times, when we have met them on an evening, leaving their workshops, covered with dirt and sweat, their countenance radiant with intelligence, and their free, bold, manly bearing indicative of their independence, we have felt proud of our fellow-countrymen, and ridiculed the idea that any band of foreigners could ever subdue them or rob them of their national freedom." But the writer recognised two distinct groups-"two classes of men"-within the distinguished workforce he met streaming out onto Scotswood Road: "The men who work in the engine shops are a highly skilled class of artisans, and in receipt of the best wages given in their respective trades. The men in the ordnance, on the contrary are not all trained mechanics. Their employment is comparatively light and easy, consisting chiefly of attending to lathes-an occupation requiring more attention than extraordinary mechanical skill." Many of these men had not previously been in iron work of any kind. They were paid 16 to 20 shillings a week "... and very contented and comfortable we understand they feel themselves to be." (2).

By the 1860s, two matters of growing national concern were the threat of foreign industrial competition and the rise of trade unionism. Neither first appeared at this time. In the early 1850s, the British commissioners to the New York Exhibition-a prominent member of whom was Joseph Whitworth-had recognised that in a variety of ways American industrial practice was already superior to that in the United Kingdom. By then unionisation of labour was increasing. The Amalgamated Society of Engineers, formed in 1851, had 12,000 members by the end of its first year. Over the next decade, fears of the decline of British manufacturing pre-eminence increased and there was a tendency to attribute a considerable share of the blame to the nature, aspirations and organisation of British working men. For instance, after visits in 1867 to France and Germany, the Teesside ironmaster, Bernhard Samuelson, concluded that continental workers were in a number of respects superior to those at home. They seemed better educated, less unionised and more peaceable, all admirable qualities from the employer`s perspective: "The workmen save their wages, buy a piece of land, which they and their families cultivate. Thus, they become attached to localities, and are interested supremely in the preservation of amicable relations between them and their employers. Strikes do not enter into their heads, though it is undeniably true, while as a rule they are better educated than the British workmen, they work longer hours for considerably less pay." (3) Clearly some of the conditions Samuelson found in European iron working communities-such as local workers` plots-were not applicable in such a densely settled, sprawling engineering community as Elswick or its near Tyneside neighbours. But as a leading and able ASE man wrote a few years later, their masters seemed to be looking for a similar kind of pliant workforce, and if the men took vigorous action, culminating in strikes, they would be looked on as "... ungrateful, insubordinate, idle fellows, who would neither work nor want; that in fact they ought to have nothing to do but to work when they are told; to leave off only when the employers choose; and to receive with thankfulness the money which is offered them." (4) For men in the engine works or the ordnance factory at Elswick such automatic subservience was becoming a thing of the past. Yet for them strikes too were undesirable. The Times summed up the matter: "The Engineers are probably the most prosperous, intelligent and closely organised body of working men in the United Kingdom, and they have in consequence enjoyed for several years a comparative immunity from strikes. Employers have rarely attempted to try a fall with them." (5) It was Armstrong`s misfortune to lead a group of Tyneside engineering employers in an attempt to defeat this exceptional band of men in a major dispute. His early experiences with working men had failed to show him how hard such a task would be.

In the early 1860s, after a long period of high demand, orders for ordnance began to fall away. This caused a short and limited dispute, which pointed the way towards more important conflicts between masters and men. In May 1862, the night shifts in the ordnance works were told by the foremen who closely supervised their work that rates of pay would be cut by 20%. A group of men left work early and were dismissed, and then about 250 men, the labour force of two of the ordnance shops, withdrew their labour. A few days later, a group of four men presented a reasoned and highly conciliatory letter to Andrew Noble in which they asked him to reconsider the reduction. He refused to do so and the striking men returned to work on the reduced terms the firm had demanded. Armstrong did not take an active part in trying to avert this brief conflict. (6) His non-intervention was formally correct for at that time the Elswick Ordnance Company was an independent company in whose conduct he had no official role.

For the time being Armstrong continued to be outgoing and positive in relationships with his men. On Saturday evening 9 August 1862, nine weeks after the strikers from the ordnance shops returned to work, he entertained about 270 members of the Elswick Engine Works Literary and Mechanics Institute in his newly opened Banqueting Hall in Jesmond Dene. Among the "gentlefolk" present were Andrew Noble and George Cruddas` son, William. The company: "sat down to a most excellent tea, together with a plentiful supply of beef, which rendered it a most substantial repast." Sir William "went round" the company exhibiting a mechanical bird like a bird of paradise, which shook it wings, moved its head and sang for a minute or two before disappearing back into its box. Replying to a vote of thanks, he said he hoped it would not be the last pleasant evening they would spend in that room. When the men left the Dene, they were accompanied by a band playing the "Keel Row" as they made their way back into Newcastle. (7) A few weeks later, there was another opportunity for Armstrong to consolidate his good relations with his work people. He laid the foundation stone for a new building to replace the existing Elswick Mechanics Institute. This had provided classes in mechanical and free hand drawing and mathematics, but, though it was one of the most successful institutes in the North of

England, it was now too small to meet the need. The stone laying ceremony was followed by a soiree attended by over 1,500 people in the Elswick pattern shop. After tea, there was a meeting, presided over by Armstrong, at which prizes were presented for mechanical drawing. A fitter from the works took the first prize. As he distributed the rest of the prizes, the chairman made a few "complimentary observations" to each recipient. The visitors were given an opportunity to inspect the workshops. A year later the "magnificent" new Mechanics Institute and Library was opened by its "... enlightened and liberal proprietor." After the proceedings at Elswick, a dinner was given at Jesmond for members of the Institute, and it was followed by a concert. (8) All this was positive and friendly, even if paternalistic, yet a trend towards alienation between Armstrong and his men was underway. The gap already opening between them was widened by circumstances beyond their control.

In October 1862, the Elswick Ordnance Company was told that it would receive no new Government orders; early next year Armstrong resigned his directorship of the Royal Gun Factory; a few months later the ordnance company was merged with the engine works. The search began to find new customers for the ordnance works. Presidency of the 1863 Newcastle meeting of the British Association was quickly followed by the beginning of the Cragside project. Others, and Andrew Noble in particular, undertook more and more of the day-to-day control of Elswick operations. In short, there was sufficient in the way of pressures, preoccupations and other factors to separate Armstrong from the labour force he had brought into being in his factories. Elswick employed about 300 in 1850, but 3,000 by 1861 and in 1864 3,800. The population of Elswick township had been 3,539 at the 1851 census but reached 14,345 ten years later, and by 1871 had almost doubled to 27,801. Already large areas of poor terraced housing were spreading across the slopes from the river up to the West Road. Conditions of life for Armstrong employees and their dependents were hard. In the early 1860s, the average age of death of Elswick members of the Amalgamated Society of Engineers was 37.5 years. Almost one third of mortality was from tuberculosis. As well as the practical difficulty of bridging the divide between masters and men, between the lives of those crowded together in the streets branching from

Scotswood Road and those who were privileged to live in Jesmond Dene, at Cragside or in the mansions occupied by other partners and top managers, there was a general trend to alienation which was probably inevitable given the huge increase in the numbers dependent on activity in the works. As the gap between him and his men widened, Armstrong`s own thinking developed in ways which helped along the process of division. Some of this came out in various public addresses.

The National Association for the Promotion of Social Science was formed in 1857 to consider the best means of uniting all those interested in social improvement. Like the British Association, each year it met in a different town or city. It produced some interesting material, but as a commentator recognised a decade after its formation, the outcome could not be claimed as an unqualified success: "The amount of discussion has, at all the meetings, been very considerable, though there is some diversity of opinion as to whether the results have materially aided in solving the more difficult questions of the day."(9) In September 1871, Newcastle upon Tyne was host to the annual Social Science Congress, and Armstrong gave an address on "Economy and Trade." His tone was as usual quiet and reasonable but he made clear that he was opposed to all types of restriction on free competition. It was less than 12 years since the publication of "On the Origin of Species", but he recognised some form of social Darwinism as a key factor in human life-"Struggle for superiority is the mainspring of progress. It is an instinct deeply rooted in our nature." Industry and trade were the foundations of the present age, and: "If regulated by no other law than the natural laws of competition, the former would...yield its best and most abundant fruits and the latter would unite all the nations of the earth in a great co-operative society..." [Might such a world also be one which no longer required armaments?] However, as he put it, "local and class" interests asserted themselves with the aim of benefiting particular sections of the community at the expense of others. He subscribed to the labour theory of value: "Labour, physical and mental, is the creative element of our nature. Nothing possesses value until labour has been expended on it ... Analyse as we will, we always come to labour as the foundation of value. Machines for saving labour are themselves the offspring of labour, and capital is nothing more than an accumulation of unused products of labour." But, just as protection (what he described as "restrictive laws on commerce") reduced the benefits which might be derived from specialisation and trade, so too particular industries were being adversely affected by trade union regulations. In the light of subsequent events, his statement of what he regarded as valid and what invalid functions of a trade union was important. In the end, he invoked the very nature of the world-as he saw it-as limiting their scope: "As societies for affording mutual assistance amongst members, these societies are deserving of all praise. As means of opposing their powers of combination against counter combinations for reducing the price of labour, they are also perfectly legitimate, but when they attempt to give fictitious value to their labour by restrictive rules, they commit the error of contending with natural laws, which cannot be violated without very injurious consequences." He did not spell out these higher principles, nor tell his listeners whom they would affect, but he believed there were natural restrictions on the proportion of the poorer classes who could rise. In his opinion, the working class "... abounds with men adapted by nature to rise above their fellows, but who are kept down by want of education and the repressive influences which surround them." On the other hand, the general prospects for this class of human beings were limited: "I hope the day will come when, with better teaching and more frugal habits, the working classes will be enabled to participate in the employment of labour as well as in the receipt of wages. Still, however, they must bear in mind that in a densely populated country like England the masses of the people cannot, in the nature of things be rich."(10)

At this time, in evidence given in Newcastle to the Royal Commission on Scientific Instruction and the Advancement of Science, Sir William made clear that, though he had been a pioneer of education to improve the situation, he had a relatively low opinion of the abilities of most workers. He explained that if one spoke in scientific language it was impossible to make oneself understood by an ordinary foreman. Asked to identify the objectives of the recently formed Newcastle College of Physical Science, in which he had been actively involved, he responded in a statement that in some parts had an almost biblical tone. When discussing the diffusion of scientific knowledge generally, he observed: "There is an almost total absence of such knowledge amongst persons who are engaged in manufactures, mines, agriculture and so on; and it is quite manifest that by communicating to those persons scientific knowledge you will enable them to work in the light instead of working in the dark, as they are at present; all their practice being rule of thumb work." For those lower down the educational scale Elswick works ran evening classes. When asked: "The work that they go through in the day is not so severe as to disqualify them from attending for instruction in the evening?" he responded: "Certainly not; not to healthy young men." He admitted that preference was given in the works to those who showed promise in the evening classes: "We are always on the lookout for those who display any aptitude and any superior progress ... we are guided by our own interest in doing so; that is the principal inducement. Of course, one would naturally like to put forward deserving young men for their own sakes as well."(11) It was all paternalistic and rather patronising, yet at the time at which he gave these opinions of the abilities of ordinary men, he and his partners were engaged in a major dispute with local workers, in which the latter proved at every turn more resourceful and imaginative than their masters.

In the first place, the men chose a favourable time for their action. The national economy had moved strongly upwards in recent years, so that male employment in Britain in 1871 was 13 percent higher than in 1861. In 1868, the index of industrial production was only 39.9% the level it would reach in 1913, but in 1871, it was at 46.1%. The unemployment rate for workers in engineering, metals and shipbuilding had fallen over the same three years from 10.0 to 1.3%.(12) For employers there was pressure to complete work in order to take full advantage of the boom, but the pool of unemployed labour on which they might draw to replace recalcitrant men had decreased. Secondly, the men did not ask for an increase in wages, which might have been passed on to customers and when trade conditions worsened would be replaced by wage reductions, but looked instead for improved conditions of work, specifically for reduced hours. Once established in the working regime, this would be less easy to reverse. When a decade earlier the Amalgamated Society of Engineers surveyed the normal working week in engineering workshops it found that the average in the Newcastle and Gateshead area was 59.5 hours. This remained more or less the standard, and the normal rate by 1871 was 59 hours. At the end of April 1871, a Nine Hours League was formed at a meeting held on Tyneside. Its target was a 54-hour week. A few prominent firms in the area, though not immediately conceding this reduction, chose to deal directly with their men, informing them that, if the nine hours was won generally, they too would conform. By this means, Palmers of Jarrow and the Stephenson engineering works in Newcastle were able to continue working. But most leading firms on the Tyne, cooperating -notwithstanding the reservations Armstrong had expressed about such actions in his Social Science address -as the Associated Employers, determined to fight the men. As the largest engineering employer in the district, Armstrong headed the confrontation on behalf of the industry. His counterpart at the League was an Alnwick born engineer, not yet 29 when the dispute began, John Burnett.

In early May 1871, the men formally asked for, and the employers rejected, a 54-hour working week. On Saturday 27 May 7,400 engineers employed by various Tyneside works came out on strike. Two months later by which time 7,500 men were out, 36% of them were from Armstrongs. Two important attempts to mediate between the two sides, the first by Charles Mark Palmer in July and a second two months later by the Sheffield MP and industrialist, Anthony John Mundella, failed. Meantime the men received support from other unions, and, belatedly also from the headquarters of the ASE. The financial help they received in fact rose week by week as the strike dragged on. Settlement of the dispute was not agreed until the second week of October, when the employers felt compelled to concede. The working week was to be cut to 54 hours, six days of nine hours. The history of this long strike is complicated and has been fully and well-told elsewhere. (13) Here, the main aim is to assess the part played by Armstrong.

He seems not to have resisted playing the leading part on behalf of the employers. One of his leading concerns was to ensure that his fellow industrialists held to their collective commitment to fight against what the men wanted. Among other things, this meant not opening their gates to returning workers without general agreement. On 4 June, a week after the dispute began, Armstrong wrote to

Crawshay of the large and long-established iron work and engineering firm of Hawks, Crawshay and Company of Gateshead, to try to prevent it falling out of line. If it was to be a "considerable affair", he thought they ought to have "a meeting of masters before you reopen your shops", for "none of us ought to take any separate action whatever". If men were allowed to return to work, "... above all things a pledge should be exacted from every man that he will discontinue his connection with the league and not in any way contribute to the support of the men on strike." He assured Crawshay: "Depend upon it no harm will be done by showing a little hesitation about re-opening the several works where the strike has taken place." Men allowed to return should accept new rules, and he already had some ideas about what they should be: "In framing the new rules I should be quite willing to concede some advantages to the men in return for their submitting to regulations which have become essential to the removal of abuses and the correction of unwarrantable laxities." To communicate his views more forcefully he planned to send his key representative-unasked for-to pay a visit: "Captain Noble will be in Newcastle tomorrow and will call upon you at your office at about a quarter past 11."(14) A few days later he contacted Noble about keeping another important employer in line. Francis C Marshall was a marine engine specialist, who after working for Palmers had a year before joined Benjamin Browne to take over and reshape R and W Hawthorn. Although from labouring stock himself, Marshall was keenly against the strikers, but Armstrong`s concern was that he was showing an inclination to act independently: "I see no harm in Marshall seeing his men so long as he makes them understand that having been compelled by the league to join the Masters, he cannot take any independent action and that we must have one settlement for all. If he takes a different course it will be ruinous and not only so but it will be keeping bad faith with his colleagues."(15) On Thursday morning, 3 August, the main firms tried to break the strike by reopening their factories but very few men proved willing to resume work on their masters` terms.

By mid August, Armstrong had persuaded himself that the employers were winning the battle, and when he wrote to Noble on the 20th he was optimistic. After mentioning recent game shooting and catches, he turned to the strike: "... my impression is that it is drawing to a close. It is now clear that any number of fresh hands can be obtained. They are coming in at the rate of about 100 a day and the only difficulty is where and how to accommodate them. By Thursday or Friday we shall have 500 boarded and lodged in the Works, the school and the Institute and I hope by that time they will begin to slip out into lodgings although the difficulty of obtaining accommodation outside is very great-partly owing to security, partly to fear of receiving "black-legs", and partly from the sympathy of lodging housekeepers with the strike. There has not been much disturbance and what spirit of violence exists is cowed by the force of special constables we have organised and by the committals which have been affected. Our old hands come in very slowly. I think however the men must begin to view the struggle as hopeless. We are getting men from Belgium, Copenhagen, Sweden and your quarter [presumably meaning Scotland]-all I expect skilled men. In fact we want no others as any number of labourers can be got from the Thames ... If the house difficulty can be got over we shall soon make an end of the affair."(16) This proved too sanguine. The loss of good men, and the inability of the employers to retain sufficient of the new men they brought in, would mean that in the end they and not their men would have to give in.

Within three weeks of the beginning of the dispute, some 4,000 men had left the area to seek work elsewhere. As the American consul in Newcastle noted soon afterwards some first class engineers chose to migrate to the United States. Responding to this loss of their labour force and the prospect of a longer term shortage of good men and in hope that they might be able to restart idle plant, by the end of Race Week-midsummer week-the engineering employers had begun importing labour from other districts and from the continent. But the workers proved able to meet such an attempt to break their strike through what the Newcastle Chronicle denounced as "social war". In mid August, it became known that the masters had sent agents to Belgium to try to engage two to three thousand men, and Armstrong had obtained consent from the Danish Government to bring over workers from its national arsenal. In turn the General Council of the International Working Men`s Association sent two men to Belgium to neutralise the efforts of the Employers` agents. It wrote to sections of its own organisation in Brussels, Antwerp, Ghent, Liege, Verviers and Charleroi. Delegates of the men were also sent to Germany and Denmark. (17) Even when strike-breaking workers arrived on the Tyne, the employers could not be sure of them. As Armstrong`s letter to Noble indicated, there were important contributions from the east end of London, and Scotland, and over 1,000 workers came from Denmark, Sweden, Belgium and Germany. At Elswick, the company schools were closed to children and converted into barracks for "blackleg" labour. Some men from the south of England were lodged within the works. Men came down to Elswick from Dundee but the strikers "got at them", persuading them to return home.(18)

Remarkably, the employers were widely opposed by those controlling key elements of the press. The Times and Pall Mall Gazette, the Spectator and the Newcastle Daily Chronicle were sympathetic to the men, and the two leading trade journals, Engineer and Engineering, were scarcely any better if looked at from the perspective of the employers. The Newcastle Journal did support the masters. The Times published letters from Armstrong as representative of the employers, but it also printed the letters it received from Burnett. As the latter informed readers of The Times, "... schools belonging to Sir William were closed to the children and converted into barracks for the foreigners. Tenants living in Sir William`s properties received notice to quit if they did not return to work; various foremen and clerks who would assent to the operation, were sworn in as Special Constables, and preparations were made to guard the different factories much the same as if they were convict establishments." On 10 August, the Newcastle Chronicle found an even more inflammatory topic. It denounced the pressures that had induced the authorities of the Newcastle Lying-in Hospital to refuse facilities to the wives of striking workers. (19)

By early September, Armstrong was losing enthusiasm, but in typically dogged fashion was still committed to the cause-as he told Stuart Rendel: "We are fighting away here very hard and see nothing for it but persevering in our present course." During the month, The Times castigated the employers for "imprudent and impolitic conduct" in refusing to negotiate with the men and for introducing foreign workers. After reading the leader in The Times of 14 September,

Armstrong was so incensed that he wrote to the editor on the same day; he reckoned that the men themselves could not have produced an article more favourable to them. The tone and content of his letter was now very different from those of a reasonable man, and perhaps the nearest he came to espousing the class struggle: "We had imagined that a determined effort to wrest concessions from employers by sheer force of combination was not a thing which found favour with the more educated and intelligent classes, whose opinions generally find expression in the columns of The Times." (20)

By early October, the optimistic outcome Armstrong had looked for was recognised to be unrealisable. At this time the highly respected Newcastle newspaper owner Joseph Cowen and Ralph Philipson, Town Clerk of Newcastle, acted as go-betweens to bring the masters and the men together. They secured an agreement in the first week of the month, and it was signed on Monday 9 October. The men obtained the nine-hour day. Andrew Noble told Stuart Rendel the employers had "... made the best of a hard job." and "we pay a fearful price for it." He reckoned that the agreement meant that effectively wages had been raised by 11.6%. (21) In spite of their best efforts and their great resources, the employers had been defeated by their own men. Notwithstanding his abilities, commitment and "perseverance", Sir William Armstrong had been out-manoeuvred by John Burnett.

When, almost half a century later, Burnett died, one of the leading trade journals described him as: "A most sympathetic man, who had gained general respect by his absolute fairness in all matters pertaining to labour ... his straightforwardness, experience and sage judgement ...won recognition from all parties."(22) Before the end of his life, Armstrong too had regained high regard from many quarters, but his experiences in summer 1871 coloured his subsequent attitudes to the increasing thousands his works employed, as repeatedly he made clear. As a colleague from his later years recognised, wherever the blame lay, "... after the strike of 1871 matters could never again be quite what they had been. The whole connection between employers and employed became far more formal and precise. A suppressed antagonism seemed to be always present, even in the most peaceful interludes. Everything has to be laid down by rule of thumb." (23)

ARMSTRONG - TRAVELLER

One of the best-known representations of Armstrong is in an oil painting by his protégé, the local artist HH Emmerson. He is sitting in a comfortable chair in the heavy stone inglenook of the dining room at Cragside, wearing slippers and reading a newspaper. Two dogs are lying quietly by his side. On the stone mantle piece are carved the words which a near contemporary described as the sentiment which filled the whole of Cragside "the kindly North-Country proverb-East or West Hame`s Best."(1) He was then in his early 70s - though he is painted looking rather younger than his years, as he apparently did. The philosophy represented by the inscription seems to have represented his thinking throughout life. In this respect, at least he was at odds with the drift of the times. In 1902 the warden of Toynbee Hall and one of his colleagues commented on the changes in holiday travelling in Britain since the Bank Holidays Act of 1871, the period coinciding with the last 30 years of Armstrong`s life. They referred specifically to Bank holidays, but many of their remarks were of wider application. "People who had hitherto taken casual holidays, and perhaps felt somewhat conscience-stricken at neglecting work, now felt justified, and began to plan the use of these days. The railways and caterers for amusement have of course risen to the occasion, and tempting advertisements crowd the walls. The effect of the Act has been to stimulate the holiday sense and awaken the curiosity of many a mental sleeper. The offer of a whole day has encouraged enterprise in those who hitherto had spent their broken bits of holiday within a few yards of their homes, and it has led those who have learnt to enjoy one day to demand a longer season. But...enormous crowds of people composed of one social class generate excitement which is unwholesome...and there is often a laxity of manner and morals, followed by episodes which are demoralizing...The tendency every year is for people to go farther afield and to make more use of the railways."(2) Such forms of "progress" can scarcely have commended themselves to a man of Armstrong`s sensitivities. Even so, both for work and to a limited extent for pleasure he too travelled widely, at any rate in his homeland.

In his youth, he lived and worked for years in London. Later he made numerous visits and spent many more weeks there in connection with the search for business for his engine works and afterwards in promoting his ordnance system. Into his late eighties he readily went up to London by train on the firm`s behalf. For many years, he travelled around the country, visiting docks, mines and factories in the main industrial areas. In contrast, early and late in life he took brief breaks from a crushing business regime amidst the delights of the Lake District. Though in these respects very much a man of the Victorian age, he never showed an appetite for one of the main indulgencies which the newly rich shared with their aristocratic forerunners and contemporaries, foreign travel. In his voluminous papers, covering the last sixty years of his life, there is record of one visit to the Continent. Only once did he travel beyond Europe. The first of these journeys was strictly for business, the second, though focussed on an engineering proposition, resulted in a fuller, interesting and published account.

The nine-hour day, conceded by Tyneside employers after a long and bitter strike and in which he had played a stubborn but apparently rather unimaginative role, came into operation on 1 January 1872. Within a few days of this, for him, unhappy outcome of this significant struggle with labour, Armstrong left home on the longest journey of his life. He returned the following month and soon wrote up an account of his experiences. First presented in four lectures later that year to the Literary and Philosophical Society of Newcastle upon Tyne, and published with illustrations and two maps two years after that, "A Visit to Egypt" provides insights into aspects of the man which contrast both with the dour, unbending leader of the opposition to the Nine Hour League, and with the more characteristically quiet, gentlemanly businessman. Indeed, it reveals features of his character, temperament and abilities scarcely seen anywhere else, and points to unsuspected talents, including a wider imagination and greater literary skills.

The ostensible purpose of the journey was that he, in company with the civil engineer, John Fowler, who two years before had been consulted by Ismail Pasha about engineering schemes for Egypt, should examine the cataracts above Aswan to see whether they could be bypassed by a canal. Stuart Rendel accompanied Armstrong to help him with translation from the French, the language spoken by better-educated Egyptians. They travelled by rail via Paris to Turin, Rome, Naples and Brindisi, where they boarded a steamer for Alexandria. After a railway journey to Cairo and meetings there, they took a train to Minieh, at which place they embarked on a dahabeah, or traditional style Nile boat, towed by a steamer. This was English built, and powered by engines made by Stephenson, as Armstrong assured his listeners and readers. They made their way slowly up river, breaking their journey at the main tourist sites. Long afterwards, Stuart Rendel recorded: "I never spent a more refreshing and enjoyable holiday than on board Sir John Fowler`s dahabeah to and from Aswan." At Assouan, as the terminus of uninterrupted Nile navigation was then styled, they stayed for about a fortnight. (3) A certain amount of survey work was undertaken, but Armstrong`s account of this essentially tourist visit-for in truth in comparison with that the canal project seems to have taken little enough of either their time or their attention-revealed a careful and understanding observer of places, scenery and people. There was a consciousness of the importance of time and history, which its author showed nowhere else, and even a sense of humour. Often real skill was demonstrated in the word pictures, which he presented. His 176-page booklet is indeed an excellent "read", but only a few highlights of its different qualities can be considered here.

Alexandria, whose harbour was then being greatly extended and improved, was "essentially a seafaring place, reminding me in many respects of Wapping." (A few months over ten years later the Royal Navy fired on the city forts there-forts defended by guns made at Elswick. It was the first event in a series, which quickly brought about effective British control of Egypt.) Armstrong and his companions arrived in the westernised section of Cairo in the evening. When he awoke, he was almost bowled over by what he saw: "Next morning, when the sun was fully up, I looked out from the door of the Hotel upon a large open space, surrounded by mansions and villas, all of a modern European stamp. Everything visible exhibited signs of European innovation, except the people, and these were far more

Oriental in appearance than the inhabitants of Alexandria. Nothing could be more picturesque and interesting than the crowds of people within view of the Hotel. There was every gradation in appearance between extreme dignity and extreme grotesqueness, and not infrequently these two qualities were combined. Stately Arabs dressed in mantles and turbans were to be seen seated on the rear of little donkeys much smaller than themselves. The quantity of apparel varied from almost nothing at all, to such a reduplication of garments as would oppress the Englishman, even in his own cold climate ... In the colour of dress, equal variety was displayed. In the East, colour is always used with skill and good taste, and the crowd before me looked like a bed of sober-coloured flowers harmoniously mixed to please an artist`s eye." His description of the "native city" was if anything even more colourful.(4)

In contrast to colour and romance, some realities of Egyptian life were difficult for a Victorian Englishman to face. In those parts of Cairo he saw there was scarcely a house without one or more slaves. He concluded that: "... in general they are kindly treated, moderately worked and become much attached to the family in which they are placed." It may have been a far too optimistic assessment of their condition. In any case, he deplored the horrible business of collecting them –"this villainous pursuit of catching slaves." Voyaging up the river they saw several large boats laden with slaves on their way to Cairo, and when he was in a Nubian village, an "especially ugly woman offered me, in perfect seriousness, a fine black child of about three years old, who seemed quite alive to what was meant, and exhibited a determined opposition to the proposal."(5)

He was skilful in his evocation of the Egyptian countryside and people and the senses of continuity and change. Nowhere is this better brought out than in his word-picture of the area around Siout more or less midway between Cairo and Aswan: "Conceive yourself standing on a high cliff, looking down upon the flat valley of the Nile, as on a green sea, sharply defined against a beach of yellow sand. Observe the opposite side, seven miles distant, bounded by a bolder coast, equally yellow, though consisting chiefly of rock; then imagine a number of dark brown mounds, rising like islands out of the green surface, each surmounted by an Arab village, enveloped in palm trees. Turn your mind`s eye downwards, upon the city of Siout, insulated by verdure, and composed of low, flat-roofed, clay-coloured houses, with palm trees and white-washed minarets rising high above them. Finally, picture to yourself, the glistening, tortuous streak which marks the Nile, flowing through the midst of the valley, and extending north and south as far as vision can reach. If you can do all this, you will see the land of Egypt as it is; and also as it used to be, save only that in the place of mounds of rubbish, capped with Arab villages, there would be great cities, adorned, not with minarets, but with the massive temples of the ancient religion."(6)

Strikingly, though critical of various things in Egyptian society, he seems not to have entertained, and certainly not to parade, ideas of intrinsic white supremacy. For instance, he recorded that as their vessel drew into Aswan they were greeted by the town governor: "... a tall, straight, handsome Nubian, of noble bearing [who] ... would have made a grand Othello if he could have played the part." Discussing irrigation by the shadoof-an obvious fascination to a man who for forty years had researched hydraulic operations-he was also impressed by the lithe, muscular bodies of those who operated them, "... and, as I looked upon their olive skins, tinted with the red glow of exercise, I became rather disgusted with my own colour, and thought what a fright I must look in the eyes of these people."(7)

Though it was almost unavoidable in such a country, unusually for him, Armstrong was obviously deeply conscious of and appreciated the burden of history. He wrote: "It takes one`s breath away to think of the antiquity of Memphis." When there, after lunch he "... stole away alone for a ramble among the tombs." The Great Temple at Karnak was "... the most imposing ruins I had ever seen..." He visited them three times, twice by day and once when they lay in moonlight. From the top of the Great Pyramid he was not only impressed by the "very fine" view of the Nile valley, but as he told his Lit and Phil audience: "I know of no situation more calculated than this to carry back the mind into the depths of historical time and to awaken solemn reflections on the wickedness and folly of mankind." Visiting the temple of Edfu, he was struck by the fact that the time interval between Karnak and it more or less equalled that from Edfu to the present. (8)

For audiences in his native city, he was adept in comparing Egyptian features with what they knew locally, or failing that by wider British standards. Thus, the native city of Cairo was very large "... containing fully twice the population of Newcastle and Gateshead."; the area occupied by the great hall of the columns at Karnak was "nearly equal to that of Eldon Square." Bringing in his own early career, he remarked that the Great Pyramid at Gizeh was "just about equal" to the area of Lincolns Inn Field. Originally the pyramid had risen to about 76 feet higher than the cross on the dome of St Paul`s. Coming to more modern analogies, they would be impressed to learn that the material already removed in the dredging which in their generation was so dramatically improving the navigation of the Tyne was greater than that excavated in making the Suez Canal. (9)

Occasionally the perspective of a western employer of labour appears in his travelogue. As he put it, in handicraft work the master was the only idle person: "He sits and smokes, while his workmen ply their trade behind him with considerable artistry, though with rude, old-world tools, and in a fiddle-faddle sort of way." On the Bahr Yousef canal, running alongside the Nile in lower Egypt, he saw thousands involved in restoration work and bearing soil away in buckets: "The multitude of carriers thus employed, look, at a distance, like a stream of ants, carrying their eggs to a new nest, and returning by a parallel route, to renew their burdens." When they visited quarries near Aswan in which the ancient Egyptians had worked red syenite, the interval of thousands of years seemed to melt away: "Everything...looks so recent that my first impulse on entering was to ask, where are the workmen?" (10) He speculated about the sort of metal tools used to cut the stones of the pyramids as well as about the inscriptions that covered them.

Unusually too, his account was marked by a quiet humour. When they visited Memphis, they had to travel seven miles across country in the saddle, and his poor little donkey threw him off in the dirt: "I quickly gathered myself up, and adopting Mr Pickwick`s policy, when running after his hat on a windy day, I tried to look as if I thought it as good a joke as the rest of the company unmistakably did." He was obviously intrigued by Egyptian women, and carefully observed them in the native quarters of Cairo: "The women mix freely with the men in the streets, and so long as they keep their faces veiled below their eyes, they care not for being jostled by the crowd. In fact, I think they rather like it. Neither are they at all particular about exhibiting their bare feet and ankles, or even a little more, for I frequently saw them trying on stockings at the shop doors; but, as to showing their faces, Oh no! anything rather than that indecency." At Aswan, in the house of the governor, he saw a good deal more, but in reporting it, he once again assumed the public attitudes of a Victorian gentleman: "... the entertainment of the evening consisted of coffee and pipes, with minstrels and dancing girls. The performances of the latter were more curious than edifying, and to see them once is sufficient." (11)

Amidst exotic scenery and despite the almost tangible burden of millennia of history, he was not a man to forget the present. He made references to power and prestige, but also to the wastefulness of Ismail Pasha, a man who, as his family had grown in power, was now no longer a viceroy of the Ottoman Empire, but khedive or king of Egypt, in which he was said to own one third of all the land. In Cairo Ismail had built a fine hotel and grand opera house and laid out public gardens-but ordinary people seemed not to care for them. The vessel in which they travelled was over provided with crew and servants: "... we had 43 persons to attend upon, and escort just four Christian gentlemen. Our store of provisions was boundless. Truly the Khedive is no niggard provider." They disembarked at some of the great sugar factories he owned. These were spaced at 40 or 50-mile intervals along the river, and each had a large tract of land that provided its requirements of cane. In Armstrong`s opinion millions had been unwisely invested in the Suez Canal; instead a railway should have been constructed up river into the Sudan, for the railway was "that greatest of all civilisers ... Egypt has made a great mistake in promoting the excavation of this canal, which has already deprived the Suez Railway of nearly all its traffic." In the light of such comments, he naturally referred to the international loans Ismail had raised-and which seven years later would bring about his enforced abdication. Given the nature of his own business at Elswick and his role some years before in negotiations with representatives of Egypt, he went on to make a rather strange comment on the Khedive`s increasing autonomy: "He has also obtained the independent right to contract loans, and create armaments, save only that he is not to have a fleet of ironclads, a restriction which I regard as much more to his advantage than his detriment."(12)

In early February 1872 Armstrong`s small party was in Nubia. From this southernmost point in their journey, they returned to Cairo. There they had several interviews with Khedive Ismail. He entertained them at dinner. Then, after a short visit by special train to Suez, they travelled back to Alexandria, steamed to Brindisi and then on by rail to England. They arrived home to snow and fog, a journey`s end which, as he put it, made them feel "... that if any form of idolatry be excusable, it is the worship of the sun." (13)

Although Stuart Rendel noted that their visit led to complete plans being prepared at Elswick for what he called a "ship-railway" across the blockage to navigation at Aswan, vessels being drawn up an incline by hydraulic power provided by turbines driven by the cataracts themselves, and descending by gravity on the other side-a "perfectly practicable scheme" as he called it-this engineering project was never carried through.(14) Seven years later Britain and France were prime movers in bringing about the abdication of Ismail, and in 1882, after a brief conflict, Egypt effectively passed under British control. In December that year, when the Institute of Civil Engineers entertained the leader of the military and naval expedition to Egypt, Lord Wolseley, to a celebratory dinner, it was presided over by Armstrong. (15) This single occasion apart, it is intriguing that, despite the great impact that his experiences in the Nile valley had on him, in his voluminous correspondence over the rest of his life, he seemed never to mention it again.

CRAGSIDE - MAKING AND BEAUTIFYING A GREAT HOUSE

In 15 years from 1870, the ideas of the young architect Norman Shaw and the growing wealth and continuing drive of William Armstrong together converted a modest country retreat into what was widely proclaimed as one of the architectural wonders of the Victorian age. After training in the architectural schools of the Royal Academy, Shaw spent two years on the continent before serving for six years as assistant to established architects. Then, after being partner with WE Nesfield until 1868, he practiced on his own account. Overall, a modern architect has described Shaw`s buildings as "... curiously timeless," having "a relaxed quality that contrast absolutely with the gesturing of so much Victorian design." (1) He soon gained a reputation for his country houses. His first important project was Leyswood, near Groombridge, Surrey, designed in 1868/69. Its half-timbered construction, gables, turrets and occasional steep roofs, and bold, tall, finely shaped chimneys, made it "picturesque", but with a trace of "Gothic" feeling. It is unmistakably a close relative of the house he was to sketch out for Armstrong only a year or so later, and of which fine drawings were published in Building News in spring 1872. What seemed relaxed in the setting of the Weald looked very different in the moorlands of northern England. The first steps towards the transformation of Cragside into a great country house were taken in 1869, a year before work on the Northumberland Central Railway was completed. They were linked with an unusual problem in Jesmond Dene.

In the course of a competition for the decoration of the Palace of Westminster the painter John Calcot Horsley produced a huge painting of "Prince Hal taking the crown from his father`s bedside." The government declined to buy it, but Armstrong did. His intention was to display it in the Banqueting Hall in Jesmond Dene, a place built for him by Dobson at the beginning of the 1860s. Although its windows provided "a series of lovely glimpses" into the Dene, this hall proved deficient in a number of ways. It was not well lit, and as it lacked large stretches of unbroken wall space, it could not take such a big picture as "Prince Hal". Accordingly it was decided that an extra gallery should be built, and at Horsley`s suggestion, in late summer 1869 Armstrong invited Norman Shaw to visit Tyneside. He designed a new display area, which was subsequently provided at the Banqueting Hall, but before this was done, the contact had already led on to bigger things. Having talked about his idea of expanding Cragside, Armstrong took Shaw to it for a weekend. Allegedly, it was while his host went out with a shooting party that Shaw, left alone, sketched out the broad lines which future expansion there followed. Over the next two years, a dining room and library were built onto the northern side of the original house, and by 1872, the great west facade was more or less complete. In spring that year, the tower was under construction. (2) Over the next few years, much more was inserted into the space between this house of 1872 and the hillside, including archways, a long, top-lit picture gallery on the second floor, gables and a second tower. In the early 1880s, a south east wing was added at second floor level, including as its main unit a large drawing room, again top-lit and with access from the picture gallery. By 1887, the house was more or less complete, looking very much as it does today, except that the tower to the right of the archway leading from the south front into the kitchen court-the Gilnockie Tower-was at that time topped by a glass-roofed observatory. Over the next few years this was replaced by gables. The sturdy but square, rather drab original country house built in the early 1860s was fully incorporated into this greater house but its whole character was changed. Now it was, as a contemporary account put it, a mixture of "Gothic" and sixteenth century styles, a place of "... many gabled picturesqueness , and of the charming effect of its quaint stacks of chimneys, and its red-tiled, high-pitched roofs."(3) This striking exterior was matched by the magnificence of its interiors. The massive extensions to the house were made by Armstrong`s men, partly under his "immediate superintendence" or that of Bertram, his agent. As well as designing the buildings, Shaw was responsible for major internal

Cragside house 1887
(Source. Monthly Chronicle October 1887)

features. In August 1871, during the engineers` strike, Armstrong still found time to comment on progress at Cragside when he wrote to Noble who was now embarking on his own major reconstruction programme at Jesmond Dene House: "As to the Parquetries, there is to be very little of it at Cragside and as yet I have no drawings to send you. That which was used for the Reception Room at Jesmond was all made abroad, but Shaw was the man who arranged the contract. Your new house in the Dene is beginning to look very well and as the Joiners` strike seems now to be quite over I trust you will have no stoppage with the interior."(4) At Cragside, no expense was spared to provide what was regarded as the best. In the fine library the upper parts of the windows contained a stained glass representation of the "Story of St George and the Dragon" by Morris and Company, and the chimney-piece was of the finest Egyptian onyx, "... set in a framework of Emperor`s red marble." The massive-to modern eyes perhaps monstrous-inglenook fireplace in the drawing room was of elaborately carved Italian marble.

In this large programme of work, Shaw seems to have been indefatigable. His relationship with Armstrong was good, though they did not always agree on the way forward. For instance, in mid October 1884 he sent him tracings for "the new Tower." He was clearly used to dialogue not only about architectural details but also in relation to the mechanical and engineering side of things-Armstrong after all had been president of both the Institute of Civil and the Institute of Mechanical Engineers. Now Shaw told him: "My only doubt is whether it [the tower] might well be made a foot or two higher. I have tried to indicate how the back will come out in a small sketch, which is suggestive, but not absolutely correct in one or two points. The difficulty is to arrange the corner stair turret over the top of the new dairy. I don`t see any trouble about it as we can get abundant abutment from the rock to the laundry wall from an arch high up above the glass roof." Apparently, Armstrong wanted something less fully finished on all sides than Shaw did, for a little later, thanking him for "your chatty letter", the architect went on: "I am sorry to say that for once I am unable to agree with you anent the upper part of the Tower, chimney, etc. I think it is hardly correct to say that the back part is only seen by servants. Of course it is mainly seen by servants from the courtyard, but it is tremendously seen by everyone from the hillside at the back. I think the back must be a very favourite walk (I know it is mine) and there you see the whole of the east side of the Tower etc., in undiminished glory." Less than a week later, in another letter, he agreed with Armstrong about another facet of the design. (5)

In one letter, Shaw noted that though Armstrong had remarked to him that he never asked for money, he was going to do so now. He went on to explain how difficult it was to be sure of costs, a problem which seems to have resulted in part from Armstrong`s ample purse and partly from his own manner of working: "You see I am not like a builder with a weekly meeting of creditors outside my office door. Have you any idea of what the Drawing Room has cost, including that chimney piece? ... It was rather a special work and the time it took was considerable." A few days later, he revealed how much the chimneypiece had cost. Writing with thanks for a cheque for £200, he reckoned this was at the rate of 10% on the cost of the work. (Usually his commission was 5% of the cost of work) His out of pocket expenses from January 1882 to September 1883 had been £21 3s 8d -"say £21". He wrote: "So when I say I am content, I mean it, and thank you very much for all your kindness." In another letter, he remarked, "I`m very glad you are prepared to give me a good character! It is worth something in these queer times."(6)

As he built and massively expanded Cragside over a period of 25 years, Armstrong attended to the task of making sure that the whole of it matched the scale of his effort and his wealth. For the interior, an outstanding businessman in the Victorian age needed not only a library, but also fine furniture and furnishings and an art collection to delight himself and his guests. All those who knew him recognised that a key factor in Armstrong`s achievements as inventor and engineer was his emphasis on the practical, and an associated, outstanding ability to concentrate on the task in hand or the problem he was struggling to solve. Such qualities contributed to the success of his engineering business and thereby to his fortune, but also to the shaping of Cragside. Contemporaries liked to emphasise that his home, with its pioneering conveniences, such as telephones, electric lighting and hydro-electric power, was like Elswick a triumph of science. For one writer the only modern mansion in the border country of comparable interest was Abbotsford-but as he stressed, whereas the latter "... rose under eye of the great master in the domain of fiction, ... Cragside has risen under the eye of as great a master in the domain of fact." Nevertheless, this down-to-earth purposefulness had its disadvantages. The schooling he provided for some of the young people of the west end of Newcastle, although it received praise from such a high authority as Thomas Huxley, seems to have been confined to the strictly practical. It did not aim to stimulate a taste for the riches of the mind that the arts could provide for those who were otherwise limited to lives of labour in an environment of blacks and greys. Armstrong too seems to have lacked a sense of wonder about the beauty of the world, and a love of music. There is little evidence that he took real joy in art-though in its enthusiasm one northern magazine in describing Cragside in 1887 assured its readers that: "Here is gathered together a collection of works of art such as only cultivated taste combined with great wealth could make possible."(7) In fact, the circumstances of the times helped to make Armstrong an art collector of some distinction, though even here the practical and utilitarian were by no means absent.

Cragside was a wholly new great house. It was appropriate both to its newness and to the status of the man who owned it that it should not only have finely finished rooms but that they should contain furniture of high quality and art of a type then deemed distinguished. In 1886, in the fashion of the times, TF Bulmer was unsparing in uncritical praise of "this lordly mansion" containing as it did "... many rare, and costly treasures of art and literature, which bespeak the wealth and refinement of the illustrious possessor of this fair and stately pile." It had "... rooms innumerable, each one perfect and replete with every appointment that wealth and taste can suggest." In the Library, "the book shelves... are breast high, and contain volume upon volume of the highest class literature. Arranged on shelves above the books are vases, plaques, and pottery of rare beauty and on the walls hang many valuable pictures." Here and in most of the principal rooms the ceilings were richly panelled in wood. The Picture Gallery contained not only "many choice and valuable paintings", but also "a well-arranged collection of conchological and geological specimens." The Drawing Room was the "appartement de luxe." Above all it was distinguished by a "superb mantelpiece of richly-carved marble"-the feature which many from a later generation would describe as almost grossly overdone. "Placed around the room at all points are numerous articles of vertu and of art." There were examples of "rare pottery", "many valuable paintings by the best masters hang on the walls of this room," and in the middle was a table made out of the oaken piles from the old bridge built across the Tyne at Pons Aelii, the ancestor of Newcastle upon Tyne. (8) In such a setting, it must have been difficult for a late Victorian topographer to remember-and still less to mention-that the very existence of this wonderful place depended on the hard labours of many thousands of men in the most unhealthy of conditions a little way to the west of that Roman crossing.

In gathering together many of the articles of fine art which embellished Cragside, Armstrong`s aspirations, experiences and achievements fitted the times very well. Looking back only a year after Bulmer`s unrestrained enthusiasm, and in a wide survey published to coincide with Victoria`s Golden Jubilee, one art historian recognised that in this department of national life, as in so many others, her reign had seen dramatic changes: "The growth of wealth, the increase of the leisured class, the subtle influence exercised by the writings of various men of genius, with Mr Ruskin at their head, have combined to increase enormously the demand for works of art ..."(9) Shortly after the end of the reign, another man commented on the changes in the art market: "Towards the latter part of the first half of the nineteenth century an entirely new race of collectors gradually came into existence; they were for the most part men who had made, or were making, large fortunes in the various industries of the midlands and north of England and other centres. They were untrammelled by "collecting" traditions, and their patronage was almost exclusively extended to the artists of the day." Frequently as these new men acquired their pictures-the author of the article referred to 11 instances between 1863 and 1878-there were important "dispersals"of these and other collections. The process had been well illustrated in the case of the pictures collected in his home in Edgbaston, by the steel pen manufacturer, Joseph Gillott. After his death early in 1873, his collection was sold for almost £170,000. (10) It was in the latter part of this "dispersal" period that Armstrong became a collector.

A number of characteristics mark the process of assembling the Cragside pictures. As suggested above in the retrospect of Victorian collecting, Armstrong chose above all to buy works by contemporary artists. [Speaking in particular of three paintings which he describes as "showpieces" of the Armstrong collection, Girouard suggested, but provided no evidence, that they probably represented Norman Shaw`s taste rather than Armstrong`s, for the latter "...inclined more towards landscapes and the sentimental, animal or anecdotal vein"(11)] An interesting variation on the contemporary theme was that Armstrong patronised artists working in his own region. Although he did in some cases purchase portraits, most of his pictures were landscapes. There was a noticeable element of sentimentality in some of them. He added to his collection until late in life, but the bulk of his collecting was undertaken over seven or eight years from 1869. Throughout, he showed considerable interest in art as an investment, but at the same time the letters he wrote home about his visits to studios and to sales, convey as an undercurrent his doubt as to the inherent value of artistic expression as "real work", and therefore scepticism about the prices being asked, and which he had been compelled to pay. This correspondence with Margaret Armstrong also revealed him, almost apologetically, explaining to her why he spent so much on this or the other picture.

At the end of his life, possibly in the last year or so when he was physically weak but remained mentally clear and active, Armstrong composed what he called an Inventory of Heirlooms. In this, he indicated that he began collecting in 1869 when he seems to have made at least four purchases. Three of the paintings were bought from dealers at 40 guineas each; the other "A Scene near Windsor", painted 20 years earlier by Joseph Pettit, he purchased from Christie`s for 300 guineas. A few years later, the emphases of his purchases were two fold. On the one hand he acquired a number of what were then regarded as modern masterpieces either from London sales or directly from the artists; on the other he bought regional works at lower cost. It was in this period that he began to buy from Henry Hetherington Emmerson (1831-1895), one of the artists centred in the little Northumberland fishing village of Cullercoats. Perhaps the first painting Armstrong bought from him was of his 3-year-old daughter, Edith, for which he paid 100 guineas in 1874. Over the following two years he acquired at least five more of Emmerson`s paintings. But this was also the time at which he emerged on the national collecting scene as a purchaser of significance. Frequent visits to London, perhaps to the embassies of countries interested in his armament system or routine attendance at the firm`s London offices, provided opportunities to keep close watch on the state of the art market. His letters home recorded the progress of his collecting campaigns.

In April 1873, writing from the Athenaeum, he reported on the first day of the art sales, his hopes for greater success tomorrow, and fears lest the cost of his victories became known: "I only bid for one picture and got it. It is a landscape by Muller, not large but very fine, price 600 guineas."[William Muller had died in 1845, aged 33, overworked and dejected by a lack of sympathy.] He looked ahead: "I reserve my strength for tomorrow when the most important pictures will be sold. I fear there will be a severe competition for John Millais' "Jephthah"["Jephthah`s Daughter"] which is exciting great admiration. It is so very fine that I must have it even at the £4,000, which

Emmerson said I would give. But, whatever I give, I wish to keep as secret as I can." In the hope of making assurance doubly sure, he added a PS: "Please put this note in the fire."(12) Whatever the reason, at this time Armstrong failed to win the "Jephthah" which he coveted; and Margaret did not burn his letter.

Almost a year later he visited the Holland Park Road home and studio of Frederick Leighton, which may have particularly attracted him because of its Arab Hall, whose origins lay in the artist`s own 1868 visit to Egypt, three years before his own. On the same day, he went to see Jules Dalou, the distinguished French sculptor, who after being outlawed by the Commune, had found refuge in England. Dalou had produced the terra cotta work, which had been talked over at Cragside when Emmerson visited them. This time he was able to reassure his wife: "I escaped without buying or ordering anything, though I saw some tempting pictures at Leighton`s."(13) By autumn that year, trade depression was affecting the sales rooms, but Armstrong remained active: "The sale of water colours at Christies today has been at once the most important and the flattest that has occurred for several years. The drawings have been equal to those of the Gillott sale [less than two years earlier] and have not produced half the prices. Stagnation of trade is blamed for it, but the time of the year, before the opening of the Academy, has something to do with it." He went on to list his acquisitions. In the process, he indicated how many people from the art world he now knew, but remained tentative in justifying this sort of spending to Margaret. "I have bought seriously, but have made great bargains. I have bought a Turner, "Dunstanburgh Castle," of his very best period for 815 guineas-a splendid drawing highly praised by Mr W Boxall [William Boxall 1800 -1879, who had been Director of the National Gallery for nine years to 1874], Crawleay (??), Emmerson, and other good judges. Watson [presumably JD Watson, of the Cullercoats group] the artist knows the picture and was enthusiastic about it when I last saw him at Cragside." He had also bought "... a magnificent Copley Fielding [AV Copley Fielding 1787 - 1855, water colourist in landscapes] and a most decorative and admirable drawing by Burton [FW Burton 1816 - 1900] the present Director of the National Gallery. These three important drawings have cost me collectively 1,800 guineas, which although a large sum is small for such first class drawings, and is, I am confident, well-laid out as an investment. Emmerson is delighted with them." Next day, if the sale was equally flat, he hoped to get two oil paintings, a Phillips and a Cox. ["A Flower Girl" by John Phillips and, probably David Cox`s "Lancaster Sands"]

In spring 1875, prices remained depressed, but it was at this time that Armstrong made important purchases. For 900 guineas, he purchased two paintings by Millais, the "Jehpthah" he had failed to secure two years before and his Scottish landscape "Chill October". Once again, he apologised to Margaret about the cost, but in his pleasure at success was excessive in his assessment of the value of what he had purchased. It was "... a big price but much less than they were expected to bring. The one is unquestionably the finest figure painting and the other the finest landscape that has been produced in the present generation." He had bought more, a Hook [James Clark Hook 1819 to 1901] and a Leighton, and "I was also induced by strong advice but rather against my will to buy a very fine early Turner." Of the day`s purchases he added "a heavy lot they are but I suppose I may regard them as no bad investment. Let us have them down to Cragside before you say much about them or I am sure to figure in the newspapers as an important purchaser at this sale if it is talked about while the sale is attracting attention."(14) Two days later, he told Margaret that The Times had his name as the purchaser of the two Millais paintings and the Turner. That day, "a very noted person" had offered him £5,000 for the Jephthah alone. He had "been in great doubt whether I should let it go but Agnew [presumably William Agnew 1825-1910, of the family of art connoisseurs and dealers] says it will pay for keeping so I may as well have the satisfaction of holding it ... I have written to Emmerson giving him the news." A little later, he appeared to be still in need of reassurance, writing to Margaret, "Mr Shaw is immensely struck with the pictures, especially the Jephthah." He even drew some support from Millais, who had been to see his pictures packed for transfer to Cragside: "He says they are his two best pictures and that he is very glad they have passed into my hands ..."

Amidst all this excitement, there remained the practical man`s suspicion of the value of things not produced by hard physical labour or costly machines, and not directly useful. He pointed out how high some prices now were by referring to the work of David Cox, who died in 1859. Cox had never received more than £100 for one of his pictures; for his "Hayfield" a dealer had paid the artist £50 in 1850. His work now commanded much higher prices: "Fowler [presumably his engineering companion from the Egyptian trip four years before] bought the "Hayfield" by David Cox at the late sale of watercolours [Quilter sale] for nearly £3,000, the highest price given at the sale. It is a beautiful thing but what a price for a drawing that does not represent more than a month`s labour."(15)

Having acquired his collection, Armstrong was happy to allow others to see parts of it. In 1878, "Chill October" was sent for the Paris Exhibition, but this was also the year in which he found that one of his landscapes was not genuine. He had sent a picture to be exhibited at The Academy of Arts, but when he acknowledged receipt, N Horsley informed him: "...circumstances have since occurred respecting it which not only prevent me exhibiting it, but which I know well would make you desire more than any one that it should not be exhibited." Two days later, Horsley explained that when the Turner arrived, he and his colleagues "were unanimous in feeling and believing that he never painted a square inch of it." The painting had been bought from a Mr Lynam, who had been cagey when Horsley had spoken to him about it. Armstrong had paid £50; it had previously been sold for only £10 by a collector who had realised it was not genuine. Horsley tried to soften the blow: "I should be quite relieved to find that you had bought the picture simply for liking it and without any warranty that it was an original Turner! This would put everything square."(16)

Although the pace slackened, and there seems no evidence that he continued to attend London art sales, Armstrong collected more pictures over the years. A high proportion of his later pictures were from North East Coast artists, including more works by Emmerson, a landscape by Edward Train, and in the early 1890s a number of paintings by John Turnbull Dixon, an amateur, who worked with his brother David in the family drapery business in Rothbury. David Dixon became Armstrong`s librarian.

Altogether, there were a large number of paintings in Cragside, well over fifty, possibly a good deal more. (17) They fell into a number of distinct categories. There were portraits of the owners, their relatives and friends - three oil paintings of Armstrong himself, by Emmerson (1880), George F Watts (1887) and Mary L Waller (1898), and in the library John Calcott Horsley`s 1868 portrait of Margaret Armstrong. There was a good portrait of James Meadows Rendel. In another group were pictures of sentiment, almost of sentimentality - of Emmerson`s daughter aged three, a "Young Girl with Flowers", and two of dogs, both by Emmerson, "Faithful unto Death" and "Waiting for Orders." There were local landscapes such as Emmerson`s "Gilnockie Tower in 1530"(c 1880) and John T Dixon`s 1891 "On the River Coquet near Shilmoor" as well as Turner`s "Dunstanburgh Castle." By far the largest class was that of landscapes by artists both renowned and obscure.

Cragside, with the benefits of its wonderful and peaceful setting, "modern" conveniences, and lifestyle reflecting the wealth that had created and now maintained it, was highly attractive to visitors. These were not then ordinary citizens, though they too were allowed into the grounds on Thursdays between 10 am and 5 pm, (18) but those the owners chose to entertain there. Here, or sometimes at Jesmond, Armstrong entertained many colleagues, potential customers and representatives of governments and army and marine ministries from Britain and worldwide. Some of these occasions were for private conversations; some were house or shooting parties. There were overnight visits and longer stays, business meetings and holidays. Inevitably, William Armstrong featured large in both the events and in the reports of them: it is well to remember that Margaret Armstrong often played an important part. The list of visitors was large and it is possible to give only a flavour of its range.

In September 1883, Captain John Fisher spent some time with his cousin in Northumberland. At the end of that month, this mercurial future First Sea Lord spent a day at Cragside. (19) Early in February 1889 George Hamilton, Salisbury`s First Lord of the Admiralty, made an official inspection of Elswick. In June that year, he too came to Cragside. Also in 1889, Joseph Chamberlain, now estranged from Gladstone and leader of the Liberal Unionists, visited Armstrong. Early in May1887, the Duke of Cambridge was on Tyneside to open the great Jubilee Exhibition. On the evening of 11 May, Armstrong gave a banquet in his honour in the Banqueting Hall, Jesmond Dene, and afterwards, the Duke stayed in Newcastle as his guest. There were visitors who were nominally more eminent. The Billiard Room at Cragside contains a portrait of the Shah of Persia, Nasir-ed-Din. This commemorates the night he spent as a guest there on 23 July 1889 after arriving from Edinburgh with "a large suite." Next day, he made what was reported as a "complete inspection" of Elswick works. A few weeks later, it was announced that he had presented his portrait and signature to Lord Armstrong. (20)

Among those who were neither business contacts, nor in government, and not associated with either the British or foreign royal families, were friends and social and intellectual contacts. A prominent member of this group was Thomas Henry Huxley. When he and Armstrong first met is not known, but their common interest and involvement in the British Association probably provided the occasion. A relevant factor in the warmth of their relationship must have been that as a boy Huxley`s great desire had been to become a mechanical engineer. In 1869, Armstrong was expecting a special guest at Cragside for Christmas, and asked Noble to help to entertain him. It was an indication of the lengths to which business responsibility might be extended. On Thursday 23 December, he wrote to inform, or possibly to remind his colleague: "Huxley is coming on Saturday [Christmas Day]. Hold yourself engaged to meet him on Sunday."(21) Regrettably, no record of the conversations held during that Cragside Christmas seemed to survive.

Almost five years later, another visit from the Huxleys threw the usually well-ordered life at Cragside into disarray. Again Armstrong asked for Noble`s help: "The Huxleys are here. I cannot find the letter announcing the time of their coming but I am afraid I have made a mistake in the matter, and the result is I cannot go to Fowler`s [presumably the civil engineer] as intended next week. I don`t like to ask Huxley how long he is going to stay and I therefore apply to you for such information as you can give me on the subject. Am I not right that he and his wife and daughters are coming to you from here before he and his wife go to Scotland. If so what are the dates as you understand them?"(22)

From his youth Huxley suffered from occasional illness and severe mental and physical depression. Perhaps this provided the opportunity

Armstrong took during summer 1876 to talk with him about Noble`s health. It led to yet another letter in which he tried to manage his way of life. The tone makes it difficult to realise he was writing to an intelligent, highly placed man of 45. "Mr Huxley says that the best man in London to consult for Rheumatism, Neuralgia, Gout and all complaints of that class is Dr Garrod whose address (according to my Directory for 1874) is 10 Harley Street. W. You should write and make an appointment with him as he is in great practice. Pray make a point of seeing him whether for the moment you are better or not and be sure you are perfectly candid with him as to your habits and mode of life."(23) In late summer that year, Huxley and his wife visited the United States, and the closeness of his relationship with Armstrong was indicated by the fact they left those of their children who were unmarried at Cragside. (24)

In 1872, ill health forced Huxley to take a long holiday in Egypt, a few months after Armstrong had been there. Twelve years later, and ill again, Huxley was wintering on the Bay of Naples. There, a most unusual letter from Armstrong caught up with him after it had been inexplicably delayed for over a month. It communicated a strange dream. An interesting response was written by Henrietta Huxley: "It certainly was a remarkable dream. My husband has certainly not undertaken to drive any other person`s engine, being scarcely able to drive his own corporeal one. I must say that reply of his to your offer of the £500 was brilliant: "Do it at once and take the glory", and evidently you would have succumbed but for your waking at the very time. He has not invested in any gold mine having nothing to invest, which is about the greatest safety against loss a man can well have." She went on to describe their visit to the ruins of Cumae: "We drove there through Pozzuoli where we saw the Temple of Serapis that wonderful example of the subsidence and rise of the land, for halfway up the pillars have been bored by sea creatures. Mr Huxley says the land is again subsiding, though very slowly. I cannot give you an idea of the glorious view we had after climbing to the top of the old acropolis of Cumae. Before us lay the blue sea, with a long sweep of curved sandy coast to the north. Across in the north east, was the long stretching wall of the Apennines, the summits of the chain that lay further back all covered with snow. On the opposite side was Cape Myceneum and

Procida and at our back gaunt hills. All this in a brilliant sunshine and blue sky." (25) At that time, Armstrong and his Elswick colleagues were responding to pressures from the Italian government with plans that, within a few years, resulted in construction of a new gun works at Pozzuoli, in the very midst of the idyllic scene Henrietta so vividly painted for him.

In late summer 1885, in his 75th year and in some ways at the height of his own achievements, Armstrong mentioned to Noble that he had read in that day`s paper that the 60 year old Huxley had made up his mind to live in Italy as his health had broken down. (26) In fact, he retired from the ferment of life in London to Eastbourne. Some years after her husband`s death Henrietta would again be in contact with Armstrong.

SHAPING THE CRAGSIDE ESTATE

By choosing a bleak hillside as the site for his country home, Armstrong not only made available a more or less blank sheet for its development but set himself an enormous task. Helped by his wealth, but also by his imagination and resolution, he assembled the expertise and huge manual labour force which long before the end of his life had transformed the original wilderness into what was now sometimes described as a "wonderland". Apart from some letters there is scant evidence to enable one to come to a reasoned conclusion, but, given Margaret Armstrong`s known enthusiasm for gardening, it seems probable that her role in shaping the character of the Cragside estate has been underrated.

Early photographs and sketches show that in 1865 the solid first house was situated amidst bare slopes. It was approached along a road edged by a stone wall. Five years or so later apart from a little vegetation on the slope which ran down into the courtyard on the south front, and a few conifers behind, the bare surface and occasional big boulders Armstrong and his companions had found when they walked over the site in late summer 1863 remained. (1) But by the time of Norman Shaw`s early planned extensions, the first elements of the new gardens were beginning to be outlined. Sketches by Shaw included in the Building News in spring 1872 had trees on the hillside above the house and the rudiments of a rockery on the slope immediately below its west front. Even so, the accompanying account made clear that the environs of the house were undeveloped: "Nothing can exceed the beauty of the surroundings, varying from a rich dell in the bottom of the valley-the Debdon Burn-filled with every variety of rare tree and shrubs, all in full vigour, up to the boldest rocks and moor land on the hill top."(2) Over another 12 years, creepers climbed up and covered the south wall of Lady Armstrong`s sitting room and the room above, the south side gardens were more fully developed and thick woods, mainly of conifers, by this time covered the lower parts of the slopes above the house, though leaving space for some rocky outcrops, one topped with a chimney-like tower.

Over many years, Armstrong supervised the processes of elaborating the huge estate he had acquired and had added to by further purchases. By the mid 1880s, the hillside on which the house stood was covered by what a contemporary described as "an endless variety of trees and flowering shrubs" among which rhododendron and azaleas were already of special note. (Before the end of his life, he was reckoned to have planted about 7 million trees and shrubs on the 1,200 acres that formed the core of his wider land holdings.) Growth of heathers was fostered by carrying in "many hundreds of loads" of sandy soil and peat from the nearby moorland. Miles of walks and carriageways were built, being so aligned as to allow for a comparatively easy rise to the top of the hills. However, on the hills Armstrong kept some areas clear to accommodate a range and targets where experiments could be conducted with shells brought up from Elswick; several small guns were kept in a "gun-house". To the east, he had damned the Black Burn to create two considerable lakes, and in the Debdon valley on the west side of the hills, dams had produced two other lakes, which now "teemed" with fish. Debdon Burn had been provided with various cascades, footpaths and "rustic" bridges in the shade of the trees. Towards the house, this burn ran between "perpendicular cliffs of great height, wooded to the top." This was the so-called "Gorge" over which a steel bridge was later built. Towards the western edge of the main part of the estate, near the road to Alnwick-and therefore a considerable distance and an uphill walk from the house-was a "park" with fine Alderney cattle and some gardens. The latter already included an "Italian Garden", an "orchard house", conservatories and a fernery "all of which are kept in the most perfect order". The account should have added that, as with the restored gardens today, these enjoyed a wonderful outlook across the Coquet valley, over the eastern fringe of Rothbury and on to the highly distinctive outline of the Simonside hills. (3)

Naturally, everything was in excellent order. Early, Armstrong had even built a small but splendid clock tower on a site high above the gardens so that the time could be conspicuously displayed, thereby ensuring a reliable working routine for his large body of estate workers. All in all, it was grand and magnificent; a wonderful statement of what imagination and purpose, supported by mass labour, a generous purse and large-scale expenditure could do in reshaping and re-clothing nature-a rural equivalent of what had been achieved in Cragside house-or, to take a mundane instance, at Elswick. But, however wonderful, both house and grounds lacked delight. In comparison, some 11 miles away at Wallington Hall the Trevelyan family enjoyed a smaller, very different sort of garden. Here was intimacy instead of massed effect, gentle beauty rather than grandeur. The great glasshouses at Cragside supplied the house with fruits almost all Britons had to procure from other, warmer lands; at Wallington a much smaller, but more attractive main conservatory was filled with the colour and fragrance of fuchsias. Cragside was shaped by an engineer, who was an eminently successful businessman, and nowhere could one expect to find the classical lines, and the simple sentiment which adorned the charming little pool in the Wallington conservatory: "When wearied and over wrought by study or affairs of business, repair to these haunts and refresh your mind by a stroll amidst the flowers."(4)

At Cragside, Armstrong seems to have been a good employer, if the length of service of some of those who worked for him can be taken as a guide. Bertram, his agent, was with him at the beginning of the whole project and still there after his death; by 1901, Henry Hudson, head gardener, had been at Cragside for 35 years. Willie Mavin, a mason, was in the first gang of workmen engaged in construction of the house and survived to serve Armstrong`s successor. William Crossby, foreman workman, came to the estate in 1864 and like the gamekeeper, William Avery, who joined in 1877, worked at Cragside to beyond Armstrong`s life. Some of these men and their families lived in houses and lodges on the estate, Avery in the lodge at the Reivers` Well, then the main gateway, Crossby at Debdon Burnfoot Cottage, which by the early 20th century was the only building dating from before Armstrong bought the property. Many who worked in the house-some 22 in all according to a surprisingly low estimate from the early 1880s-lived in various cottages around the estate. (5) A much bigger band of workers-those "on the hills or in the grounds and gardens"-some 170 in all in 1886-were largely housed in workmen`s cottages which Armstrong built in Rothbury.

Not all who have written about Cragside have been appreciative of the taste of its creator. Two, a century after Armstrong first met Shaw, described the house as "a pretentiously romantic assemblage of English and Germanic elements..." Consistently enough, they thought the estate cottages "... self-consciously pretty, like a Victorian illustration to Hansel and Gretel."(6) But these cottages were convenient and reasonably comfortable. When they were newly built, few men from working class districts on Tyneside saw either them or the other "model" housing Armstrong was said to have built for his employees. If they had done so, they might well have wondered why those who laboured in his country home were so much more favoured than were those toiling at Elswick. Meanwhile the Cragside workforce, by far the biggest in the area, was an important factor in halting the decline in the population of Rothbury township. From a low in 1861 it revived and by the end of Armstrong`s life was two thirds greater than when he took over the estate.

By the latter part of the 1880s, the grounds of Cragside were already celebrated. An account of autumn 1887 summarised the beauties that had been created. The prose is sometimes over lush, but the author managed to provide some unusual insights: "Every natural advantage has been greatly utilised or improved; even natural disadvantages have been conquered and turned to good account. On the steep sides of the hill, walks and drives have been formed which lead by easy ascents up to the house and the hilltop which rises behind it. From this hill top, where stands the huge solitary boulder called the Sea Stone, we look down on Cragside, and upon the town of Rothbury lying in the Coquet Valley, with Simonside rising high above. Close by us are the two new lakes formed by the engineering skill of the genius of the place, probably upon the sites of where ancient lakes once gathered, while away to the east we see the North Sea gleaming in the distance. Descending again, we may admire the formal beauty of the trim Italian Garden, or the wonders of the Orchard Houses. In these latter, dwarf fruit-trees are grown in large pots which turn on pivots, so that each side in turn enjoys the ripening influence of the sun, or the whole can, by hydraulic power, be wheeled out into the open air with the gangways on which they stand. Then there are the noble Conservatory, the Fern Grotto, and the spacious grounds where flourish in bewildering profusion the rarest and most beautiful trees and shrubs. Or again, we may descend still lower, into the deep ravine of the Debdon Burn, and follow the windings of the stream-the wooded cliffs towering over us on either side and forming a veritable fairy glen of most romantic beauty."(7) All in all it was an idyllic picture, and it seems clear from the almost contemporary watercolours of Emmerson, or paintings by Armstrong`s friend, John Adye, that it was a description that did no more than justice to the transformation of landscape which had been achieved.

Over the years, more and more land was added to the large area that Armstrong already owned. Much of it furnished shooting. Whatever the other pressures, while he was able, the game bird season had his attention. In a letter to Noble in August 1871, when deeply involved in the engineers` strike, he nonetheless wrote at some length about shooting: "We have missed you sadly all this week and I cannot sufficiently express my regret that calls of duty which you are always so ready to obey should in this instance have deprived you of an enjoyment which can only be had at this particular season. We have been very unfortunate with our visitors. Campbell and Majendie were the only two that came and the latter was obliged to leave after only half a day shooting to attend the investigation of the great gun cotton explosion at Stow Market. For my part, I have only been able to shoot three and a half days having to be so frequently in Newcastle but we made great bags. Putting all the times of shooting together they represented five days with 2 guns and we killed 104 brace. Campbell is scarcely as good a shot as I am and how the deuce we got so many I hardly know. One day when I was absent Pease took my place and got 20 brace to his own gun."(8)

Eventually Armstrong owned about 14,000 acres around Cragside, of the order of ten times the original, core and enclosed section. He accumulated this from various sources, and rented out some of what he bought. The Trewhitt estates in the area were put up for auction in 1878 but were withdrawn when the price offered reached only £42,000. Later they were purchased by Armstrong. Correspondence from 1884, by which time his investment in the major improvement of the house was more or less complete, provides insight into the processes of acquisition. Early in March, he received a letter from L Snowball of Dudley, Northumberland about possibilities near to the core area of the estate. Snowball had been informed by Mr Tennant of Thrum Mill that on next Lady Day he was prepared to hand over what he at present occupied under the Duke of Northumberland. In addition to the mill itself, this included 35.5 acres of land. For this Tennant was paying an annual rent of £99 and 4 shillings - which included drainage charges. During the 1880s, Armstrong bought lands in the township of Snitter, until then owned by the Duke of Northumberland. He also acquired two of the three Great Tosson farms, owned part of Thropton township and in 1883 bought Cartington, where four years later he partially restored the castle. In his lifetime, the hill farms were mostly stocked with sheep, largely Leicesters or Cheviots. On the Thropton section of the estate an allotment system was adopted, lettings ranging from three acres upwards. (9)

In building up and running his estate, Armstrong was assisted by able and apparently dedicated men. Bertram, his agent, was clearly a key man; so too was Thomas Allan of Snitter, a person of some distinction, a "well-known agriculturalist" and for many years chairman of Rothbury Board of Guardians. In 1865, he helped Armstrong make a valuable contact. Compared with the contemporary hearings and trials of the Armstrong and Whitworth Committee, or the search for business to replace orders from the British government, the matter was of trivial significance, but among other things, it provided yet another proof of the meticulous thoroughness with which Armstrong took up any issue. He contacted Noble from Cragside: "Mr Allan has met with a little horse which he thinks would suit you very well. It belongs to a very respectable farmer at Felton. Mr Allan describes it as fourteen and a half hands, good looking, not very fast but reasonably so and altogether a likely hack to suit you. It is a mare, price £30, colour brown. Mr Allan, who has been all over the country and even at Newcastle on this business, wishes you to see it and proposes that you should meet the owner with the mare at Morpeth on Tuesday or any other day you may arrange with the owner whose address is `Mr Rowe, Moleshaugh, [Mouldshaugh] near Felton, Morpeth.` There is an objection that the mare has never been in harness. You had better write to Mr Rowe on the subject generally." He added a P.S "I think you could not lose much if it did not suit you."(10)

In June 1884, Allan wrote to Armstrong about game rents and the insuring of the land he was adding to the estate: "As you informed me that Captain Noble would have the sporting on the south side of the Coquet, I presume the rent will be paid by him." This was followed shortly after by a letter indicating how much Armstrong was acquiring well away from Cragside, in the area south west of Rothbury. "There is a good deal of your lately purchased property not insured in your name. Tosson West Side, Wolfershiel [both purchased the year before] Allerdene, and Mr Readhead`s farm here. May I take steps to have this done in the same way as all the other farms and in the same office? Your reply will oblige." Allan seems to have taken the initiative in trying to rationalise this piecemeal process of extension, by November telling Armstrong: "I should like to meet you at your convenience to point out and explain from a tracing I now have of the proposed exchange of land between Tosson and Spylaw farms." At this time, Armstrong was communicating with Noble about the shooting tenancy of about 2,400 acres of land, of which 1400 was moor and the rest field land. He had asked a Mr Gow (?) what he thought the rent should be, and although the latter could not say definitely without going over the ground, he thought it should be between £80 and £100. For a colleague and trusted friend that was enough for Armstrong - "What say you £90 as a mean?" (11)

As seen above, for a number of years parts of the estate were used for testing guns or their accessories, apparently both artillery and lighter weapons. When he told Noble about some of these experiments in spring 1878, it seems from the context that he was probably testing the Gatling machine gun, which Elswick was producing under license: "I had an adventurous morning in getting to the gun house and back. I was several times up to the middle in snow and had some difficulty in getting out and on one occasion only did so with the loss of my leather leggings....the bullets seemed to strike very fair, but it was snowing so hard and the target so plastered with snow that it was impossible to see the holes and count them. I therefore left Bartram to do this and I will hear the result tomorrow." A few days later fog made firing impossible, but late that same year snow was again the enemy: "Although I have been terribly impeded by a succession of snow storms I have succeeded in firing the 12 time fuses this morning and the results are very satisfactory."(12)

Some of these activities on his expanding estate impinged on others. For the most part, those affected were the ordinary people of the Rothbury area, and they had little reason to complain, for new fences or the sounds of game shooting or even the less common and much louder noise from the testing of guns, might well be regarded as the price they had to pay for employment opportunities or merely a minor inconvenience to set against the owner`s generosity to the local community. Neighbouring landowners might look at the matter differently. From the eastern edge of the Cragside estate, the large but sparsely peopled parish of Longframlington stretched out towards the Morpeth to Wooler road. Its southern part along the Coquet, included Brinkburn. About one fifth of the parish in the west was in the 1870s described as "wild and dreary moorland". Even though very few people lived here to be affected, his experiments annoyed one who could make his feelings known. In 1884, he received a complaint through Snowball from D Fenwick, who lived in Embleton Hall on the northern edge of Longframlington village. Fenwick was uncomfortable about the shells Armstrong had fired. One had been found on the moor two weeks before when Snowball was with him, and he now wrote about a further incident: "We picked up another shell yesterday just below Shirlaw Pike and this time an unexploded one; it is rather beyond a joke....I don`t want to be disagreeable but I don`t fancy being bombarded for nothing."(13)

Fortunately, Armstrong used his large estate for purposes that were more benign. One of these made Cragside a world pioneer of a new technology, though it represented an application of interests he had developed many years before. In his early thirties, he had moved on from researches in hydraulic power to experimental work on electricity. Over a quarter of a century later he used his ideas, experience and aspirations, and the expertise of others with whom he was closely associated, in applying electricity to domestic use. In the last decade of his life, he also returned to a deep and productive involvement in electrical experiment.

During summer 1865, less than two years after the first 20 acres of his new estate were acquired, and construction of the first "Cragside" house began, Debdon Burn dried up. Reacting to this, the following year Armstrong had dammed this stream above the house, to form Tumbleton Lake. Below this artificial lake, he put up a small building containing a hydraulic pump that delivered water to a tank serving the house, driving a hydraulic lift and powering the kitchen spit. By 1870, he had a second dam on the Debdon Burn, this time west of the Alnwick Road and forming Debdon Lake. A few years later, a second power house was built downstream, in this instance having a turbine that drove a dynamo. For a time power generated here was used to operate machinery in the estate joiner`s shop. Then in 1878, there came a much more important development when Armstrong became associated with Carl William Siemens in providing Cragside with the first hydro-electrically generated lighting anywhere in the world.

In a letter written early in June 1878, Armstrong asked Siemens a number of questions about possibilities for lighting his dining room and library. Responding Siemens assured him that such an application "... would be the first of its kind and therefore very interesting, and I should be happy to assist..." Answering Armstrong`s questions "seriatim", he laid out both the possibilities and the limitations of the technology of the time, depending as it did on light produced from an electric arc: "1. In order to get the effect of 600 naked candles you would require two Electric Candles giving 600 candles power each so that half the light may be lost in the opalised glass lantern. 2. One of our smallest Dynamo Electrical Machines (weighing under 2 cwt and costing £70) would suffice for this purpose. Such a machine would, in producing 1200 candles power consume 2.25 HP, but the motor should possess some surplus power (say from 3 to 3.5) in order to start the light, when the carbon points are touching one another and consume extra current. 3. The division of the current into several branches is a problem which has not yet been solved quite satisfactorily. It has occupied my attention for some time and experimentally I have succeeded in doing it, but am still without working results in dealing with several lights. The same end would be obtained in making a number of Dynamo Machines work an equal number of separate lights, but the drawbacks are that small dynamo machines work with less ...?... than large and are more liable to heat. 4. The only cause of unsteadiness in the light is in the Carbon points which are not yet as perfect as might be. I have now arranged special apparatus for making these Carbon sticks and hope for good results. It will always be necessary however to have several lights in the same apartment. In short, the Electric Light is now sufficiently perfect for the production of large effects of light but it is still in the experimental stage for domestic purposes."(14)

Armstrong decided to go ahead. In late November 1878, at the same time as he described the deep depression and wage reductions then affecting the basic industries of Tyneside and Wearside, the local correspondent of the Mining Journal reported that "by the interposition of a turbine, by means of which the requisite revolutions are given to a dynamo-electric machine", Sir William had been able to use power from the outfall of a lake to produce electricity and carry it 1.5 miles to illuminate his Cragside picture gallery. He hoped to use it for other domestic purposes as well. (15) But as Siemens had made clear, his technology was by no means perfect. There was a high consumption of carbons and difficulty in relighting the "candles" if the arc was accidentally "blown out". Fortunately, by the time these arc lamp appliances were installed at Cragside, progress was being made in developing an alternative approach to the problem of electric lighting. This was the incandescent lamp using a carbon filament enclosed in a vacuum in a hermetically sealed glass vessel-eventually the "light bulb". Edison was one of the inventors of this process, and would receive much of the fame. The other pioneer was Joseph W Swan who in 1879 produced an incandescent lamp in his home laboratory in Gateshead and next year publicly exhibited the first successful carbon filament vacuum lamp bearing his name. (16)

In December 1880 Swan`s incandescent lamps were installed at Cragside. A few weeks later Armstrong wrote to the Engineer to give its readers news of what had been done. To a coal age readership, the most remarkable sentence in his letter must have been the one in which he summarised the source of his power: "The brook, in fact, lights the house, and there is no consumption of any material in the process." The Siemens "dynamo-electric machine" and the turbine now supported 45 lamps in the house, "... but as I can switch off the current from room to room, I never require to have more than 37 in light at once." In the library, some lamps were placed on vases previously used as stands for kerosene lamps; in passages and on stairs "... the lamps are for the most part used without glass shades, and present a very beautiful star-like appearance, not so bright as to pain the eye in passing, and very efficient for lighting the way." Arc lights gave more light but they could not be serviceably distributed through the house, and compared with them the incandescent lamp was free from "disagreeable attributes". "It is perfectly steady and noiseless. It is free from harsh glare and dark shadows. It casts no ghastly hue on the countenance, and shows everything in true colours."(17)

Although the power for the Cragside electric lighting initially came from the dams on the Debdon Burn, Armstrong soon decided to provide himself with a much greater head of water to drive his turbine. Accordingly the Black Burn, crossing the former moor land to the east of the steep slopes which overlooked the house, was dammed and its waters channelled into two new, high-level reservoirs, the Nelly`s Moss lakes. From here, the water fell to the newly built Burnfoot Power House. This head of water not only generated electricity for lighting the house, but also was used for miscellaneous other duties around the estate. For instance, by the mid 1890s it powered compression in the silo at Crag End Lower Farm, 190 feet below the lake. (18)

There was another early outcome of the successes with the incandescent lamp. It took some of Armstrong`s attention back from Cragside to Tyneside. In 1881, he joined Swan, and two other prominent local men, Dr Robert Spence Watson, educationalist, industrial arbitrator and Liberal organizer, and John Theodore Merz, a man involved in the alkali industry on Tyneside, but later much more widely known as one of the most learned of all historians of science and belief in the nineteenth century. Together they formed the Swan Incandescent Electric Lamp Company, which built a factory at South Benwell very close to Elswick. However dispute soon followed with Edison over patent rights, and this led in October 1883 to the creation of the Edison and Swan United Electric Light Company Ltd. Before the end of the decade, manufacture of electric light bulbs had been moved to Ponders End, Middlesex. (19)

NEW MEN, A NEW COMPANY AND SHIPBUILDING

Of the seven partners, who on 1 January 1864 signed the deed of co-partnership in Sir W G Armstrong and Company, Lambert died in 1867, and George Cruddas in 1879. Stuart Rendel became an additional partner. Within the small group that controlled the rapidly expanding company, there was by no means always harmony. Much later, Stuart wrote that for years Noble tried to dislodge his brother, George Rendel, from his central position in the company. (1) This was a contention for which there was scant evidence, but unquestionably, Armstrong came to regard Noble as his most dedicated lieutenant. Over the years he became dissatisfied with Percy Westmacott`s commitment to the commercial engineering work of the firm. By the early 1880s, it was clear that it was time for important changes.

In November 1880, Armstrong passed his 70th birthday. Although he might now reasonably expect to be less involved, for the time being at least he remained fully active in research and development, and in ensuring the company maintained a high level of competitiveness. Soon there was a crisis in the company affairs. It had two main roots. One was the temporary loss of two key men, Stuart and George Rendel. In 1880, Stuart fought and won the parliamentary seat of Montgomeryshire as a Liberal, and was obliged to relinquish his interest in Sir W G Armstrong and Company. He argued that he was more useful as an MP, and was already working to secure a peerage for Armstrong. (He soon reported that he had spoken to people in the party about this, and eventually the idea would be brought to Gladstone. Those with whom he had discussed the matter knew he was acting without Armstrong`s knowledge.) During 1882, George Rendel resigned from the firm to take up a newly created post as a civil lord at the Admiralty.

Armstrong retained an unquestioned headship. This was shown in a letter Stuart Rendel wrote in May 1881 to Andrew Noble about his own circumstances: "I made no terms with the Firm. I left myself wholly at their mercy. I think Sir William took a strong step in excluding you and George and Hamilton [his own younger brother] from any voice in the question whether I should ever be readmitted or not."(2) Of all the partners, only Noble was at the height of his great powers and completely committed to the firm and to Armstrong personally. New men were badly needed, for the pressures on top management could be expected to become even more burdensome as expansion of operations in various directions was seen to be desirable. The firm had enjoyed considerable success in warship design, but could not build its own vessels. From early days, there had been some serious disagreements with Mitchell, who undertook this on their behalf, but even so, there gradually developed an idea of a closer association with his company. (3) Rather surprisingly, this involved the possibility of building a major yard at Elswick designed specifically for construction of naval vessels. There was expansion in other directions. Early in 1883, there came an important acquisition of both plant and talents in the form of the London Ordnance Works of Southwark. This had been built up by Josiah Vavasseur, who now became a close associate, taking over the London office, previously run by Stuart Rendel. Steel manufacture was seen as another desirable new line.

These acquisitions, extensions or plans required capital. Yet some of the partners in the existing, private company were withdrawing; others were taking money out of the business. The most common way in which the latter happened was by investments in property and land, as with Armstrong at Cragside, Noble in Jesmond Dene House and William Cruddas, George`s son, at Haughton Castle in the North Tyne valley. George Rendel had a villa on the Bay of Naples, and Stuart was gaining a reputation for his accumulation of fine houses - in addition to lavish spending to secure his parliamentary seat in Wales. In such circumstances, why not bring in men with expertise in the planned new lines of business, and at the same time raise additional capital by converting the partnership into a public limited company?

In 1882, Armstrong and his colleagues began to move towards an amalgamation with Mitchell. This would form the centrepiece of a limited company. It seems possible that the first suggestion came from Noble in February, at which time Armstrong wrote to him from the Athenaeum: "Your proposal is not at all distasteful to me in principle but there will be much to say as to the practicability of carrying it out. All that must stand over until we meet."(4) Three months later things were taking shape. (By now Armstrong was thinking imaginatively about what lay even further ahead, for he already contemplated the advantages to be gained from a link with a traditional enemy as well as with Mitchell: "I have had an encouraging interview with Radcliffe and discussed the subject in all its bearings. He strongly advises our endeavouring to effect the Mitchell idea. GR [George Rendel] also fully approves of it. It has since struck me that it might be possible to effect a similar arrangement with Whitworth. I fear he is an impracticable man, but if it could be carried out, the result would be one of prodigious strength. Think about this and let me know while I am here.") By the time he wrote to Noble from Elswick on Saturday 11 November, the Mitchell matter at least was on the edge of completion. He would travel up to London on the 4pm train that day and would be at Radcliffe`s office on Monday at 10.30am. Thompson [presumably from Dees and Thompson, his former law firm] would be there as well. He explained, "... as I am desirous of getting everything settled then and there so as to get the prospectus out without further delay I fear we must have you there also ... I will tell Mitchell if he wants a part in final arrangements he must be in London on Monday."(5) The merger went ahead. Next year Sir W.G Armstrong, Mitchell and Company Ltd made a good start on two new sites on the east side of the Elswick Ordnance works. One was for a new steel works, the other for a naval yard. The latter had developed from an involvement in warship construction, which had begun 15 years before.

From the time of his interest in applying hydraulic power to coaling operations and his first experiments with guns, Armstrong had close contacts with the Royal Navy. From 1859 to 1863, his breech-loading gun was used in British warships. After that, in the long campaign to regain recognition from the armed services, relations with the navy formed an important part of the struggle. Eventually, it was a change in policy at the Admiralty that marked the breakthrough, but his guns had already been sold to foreign navies. The company gradually made its way into warship construction and long before the end of his life, his company would, in some years at least, rank first among British shipbuilding companies.

As early as May 1863, three months after he resigned from Woolwich, there had been a press report that the Elswick Ordnance Company would begin iron shipbuilding, one way in which it might find its way out of a very real predicament.(6) There were other possible or reported links. By the end of the decade the Clydeside firm of Napier were in consultation about gunboats and their armament. A few years later, it was reported in Glasgow that Armstrongs contemplated building small ironclads for use in shallow waters, for which a yard would be developed near Greenock.(7) In fact well before this Armstrongs had moved more definitely in this field, but much nearer Elswick. As well as testing its guns in various isolated places, they were sometimes mounted on floating platforms. From this there evolved the idea of a gunboat; in the first instance no more than an unsophisticated vessel armed with a single large Armstrong gun. The first was designed by George Rendel and built during 1867 for the Royal Navy. Named Staunch, it was wholly without armour, 79 feet in length, 25 feet broad and with a displacement of 150 tons. In its forepart was a 12.5 ton, 9 inch muzzle-loaded gun. (8) There was some difficulty in securing payment from the Admiralty, but this small, simple vessel marked not only a first step in naval design but also the start of an association with the well-established shipbuilder, Charles Mitchell of Walker on Tyne.

In 1840, John Coutts had set up a yard at Low Walker to build iron ships. Two years later, Charles Mitchell came from Aberdeen to work for Coutts. By 1852, he had his own yard next door. Having supplied the Admiralty during the Crimean War, very soon afterwards he was busy building ships for the Russians. In 1862, he was invited to undertake modernisation of the Imperial dockyards at St Petersburg, where he very successfully built ironclads. Armstrong arranged for Low Walker yard to build the Staunch. Over the years, the association between the two companies expanded and became closer. Even so, for well over a decade, shipbuilding remained a relatively small part of Armstrong business. After Staunch no new vessel was completed at

Walker on Armstrongs` account until 1871, and throughout the 1870s it built only one 4,500 ton troopship for Britain. It did however complete more Elswick designed gunboats. Two of these were supplied to the Royal Navy, two were built for the Netherlands and the other eight-the so-called "Alpha" boats as the Greek alphabet was used to identify them-for China. By 1876, the "Alpha" gunboats then being built were twice as big as Staunch. Next year two more of them were of 425 tons, and, in contrast to its single 12.5 ton Armstrong gun, they had a 38 ton gun, two nine pounders and two machine guns. Staunch carried up to 15 tons of fuel; the maximum load on Gamma and Delta was 60 tons, which would provide them with 12 days full steaming. In short, though designated gunboats, in size and complexity they were becoming more complicated warships. (9) Armstrongs continued to build their gunboats at Walker - three more for China in 1881, and in 1882 and 1884 six for Britain. At this point changing circumstances hastened a fuller involvement in warship construction. The three relevant factors were their own progress in design, increasing tonnages and a change in the balance of power at sea.

Over 13 years to the end of 1879 Armstrongs launched only 13 fighting vessels, amounting in all to 4,500 tons. Then there came a change of scale and of tempo. George Rendel, who had demonstrated high ability in development of ordnance and above all in applying hydraulic power to the operation of heavy guns, before becoming involved in gunboat design, now took another major step forward, by designing a protected cruiser. This would carry heavy guns, constitute a small target and be relatively cheap to build - and to buy. Unlike the gunboats, it would be capable of high speed, be more seaworthy and have a longer range. (10) His first cruiser Arturo Prat, was ordered by Chile, and laid down at Low Walker early in October 1879. Six months earlier, Chile had declared war on Peru, initiating the War of the Pacific. The next step involved two cruisers of the same class for China. These vessels were of 1,350 tons displacement, 210 feet in length, powerfully armed, and could steam at 16 knots. Although described as un-armoured, a light steel deck and the bunkers that held their coal provided them with some protection. In the event, Chile decided not to buy the Arturo Prat, and in 1883, it was sold to Japan. Already George Rendel had embarked on a bigger, more powerful version of his first cruisers; in spring 1881 the 3,000 ton, 270 feet long Esmeralda was laid down for Chile. In speed trials, it exceeded 18 knots. It too had a steel deck which "sheltered the machinery, boilers, magazines and other vital parts... [shelter for the crew was not mentioned]". As the Director of Naval Construction of the time, Nathaniel Barnaby, later put it, Esmeralda both changed the situation of sea power and "... made the fortune of the Armstrong firm."(11) It was an opportune time for such an innovation for it was now widely recognised that changes in the balance of European naval power demanded vigorous action to build up the Royal Navy.

The cruiser Esmeralda 1883.
(Source: Encyclopedia Britannica 1902)

In the six years, 1874 to 1880, during Disraeli`s second administration, 11 armour-plated warships, of a total 85,000 tons were laid down or bought. Over more or less the same time, the French navy was provided with 17 ships of this class, amounting to 128,000 tons. (12) Additionally, in the later part of this period the French very considerably increased their naval expenditure. Writing in 1884, Barnaby provided what was effectively a Royal Navy justification and manifesto for continuing large-scale spending on warship construction: "There is a growing necessity for high speed. Commerce increases its speed, and war must at least equal it. High speeds and fair fuel endurance require large coal supplies. The ship with high speed and large coal supply is already a large ship. To protect such a ship efficiently with armour demands the highest quality of protective material over considerable areas. There is then a further demand for powerful artillery for the purpose of dealing with such armour in an adversary. The attack is constantly developing new methods, and demanding not only the adoption of its weapons but also the creation and adoption of corresponding defences against them. So it comes about that nothing but a large and costly ship can take first rank in a regular war navy." Self-defeating as such an argument may seem in distant retrospect, the Pall Mall Gazette took up the theme, running a series of articles entitled "The Truth about the Navy". They provided a much more emotive argument for larger expenditures. The charges of inadequacy they made were supported by remarks from what were said to be high authorities. These included naval constructors, politicians, and Sir William Armstrong. (13) In fact long before the articles appeared Armstrongs were committed to making warship construction a major part of their operations, and themselves one of the largest private builders.

Although after 1880 the tonnage of warships launched at Low Walker for Armstrongs fell away for two years, it was obvious that the longer-term prospect was for further increases. Over the 18 months to spring 1881, they started work on four protected cruisers, with a combined displacement of over 7,000 tons - 1,400 tons more than all the naval construction they had undertaken since 1867. Should the firm continue to pay Charles Mitchell to build its naval vessels? Other serious problems were in design and oversight. For two reasons the position of George Rendel had changed. One was personal. After the death of his first wife in 1878, in 1880 he married an Italian for whom life on Tyneside seemed harsh. More important, in recognition of the eminence he had attained in this field, in 1882 he was appointed an extra, professional, civil lord of the Admiralty. As such, it was necessary for him to resign his interest in the firm in which his designs had been so important. Bit by bit it was recognised that these various changes provided an opportunity for an expanding warship construction programme concentrated in a new, specially designed naval yard at Elswick, operating under a new, specially trained naval constructor. A final, quite different type of factor was a change in conditions of navigation on the Tyne. This too involved the resources of Elswick.

In 1866, the old Tyne Bridge was demolished by the Tyne Improvement Commission. It was replaced by a temporary bridge, but work soon began on what would be known as the `Swing Bridge`, for it could be opened to allow the passage of vessels. Constructed by the Elswick Engine works, this was opened without ceremony on 25 June 1876. The new bridge transformed the commercial situation of riverside industries above Newcastle, and above all that of Elswick. Significantly, the first vessel to pass through the swing bridge was an Italian transport, Europa, which came up to the Armstrong wharf to collect a 100-ton gun. Gradually a rational plan emerged for the future of the firm`s interest in shipbuilding. At the Tyneside Exhibition in 1882, Armstrong spoke publicly of a possible amalgamation with an "eminent firm". By November Sir WG Armstrong and Company had merged with Charles Mitchell and Company to form Sir W.G. Armstrong Mitchell and Company Limited. Three months later the Tyne Improvement Commission was informed that the company intended to build at Elswick ships: "... of the greatest dimensions which can safely be passed through the bridges." (14)

The Elswick Naval Yard was laid out beyond the eastern end of the existing works on a site that until then had been occupied by wood yards. The keel for its first warship was laid in September 1884, and nine months later this vessel, a 1,552-ton "torpedo cruiser" was launched. Both Panther and her sister ship, Leopard, were built for Austro-Hungary. The next six vessels were protected cruisers, one for Italy, one for Romania-whose independence from the Ottoman Empire had only been confirmed in 1878-and two each for Spain and China. In the mid 1880s dredging undertaken by the Tyne Improvement Commission at last removed Kings Island from the Tyne alongside the Elswick works, making available deep water off shore and wider room for launching, and thereby the construction of larger vessels. This was followed by the building of by far the largest, most complicated vessel Armstrongs had yet built, a 10,500-ton battleship for the Royal Navy. Armstrong himself was in the Elswick yard for the laying of the keel for HMS Victoria on 30 July 1885. The fourth warship in the new yard, it took longer to build than earlier, smaller vessels, and after it was launched in early April 1887 did not leave the Tyne for another year. Five years later, in manoeuvres off the Syrian coast, as a result of a failure of judgement by the Commander in Chief of the Mediterranean Fleet, it was rammed by the battleship Camperdown, and sank with the loss of 321 of her crew.

During the late 1880s Elswick built protected cruisers and torpedo gunboats for Britain and the Empire. In the mid 1890s, it also turned out two of a new category of vessel, the destroyer. But, throughout the whole of Armstrong`s life, most of its work was for foreign navies. Of the 191.4 thousand tons of warships built at Elswick during the yard`s first 16 years, only 31.5 thousand tons were for British or Empire fleets. The three "ABC"navies of South America - Argentina, Brazil and Chile - together accounted for 43.4 thousand tons. Even more impressive, 79.7 thousand tons were supplied to Japan and China. (15)

As designers and builders of naval vessels, Armstrongs earned a high reputation. Even so, it was by no means always a profitable section of their activities. In the last year of Armstrong`s life no naval vessels were launched at Low Walker and only 17, 296 tons at Elswick. That year gross profits in the Walker yard-on mercantile tonnage-were £18,000, and in the Elswick naval yard £3,000. In striking contrast the Elswick engine works and foundry earned £84,000, the steelworks £85,000 and the ordnance department £395,000. Yet it is important to recognise that these very different levels of profitability oversimplify the situation. For instance, a good deal of the profit of the steel works, and still more of that in the ordnance department resulted from orders derived from the shipyards. In the case of ordnance, wider sales were also influenced to an unknown, but probably important extent by the fact that Armstrongs used its guns in the warships they built. [The Whitworth company remained a competitor, and from 1888 Vickers made heavy ordnance, but Armstrongs retained first place in the early 90s-in 1892 the five largest guns made for the Royal Navy came from Elswick.(16)] 1900 was an exceptional year in another respect. The invasion of Natal in October 1899 by forces from the Transvaal and Orange Free State initiated the Boer War. Over the next two and a half years, British arms firms were unusually busy, but the nature of their enemy meant these orders were above all for field guns and ammunition, not for warships.

Just as there was dispute among Armstrong`s partners before the formation of Armstrong Mitchell, so too, in the mid 1890s before he relinquished the nominal headship of the company, there was renewed and sometimes heated disagreement about the direction ahead in shipbuilding. In commercial engineering and in ordnance, Armstrong, Mitchell was, or, in the latter instance, with the opening of its steelworks became, fairly self-sufficient. In naval shipbuilding, it achieved impressive results, but remained unbalanced. It did not make mild steel plates or angles, and had to buy these from commercial steel firms. Not until after the end of Armstrong`s life could it make armour plate. Until then it was dependent on purchases from one or other of the three Sheffield armour firms, two of which were already rivals in naval construction and the other would soon become one. Most blatant deficiency of all, it could not provide the engines to power its warships.

The engine for Staunch came from Stephensons, and Hawthorn Leslie of Hebburn was the major supplier for their expanding programme of naval construction from the late 1870s onwards. As early as spring 1887, less than two and a half years after its own first keel was laid, a visitor to Elswick from The Graphic, was told it was the intention of Armstrong, Mitchell "...to become manufacturers of marine engines upon an extensive scale." A site was said to be available. (17) In fact the engine plant was not built until 20 years after Armstrong`s death. Meanwhile a large number of the marine engines for their warships were bought from Hawthorns or the Thameside engineering works of Maudslay, Son and Field and above all from Humphrys Tennant and Company. In the 1890s, as activity grew some of those associated with the shipbuilding division of the company began to press for control of marine engine capacity on the Tyne. This reopened old controversies about their association with Mitchell.

Charles Mitchell died aged 76, in summer 1895. For thirty years his managing partner at Low Walker had been Henry Frederick Swan, who when the merger with Armstrongs occurred became a managing director of the new company. Over the years, Swan gained a high reputation as a designer and builder of merchant vessels, particularly oil tankers. By 1895, Low Walker had built over fifty tankers, and when Swan died 13 years later, it was reckoned that nearly half of all "ocean

Bird`s eye view of Elswick works and community 1887.
(Courtesy BAE Systems)

oil carriers" then afloat had been built there. (18) Long before his association with Armstrong, Mitchell had helped two of his managers to start a yard at St Peters. This was moved in 1873 to Wallsend where Henry Swan`s brother Charles was put in charge; during the same decade Charles Mitchell and the two Swans became members of the board of the Wallsend Slipway Company. The first of these two ventures became Swan, Hunter, the second evolved into the Wallsend Slipway and Engineering Company. The engine making capacity of the latter provided the grounds for dispute within Armstrongs in the late `90s.

As with the situation some 15 years earlier, when construction of a steelworks and new yard were in contention for the available funds in the new public limited company, so in the mid and late 1890s there were competing contenders for capital expenditure. Henry Swan favoured acquisition of Wallsend Slipway-"a first class establishment"-

and thereby of marine engine capacity to remove "... what at present is a most prejudicial state of things." He persuaded Noble to visit the Slipway Company and believed he was impressed. He wanted Stuart Rendel to do the same, but Rendel was gathering support for the opposition. In the opinion of Josiah Vavasseur, control of their own armour plate capacity was a greater priority than manufacture of marine engines, and he reported that their new Whitworth colleagues were opposed to the Wallsend scheme. This was scarcely surprising, for, if given a go-ahead, a new armour plate mill would be located at Openshaw. (19)

Well before the end of Armstrong`s life, Armstrong, Whitworth and Company, of which he was still nominal though no longer effective head, had become one of the world`s leading shipbuilding companies. It was eminent in both mercantile and naval construction. To the Royal Navy it contributed a professional Lord of the Admiralty (George Rendel) and three Directors of Naval Construction. In fact, for 39 years to 1924 the men who occupied the vital position of DNC in British naval construction had either been trained by, or employed at Elswick. Such a record was yet another example of the extraordinary ability of Armstrong, or the senior colleagues he had initially chosen, to pick exceptional men for key positions.

William George Armstrong, 1883.
(Source Newcastle Monthly Chronicle January 1889)

PRIMING THE PUMP: BUSINESS HOSPITALITY AND ADVOCACY

During the Crimean War, armaments had been made to supply an urgent demand. In times of less intense pressure, it was possible to stimulate demand and to try to ensure that the weapons bought were those produced by one company rather than by others. There were two main ways of achieving these objectives, though they were largely complementary. One was to entertain a likely purchaser or their leading representatives, taking the opportunity provided to negotiate or persuade. The other was to take the initiative in visiting and inducing governments to buy a particular weapon system, through interview with the decision makers, or, by statements, articles or other means, to convince the public of a need to press for increased spending on armaments as essential for adequate national defence. Through the last forty years of the century, Armstrongs were active in these fields, and their head proved a dedicated and skilful player on their behalf.

From the early stages of involvement in ordnance, he entertained those with whom he had business dealings. Sometimes the arrangement seemed of questionable propriety, as when he brought the Ordnance Select Committee to his Jesmond home. On Friday 29 October 1858, less than three weeks before it chose his gun in preference to all others, he informed Margaret Armstrong-in a rather peremptory manner, which seems to have been by no means exceptional-that members of the committee would be in Newcastle the following Wednesday "and will most probably dine with us on that or the following day, but of this I will give you further notice." Three years later the Select Committee was again on Tyneside, spending two days inspecting the Elswick Ordnance Works. Although by virtue of his Woolwich appointment he formally had no interest, he took in hand arrangements for accommodation: "I will invite as many as we can accommodate to stay at Jesmond. Colonel Lefroy will stay with Noble. Can we take 4? If so Noble will take Baines (?) as well as Lefroy. Please let me know by return of post."(1)

When forced by circumstances to explore the possibility of selling his gun overseas, Armstrong`s homes provided congenial environments in which he and close colleagues could meet existing customers or try to secure new ones. Again, the facilities and convenience of Jesmond were called upon. In spring 1867, he asked Noble to deal directly with Margaret Armstrong in arranging hospitality there: "Please inform Lady Armstrong if E. Pasha [Efflatoun Pasha, the Khedive`s personal negotiator] accepts my invitation to come to Jesmond" (2). Now he also had Cragside, and it was quickly pressed into service. As early as September 1866, writing from the Athenaeum, he told Noble of his intended journey home and about plans for Efflatoun Pasha, with whom their relationship, though a business one, was warm. Armstrong had dined with him the previous evening: "He has now the run of this Club and attends the smoking room nearly every evening. The Club is at present free to the senior United Service people and old Halsted amongst others finds his way to the smoking club where he holds forth in his usual strain upon the Whitworth and Armstrong subject. He gets heavily snubbed by Percy but he also caught a tartar in Efflatoun Bey who I hear from Percy gave him a splendid set down a few evenings ago. Efflatoun likes the Athenaeum much better than the United Services. He says, "Here I meet with men of intellect. There I only meet with men like that "humbug old Admiral" (meaning Halsted) He is going to Liverpool tomorrow and expects to be able to leave that place for Newcastle on Saturday morning, arriving at the Central Station at 7.55. He would like to come to you for the night and proposes to go forward to Cragside on Sunday morning by the early morning train (6.13). Now I want you to take him in charge and accompany him to Cragside staying over Monday. He is a good friend and he likes you. He says he is frightened of Rendel [whether George or Stuart is unclear] who is "stern and cross" with him. I want you to take a carriage for him at Morpeth and pay all expenses which must be charged to the Firm as a matter of business. He says you promised him many pretty girls when he went to Cragside, but I don`t know how you are to keep your word in that respect."(3)

Sometimes cultivation of business was combined with hospitality for other visitors, making up house parties. His partners were also called on. Sometimes these occasions occurred in the shooting season, and guests were invited mainly for relaxation and leisure; even so, there must have been many useful discussions of particular problems or wider issues. In November 1867,ending a letter concerned with tracings of the breech ends of 9 inch guns, Armstrong mentioned to Noble: "I hope you can arrange to come here with me next Friday for a day`s shooting on Saturday. S. Rendel will be down by that time." Next year, late in August, when the firm was supplying naval guns to the Netherlands, he told Noble: "I have invited the Dutchmen for Wednesday. You and Mrs Noble and Miss Douglas (?) must please consider yourselves engaged." Three weeks later the emphasis was different. He entertained Henry Dyer, who had served on the test ranges at Shoeburyness. [Later he would join Whitworths for seven years, before becoming an Armstrong director.] The schedule of the few days before this meeting illustrated how desperately Armstrong needed a refuge, but also how even this place had become part of his pressing routine of work. On the morning of Wednesday 16 September 1868 in Newcastle he learned that the company had received an order for six 150 pounders. After this, he left for Cardiff to attend a dock opening-more probably an extension-from which he thought considerable orders for machinery were "looming". Two days later, he went up to London, where he met Stuart Rendel and Albini, before that evening going on to Newcastle where George Rendel and Dyer joined him for dinner in Jesmond. At 7 o`clock on Sunday morning, he wrote to tell Noble, "we are all hurrying off by the 8 o`clock train to Cragside." There, Cadogan and "a few other friends" would join them. In October the following year, he told Noble: "We shall be at home on Saturday evening. Will you ask His Excellency to come to my house on Sunday and stay a few days? I expect Mrs Cadogan and Lady Hawes will be there." By early 1869, he was spending one week at Cragside and the next at the works, when he presumably stayed in Jesmond. (4)

Year after year Cragside hospitality was sometimes confined to business, but often intermixed with pleasure. In August 1884, there was an exceptional occasion. The Prince of Wales and Princess

Alexandra and their children stayed there during a visit to Tyneside. The royal party officiated at the commissioning of the Albert Edward Docks, opened the Hancock Museum and visited Elswick. Armstrong reported to Noble on his shooting expedition with the Prince, "We got out at 10 this morning. Our bag is 43 and a half brace of grouse, 6 snipe and 21 old black cocks. Campbell, the Prince and myself got 21 and a half brace grouse for our bag. Tomorrow we shall go on the west side of the Alnwick road. Where shall we see you? I hope you have had fair sport. If the weather had been favourable we should have got far more."(5)

After that high point, entertaining of guests who were, or might be, important to the company continued into the last years of Margaret Armstrong`s life, and afterwards. Not all of their visitors were equally welcome. In spring 1889, when the Shah of Persia, Nasir-ed-Din, made his third visit to Europe, he spent a month in Britain. Armstrong was requested, apparently by the government, to entertain him at Cragside on 23 July and to take him over Elswick the next day. He explained to George Rendel: "Our government is competing with Russia for the Shah`s favour and is very anxious that he should receive great attention in this country. But I expect he will be a troublesome person to entertain, as he styles himself King of Kings and expects to be treated as such." In March 1894, Lord Roberts, back from nine years as commander in chief in India, was a visitor. Next year when Crown Prince Nazrullah Khan of Afghanistan came, it was reported that his tour of Elswick was almost the only time he was impressed during his time in Britain. During summer 1897, the King of Siam visited Armstrong, an event that would bring about a dramatic change in the nature and pace of life at Cragside. (6)

Armstrong and his colleagues were indefatigable in efforts to influence important decisions about military spending, even though, according to Stuart Rendel, he had initially showed indifference to promoting overseas sales. At home, over many years, he cultivated contacts with the War Office and Admiralty and in the press, speeches and articles used the progress in warlike preparations made by foreign powers-even by reference to his own company`s sales to them-to stir up demand for increases in military spending.

An example of the way he recognised that fear of war provided opportunity for sales, came in a letter from Jesmond to Noble. Concerning howitzers, it unfortunately was not dated: "We must try to push the matter through while the present apprehension of Russian interference continues."(7) In 1869, his attempt to make contact with Hugh E Childers, First Lord of the Admiralty in Gladstone's first administration, was another attempt to stimulate. Its failure and the way in which years later Childers was characterised in Armstrong company correspondence as "unfriendly to us" has already been summarised.(8) Even so Armstrong and senior colleagues were always ready to press government ministers to favour them with orders. In spring 1895, in the last weeks of the Rosebery government, when Henry Campbell-Bannerman was at the War Office, and Lord Spencer First Lord at the Admiralty, John Fisher provided an insight into this process in the course of a letter to Spencer. He wrote, "In view of the assertion of an Admiralty bias against Woolwich, would it not be desirable to mention to Mr Campbell-Bannerman at tomorrow`s meeting our memorable interview in your room with Lord Armstrong and Sir Andrew Noble, when they vehemently accused the Admiralty of giving an undue proportion of orders to the ordnance factories to the great detriment of the private trade of this country?"(9)

Attempts to secure orders from overseas were continuing and so successful that for many years in the sixties and seventies almost all their business in ordnance came from that quarter. As seen earlier, in the last 15 years of Armstrong`s life naval construction for Japan or Italy or Chile was often on a far larger scale than that for the Royal Navy. There were some notable failures. Given their history, the French were understandably reluctant to call on British armament makers, but Armstrongs were willing to try. Early in 1878, they wrote to the French Minister of Marine and the Colonies, pointing out that they had supplied hydraulic gun carriages for the Tonnere and Devastation, and, in effect, asking for more work of the same nature. A prompt but cool reply from Paris informed them that the new orders had already been placed. (10) With the Germans, Armstrong`s initially made much more headway. In 1868, Noble visited Berlin in connection with supply of guns for the first important ironclad vessel ever built in Prussia. Although Armstrong recognised they must leave him free to undertake negotiations in the way he thought best, he sent him his own thoughts on the matter: "Still however the great thing is to urge the arming of this monster Prussian ship with [the] 10 inch gun, pointing out that this is now a well tried gun and if ever there was a case for carrying such a gun it is that of the Konig Wilhelm. I think that it is doubtful policy our following Krupp into the region of experiment. He is trying first one thing and then another and can offer no assurances as to the result of extended trials. It is for us to rest upon well proved results and to stick to them and to the conditions under which they were obtained, unless forced by circumstances to a different course." In fact, in this case too, Armstrongs eventually failed, for Krupp possessed two powerful advantages. In the first place, testimony from Russian authorities at last convinced the King and his War Minister that the Krupp gun was superior to that made by Armstrong. Secondly, as Alfred Krupp explained to his Berlin representative, Carl Meyer, he was resolved to play his master card: "That the Royal Prussian Navy should not draw its guns from abroad so long as it has an opportunity of obtaining better guns at home, is for me much more a matter of honour than of financial interest."(11)

An early illustration of using news of technical advance to stimulate orders came after the 1868 construction of Staunch for the Royal Navy. In May 1869, a report in The Times seemed to provide an opportunity for promoting further gun boat orders. As proved typical over the years, Armstrong used it to draw public attention to the inadequacy of British armaments. Staunch, he stressed, was both cheap and effective: "You have recently alluded to the success of the gunboat Staunch, designed by my partner, Mr George Rendel, and I am desirous to call further attention to the value of small vessels of that description for defending our numerous ports against the sudden inroads of hostile ironclads in time of war. ...The cost of a couple of ironclad frigates would furnish a hundred Staunchs." Indeed, he even claimed that six small gunboats each armed with a big gun could cope with an ironclad. He went on to make a general point well-calculated to unsettle the newspaper`s readers: "...whatever difference of opinion there may be as to the best mode of attaining the object, [defence of the numerous seaports] certain it is that at the present time we are prepared with nothing that would have the least chance of proving effectual."(12)

A few years later, he used a similar approach to advocate fast, well-armed, but lightly armoured cruisers, such as Esmeralda. For his inaugural address as chairman of the Institute of Civil Engineers on 10 January 1882, he chose a promising subject for a major maker of ordnance and warships: "National Defence". The Times reported his remarks next morning: "Light unarmoured ships, designed by Mr George Rendel, had lately been built in this country for foreign powers, which, with a displacement of only 1,300 tons, had attained a speed of 16 knots an hour. They carried coal for steaming 4,000 miles, and had already actually steamed 3,500 miles without replenishing. They were each armed with two 10 inch new type guns, which had nearly an all-round fire, and were capable of piercing 18 inches of iron armour, and with four 40 pounders on the broadsides. It was a very serious question what could be done in the event of a number of such vessels as these being let loose upon our commerce. At present there was not a single ship in the British Navy carrying an armament competent to engage them, that could overtake them in pursuit, or evade their attack when prudence dictated a retreat." Having provoked fear and doubt in this manner, Armstrong ended: "the government should pursue such a course as would bring into full play the abundant engineering resources of this highly mechanical country for increasing the efficiency of our national defences." His paper received immediate attention, some of it highly critical. (13) He continued to pursue this theme at this time of generally rising concern about the future of the Royal Navy.

At the second Annual Meeting of Armstrong, Mitchell and Company on 1 October 1884, as the new Elswick shipyard neared completion, Armstrong told his shareholders that Esmeralda was "...the swiftest and most powerfully armed cruiser in the world ... unarmoured as all cruisers ought to be." Completed in mid July, in her sea trials she had actually reached a speed of 18.2 knots. The Times now published an article about her. It was anonymous, but later found to have been written by WH White, at that time chief naval architect at Elswick. From the chair, at the meeting, Armstrong launched into an even clearer case of naval policy blackmail than that of his Civil Engineers address. "Happily she has passed into the hands of a nation which is never likely to be at war with England....No cruiser in the British Navy is swift enough to catch her, or strong enough to take her". He recognised a "well-founded scare" about the navy but regretted that it centred on the provision of ironclads, which were not effective in commerce protection. He reckoned the Esmeralda class "will never be out of date, while ironclads often become obsolete almost as soon as made. "He wound up his remarks by bringing the matter home to the prospects of his own company, though he also managed to weave in a touch of humour: "These observations are pertinent to the occasion, because the success of the Esmeralda, and a more appreciative view of ships of the cruiser class, are obviously connected with the prospects of this company. I might extend my remarks to the unprotected state of our commercial ports, but that does not so much concern the business of our company, unless, indeed, a hostile cruiser should some day run into the unprotected Tyne. In that case, we might expect a visit from her at Elswick, unless she was stopped by the difficulty of opening the swing bridge. Our establishment is more dependent for its safety on the swing bridge than on anything Government has done for barring the entrance to the river." (14) His vigorously expressed views had the desired effect. On the same day as the annual meeting, Rear Admiral John Wilson wrote in alarm taking up his suggestion of a threat to Elswick, and a few weeks later Armstrong received a letter from Alfred Milner, then in a relatively humble job as assistant to WT Stead, editor of the Pall Mall Gazette. Milner invited him to contribute his views about naval ordnance, rather optimistically telling him not only that "an article from so great an authority might exercise a great influence" but also that: "....the objection which would be raised in the case of advice given by the head of any other private firm viz, that he had "an axe to grind" would not apply to a man of your immense business and long established public position."(15)

THE ROUNDED MAN

Over the many years during which he laboured to perfect commercial and armament inventions and worked conscientiously to sell them, Armstrong also served society well in a considerable range of other activities. One of these spheres, private at the time, later proved to be a major and worthwhile contribution to the wider good. Even this, the creation of Cragside, did not provide a limit to his services.

One field of eminence derived from his adopted profession. He was a long-term member of the Institute of Civil Engineers and the Institute of Mechanical Engineers. In turn, he occupied the presidency of each of these institutions of international reputation. As seen above, he took the opportunity this afforded not only to review the state of engineering, but also to champion his own ordnance innovations and to justify involvement in perfecting weapons of mass destruction. Later in life, he was also associated with the Institute of Naval Architects, on more than one occasion offering hospitality to some of its functions when meetings were held in Newcastle upon Tyne. In 1883, when the British Association met in York, as president of the mechanical section he considered future options for energy supply, including large-scale hydro-electric generation and solar power. Twenty years before, as president of the Newcastle BA meeting he provided considerable impetus to the debate about the adequacy of Britain`s coal reserves to support its continuing industrial leadership. It also gave him an opportunity for a survey of contemporary science, and provided important insights into his own opinions about some of the leading issues of the day.

Discussing "The Coal Supply" in 1873 in Newcastle before an audience of engineers and mining men, he moved on from an examination of energy consumption in marine transport, to share his thoughts on the application of steam power to agriculture. His ideas were stimulating, but there was one strange omission, namely the rapidly changing world situation within which British farmers were operating. Given the context, perhaps he took this for granted. Speaking on what would prove to be the very eve of a crisis in British agriculture, he tried to think his way through the application of mechanical power to "every kind of farming operation…for if the food producing power of the land has to be increased, it must be by substituting, as far as possible, the comparatively cheap power of steam, for the labour, both of men and horses." World agriculture apart, his argument was wide-ranging: "The greatly increased demand for labour in manufacturing occupations, as well as for mining and constructive purposes, will certainly diminish the supply of rural labour and increase its cost. Such a result is not to be regretted, considering how miserably ill requited farm labour in most parts of England has been; but unless the growing cost of agricultural labour and of horse work, can be counterpoised by a more extensive use of steam power, we may expect much of the land in this country to be thrown out of cultivation. Very different are the views of those who maintain that food would be more economically produced by increasing, instead of diminishing, the labour employed on the land. Such is the doctrine of those who advocate parcelling out the land in small plots to peasant holders, and who even contend that wastelands, incapable of profitable return by ordinary treatment, could, by this means, be advantageously cultivated. It would, indeed, be a retrograde step to renounce the aid of capital and mechanical skill in tillage, and fall back upon the primitive system of spade husbandry. If there be any country in the world where such a mode of cultivation is the best, that country is assuredly not England, where all the resources of science and skill are necessary to the maintenance of a large population, under adverse conditions of soil and climate, and where labour is more highly paid in manufacture than in agriculture." He returned to the problems of farming 14 years later, by which time the British industry was deep in depression. Speaking at a dinner that he gave to members of the Royal Agricultural Society, then holding its annual meeting in Newcastle, he said, "…great as are the advantages of cheap food, they must be weighed against the disadvantages of paralysing more or less the greatest of our home industries, and the casting balance of advantage is that which ought to determine the course of legislation on the subject."(1)

One of the most interesting features of Armstrong`s intellectual and public life, was the way in which his role on the national stage was counterbalanced by a continuing part in the rich life of his home region. He played a key role on numerous occasions when Newcastle entertained national organisations. One noteworthy instance, which also had an international dimension, came when the Iron and Steel Institute held its annual regional meeting in the city in September 1877. On Thursday 20 September members of the Institute visited Elswick. The works now covered 40 acres, had a mile long frontage on the Tyne and employed almost 4,000-though this was no more than 14 or 15 years before when the Ordnance works was engaged exclusively on work for the British government. In the evening, a banquet was given to about 250 members of the Institute by Armstrong. The guest of honour was Ulysses S Grant, who in the late stages of the Civil War had commanded the armies of the Federal Government and from 1869 to earlier in 1877 had been President of the United States. Armstrong proposed the health of General Grant. The Times reported that, "The General concluded a brief acknowledgement by expressing the hope that the makers of such weapons as Sir William Armstrong might long continue their vocation, and oblige the nations to keep the peace." As he made those remarks, one wonders if he remembered that Armstrongs had supplied both sides in the terrible struggle in which he had played such a prominent part.

Over a long period, Armstrong was important in the affairs of the Newcastle Literary and Philosophical Society, one of the distinguished societies for men of science, business and wider intellectual concerns, which had been set up in major provincial cities at the end of the eighteenth or during the early years of the nineteenth century. William Armstrong senior had been involved in the early years of the "Lit and Phil", and his son became a member in 1836. Ten years later, he took a leading part in its first "Conversazione", and by 1855 was vice-president. In October 1859, in consequence of the death of Robert Stephenson, he became president. Then almost 50, he remained president for over forty years. Apart from presenting lectures and demonstrations, he played an important part in steering the society. One of the most striking of these contributions came when he was in his 80s. At that time, he fiercely defended its traditional neutrality in relation to economic and political issues. This involved him doggedly insisting that the meetings of a so-called "Economic Society" should not be held in any form of association with the Lit and Phil. Having assisted it handsomely during his lifetime, in his will he left the society a £1,000 bequest. (2)

In politics, he became over the years more and more an establishment figure. In an unusually full and relaxed letter to Margaret Armstrong for her birthday in 1860, he told her about a party at the home of General Peel he had attended a few days before. There he met Princess Mary and the Duchess of Cambridge. They talked about Garibaldi, who was in disfavour with the royal party for his revolutionary tendencies. When, stoutly, Armstrong confessed to being "somewhat smitten" with the "Garibaldi fever" the Duchess turned good humouredly to General Peel, saying "Aha ...I see your friend is a radical"(3) In later life very few people could have thought of using such a term to describe him. Dougan has claimed that Armstrong was a "moderate Liberal" all his life, but Stuart Rendel wrote that Armstrong "hated" his politics when he stood and was elected as Liberal MP for Montgomeryshire. Feeling particularly strongly opposed to Irish Home Rule, in the 1886 General Election Armstrong agreed to fight Newcastle as a Unionist Liberal, supporting the Conservatives. When the results were declared, John Morley and another Home Rule Liberal were elected: Armstrong and the Conservative, Sir Matthew Ridley, were defeated. Because he received a peerage, he never again stood for Parliament, but he retained a strong aversion for Gladstone. This came out well in a letter to George Rendel late in 1888, when Gladstone was out of office: "...I hear Stuart has taken a house in Naples and is going to entertain the Gladstone family there. At present they are living with him at Whitehall Gardens, where I met them a second time at dinner the last time I was in London. I suppose you will have to invite the G.O.M (<u>G</u>od`s <u>O</u>nly <u>M</u>istake as someone interpreted the letters) to dine at Villa Maravel [GWR`s home] where I have no doubt he will make himself very agreeable."(4)

Earnings from commercial engineering and armaments made William George Armstrong a very wealthy man. Much of the money accumulated during an exceptionally long working life was invested in his two homes, their furnishings and luxurious contents and, in the case of Cragside, in embellishment and major extensions to the large area of land he controlled. Yet, although he undoubtedly lived the life of a plutocrat, he seems to have been genuine as well as generous in charitable giving. In this, as in so many other things, his home city and neighbourhood received almost all his attention. Contributions to good causes were sometimes made dependent on matching commitments from others. An example from as early as 1861 was his offer of £2,000 for a seaside convalescent hospital near Tynemouth for the treatment of scrofulous diseases - conditional on it receiving another £4,000 by public subscription within 12 months. (5) He was generous towards education, not only in the elementary and technical schools he established in Elswick, but also by fostering higher education. He contributed £100 for six years to the Newcastle College of Physical Science which was established in 1871; sixteen years later, he was one of the main contributors to the new buildings at Barras Bridge. Today, in the attractive courtyard of the University of Newcastle upon Tyne, there is a plaque recording that he laid a foundation stone on 15 June 1887. Within three years of his death, the place was renamed and known for many years as Armstrong College. Nearby, between the University and the Great North Road, he and Margaret Armstrong donated £11,500 for the building of the Hancock Museum for the Natural History Society.

When he paid the full cost of almost £30,000 for the high-level bridge which was opened across Jesmond Dene in 1878, Armstrong left the Corporation to build the approach road on the hospital ground at St Mary`s Mount, a project reckoned to cost a further £8,000. That year, he began donating parts of Jesmond Dene to the City, beginning with a section that was renamed by the grateful recipients, "Armstrong Park". Five years later, he added the remaining parts of the Dene to his gift, subject only to the reservation that during his lifetime or that of Margaret Armstrong complete control should remain with them. Three years on, there was a further gift, this time of the pictures, statues, furniture and other effects of the Banqueting Hall in the Dene.

Said to be frail as a child, Armstrong not only lived to become a nonagenarian, but also until his last three years, lived a physically active life. Fishing featured largely in his younger years, but later, though he reckoned himself not a particularly good shot, game shooting became his main sport. He was also a vigorous walker. There are two accounts of holidays in the Lake District. They indicate his prowess in this respect, but also incidentally seem to suggest that perhaps he did not find it easy to appreciate the beauties of scenery. On Sunday 3 September 1854, he wrote to Margaret from Braithwaite to report on a holiday trip with four members of the Rendel family: "I reached here late on Friday night and yesterday George and Hamilton with Edith and Emily joined me in a very successful excursion to the head of Langdale, from which point George and I scrambled to the top of Langdale Pike, 2,500 feet high, and returned to the foot in the short space of only one hour and a half. The day was sultry and I think I never was so hot, but today I feel as light and strong as possible ... The weather is magnificent but awfully hot ... Although this place is very pretty it is a desperate long way off from places of interest and if it was not for the lake and the boat would certainly admit of being tired of." Seven years later he was staying in the Lowdore [sic] Inn, near Keswick: "We have been here two days and had two capital rambles. Yesterday was really a fine day and we went to the top of Scawfell Pike, (the highest point in England) after which we climbed the "Great Gavel" [it seems this refers to Great Gable] almost as high, and had some wonderful views. Today it rains, so we shall keep near home. Tomorrow we shall go to Buttermere, over the mountain tops taking the top of Honister Crag in the line. On Saturday we expect to be in Keswick and you may look for me at Jesmond on Sunday if you hear nothing to the contrary....We have not seen a newspaper since Sunday [it was now Thursday] and know nothing of what is going on in the world.....We are all very well and can walk over 20 miles a day without much difficulty."(6)

From his physical recreations and sensitivities, it seems necessary to move on to ask - what did Armstrong believe? What motivated him, and set his work and wider life in the broader contexts of humanity, time and eternity? In short, what was his faith? Did he have a religious belief? If so, what was it? To disentangle this is not at all easy for he was one who did not readily reveal the state of his heart. Nowhere is there a clear statement of convictions, and indeed little more than scattered clues.

To many modern believers in God, in Christ, and in the values of a

Christian way of life, or for that matter for a humanist, it is almost inconceivable that any man, and particularly a man of Armstrong`s intelligence, should devote a large part of his adult life and his finest talents striving to perfect the means of mass destruction of his fellow men and of the material base of their lives. In an earlier age, there may have been many who had a genuine belief in the adage that today seems so hollow: "If you wish for peace, prepare for war." His working life apart, Armstrong was reckoned generally to be kindly, a man who did much good not only in philanthropic support for important causes but in countless smaller acts of individual charity. Did he do so as a humanist, rationalist, or from religious convictions?

As seen earlier, his presidential address to the 1863 Newcastle meeting of the British Association provided a wide review of progress in science. When, at the end of it, he referred to the work of Darwin, and the controversies it had aroused over the last few years, he made clear that he was puzzled, but inclined to sit on the fence in relation to some of the profounder issues. It would be of great interest to know whom he consulted for expert advice in this matter, but the words he used, as well as the ideas he expressed are useful pointers to his own beliefs. He began by mentioning a path well worn in his kind of work. On the one hand, "Investigations, patiently conducted upon true inductive principles, cannot fail eventually to elicit the hidden laws which govern the animated world. Neither is there any lack of bold speculation contemporaneously with this painstaking spirit of inquiry....[but] The novelty of this ingenious theory, the eminence of its author, and his masterly treatment of the subject, have, perhaps, combined to excite more enthusiasm in its favour than is consistent with that dispassionate spirit which is so necessary in the pursuit of truth." He then went further, revealing what was essentially a deist perspective - though again from an eminently "Armstrong" starting point: "Where good reasons can be shown on both sides of a question, the truth is generally to be found between the two extremes. In the present instance we may, without difficulty [!], suppose it to have been part of the great scheme of Creation, that natural selection should be permitted to determine variations amounting even to specific differences, where those differences were matters of degree; but when natural selection is adduced as a cause adequate to explain the production of a new organ not provided for in original Creation, the hypothesis must appear, to common apprehensions, to be pushed beyond the limits of reasonable conjecture. The Darwinian theory when fully enunciated founds the pedigree of living nature upon the most elementary form of vitalized matter. One step further would carry us back, without greater violence to probability, to inorganic rudiments; and then we should be called upon to recognize in ourselves, and in the exquisite elaborations of the animal and vegetable kingdoms, the ultimate results of mere material forces left free to follow their own unguided tendencies. Surely our minds would in that case be more oppressed with a sense of the miraculous, than they now are in attributing the wondrous things around us to the creative hand of a great presiding Intelligence." When he briefly mentioned how much Lyell`s work had extended the history of the human race, he added: "...but, notwithstanding this great antiquity, the proofs still remain unaltered, that man is the latest as well as the noblest work of God."(7)

For over 30 years, he was one of the Rothbury churchwardens. In the light of this, it seems surprising that the benefactions incorporated in its modern structure came not from him but from his successor. The pulpit bears the inscription, "in affectionate memory of Margaret, wife of Baron Armstrong of Cragside.", but it dates from 1901 and was given by William Watson-Armstrong. At the same time Watson-Armstrong donated the chancel screen "...in loving memory of William George, Baron Armstrong of Cragside." Perhaps an indication of why he himself did not give lavishly to the parish church is to be found in something he wrote in the early 1880s to Margaret: "Percy Westmacott is going to give £4,000 for a reredos in St Nicholas [raised in 1881 to the dignity of a Cathedral]. I think the public will hardly appreciate such a lavish expenditure."(8)

In formal terms, Armstrong seems to have been what indeed a number of those who celebrated his life claimed for him both then, and in retrospect-"a fine Christian gentleman". When the Congregationalists of the town wanted a place of worship, he allowed them to use a plot of land he owned, and on Wednesday 15 May 1895 laid the foundation stone. Though the few words he used on that occasion were unexceptionable, they seem to reveal something of the limitations of his own convictions: "I declare this stone to be well and truly laid, in the name of the Father, Son, and Holy Ghost. Ladies and Gentlemen, it now only remains for me to congratulate you upon having made a fair start in the erection of this new church, and to express a hope that it will have a prosperous and useful career."(9) It is known that Andrew Noble held daily prayers in his home for his family and servants, but there is no record that this occurred in the Armstrong homes. He was happy in the company of agnostics or unbelievers such as Huxley, and Tyndall, but it may have been their science and involvement with him in the organisation of the British Association and not their attitudes to religion that attracted him to them.

Some insights into his thinking may be obtained from his account of the 1872 visit to Egypt. On the first Sunday after their arrival Armstrong and a friend-presumably his "translator", Stuart Rendel-attended an "English" service in the hotel in which they stayed. In itself this was not significant, for then as later this sort of thing could more easily be a way of asserting national allegiance and cohesion-the sort of thing Englishmen abroad do on Sundays-in a foreign land than deep personal commitment. While in Cairo, he visited a suburban mosque, in which the so-called "Howling Dervishes" worshipped. The leader of this group was "a tall handsome man, with a very dignified bearing and a mild and intelligent countenance." Referring further to him and to his own experiences there, Armstrong gave a very "liberal" interpretation, seeming to make clear that action not belief was vital: "I feel confident that the grand old fellow who presided over the miscalled howlers [for they did not produce what he would call a howl] was not only thoroughly sincere, but was every inch a gentleman. Had he been born in a Christian country, and of Christian parentage, his devotional tendency would have taken a better form, but imbued with the traditions of his race, and excluded from all contact with Christianity, except in a degraded form, how could he be expected to take the Bible for his guide instead of the Koran. If he acts according to the light in that state of life in which it has pleased God to place him, who shall affix anathema to his name?" Though of much less significance, by implication he made clear that he shared the views of those who had no qualms about discarding the whole timescale of the Old Testament. He quoted the Rev. Barton Zincke on the age of a wooden statuette found in one of the Nile valley tombs: "Mr Zincke ...

feels constrained to assume a longer period of historic time than the chronology deduced from the earliest Hebrew records ... He argues that the Scriptures were designed to teach men religion, and not universal history, or science or anything of that kind." Another sign of his possible doubting, modern style of thinking came in a comment on the sacred island of Philae above the first cataract: "The story of Osiris is a very remarkable one, on account of a certain degree of analogy it bears to the Christian faith [in death and resurrection]." (10)

Three years before his visit to Egypt, his presidential address to the Institute of Mechanical Engineers, provided another, more general insight into his views about life and values. It did not refer to religion, but revealed him as a thoroughgoing utilitarian, and ended with an invigorating dose of meliorism. After reviewing the progress of the century since Watt's invention, he referred to the Suez Canal, and championed the material values it epitomised against other, earlier value systems: "In contemplating this undertaking, we are naturally led to compare it with the great neighbouring relics of Egyptian antiquity. In quantity of material moved, the Suez Canal is far more vast than the great Pyramid. In its moral and intellectual aspect, it is immeasurably superior. The ancient work is a useless monument of the idle vanity of a tyrant; the modern work will bear witness to the practical science and utilitarian spirit of our better times. Surely the world improves as the dominion of mind over matter is extended."(11)

In their obituary notices of him, two of his business colleagues obviously drew on each other`s recollections of Armstrong`s views of these wider issues, but the emphases of their very short references to this aspect of his life differed slightly. Andrew Noble, who had known him most closely, recognised both the roots of his great success and their strict boundaries: "His talents were rigidly limited to practical issues. It would be an overstatement to describe him as lacking in imagination, but he had no taste whatever for transcendental or speculative enquiries." Alfred Cochrane, a relative newcomer at Elswick, wrote, "His mind was at the same time original and yet strictly practical; he noticed with a penetrating observation, and drew conclusions with intuitive genius. Abstract speculation had no charms for him; he never cherished wild dreams or extravagant ideas." In that last remark, Cochrane may also have identified why a talented engineer had become one of the world`s greatest armaments makers. (12)

AN OCTOGENARIAN IN BUSINESS

In the late 1880s, dramatic changes began in the armaments industry. They were associated with fears that Britain`s leading position as a naval power was being eroded. In March 1889 Lord George Hamilton, First Lord of the Admiralty, introduced a Naval Defences Bill which provided for expenditure of up to £21.5 millions for "building, arming, equipping and completing for sea" 70 warships over a four and a half year period. This programme would include eight first-class battleships of unprecedented size. It meant that by 1894 Great Britain would have 165 warships as compared with only 62 in France, 58 in Germany, Italy 36 and Russia 30. However, the old, unquestioned primacy of Great Britain was not restored. Expansion from now on proved a never-ending process; a naval race was underway. By late 1893, there was agitation for another new naval programme. According to a memorandum circulated by Lord Charles Beresford, battleship numbers should be raised from 45 to 60, and the fleet of torpedo boats from 97 to 377 at a cost of £18 million, if Britain could hope to contend on equal terms with France and Russia. (1) Partly as a result of the increased programmes for the Royal Navy, but also because of building for other countries, particularly Japan, Armstrong profits increased rapidly. They were £244,000 in 1889 the year of the Naval Defences Act, but in 1899 and 1900 averaged £662,000.

Expansion in naval construction, and the increased profits made by established armament firms helped bring about a major realignment of the industry, as new armament groups were formed. In 1888, Vickers, the Sheffield firm that had supplied steel to Armstrongs from their early days, produced their first armour plate and heavy guns. Nine years later, they acquired the Barrow shipyard from the Naval

Construction and Armaments Company. In 1899, their Sheffield near neighbours, John Brown, obtained their own, major shipbuilding branch by a link with the Clydebank Engineering and Shipbuilding Company. The final stages of this national restructuring process took shape in the few years following Armstrong`s death. By 1901, the Scottish steel and engineering company, Beardmore, had begun a wholesale extension of its business with armour and heavy gun manufacture at Parkhead and a major new naval yard at Dalmuir. Finally, in 1903 the third Sheffield armour plate firm, Charles Cammell, absorbed Laird Brothers of Birkenhead. Until the late 1880s, Armstrongs had been unique in controlling steel, ordnance and shipbuilding capacity; by 1900, there were two additional "complete" armaments groups, and the next few years would add two more. Though now in his eighties, Armstrong continued to be interested in these changes, and was involved in decision taking, and even to a considerable degree in negotiations.

He was present at the launch of the Japanese warship Yashima on 8 February 1896. In his remarks he said: "Whatever may be the destiny of this splendid ship, we may be sure that she will be handled with the ability, the skill, and the courage recently displayed in the Japanese navy and that she will prove worthy of the highly civilised and progressive nation to which she belongs." His words were greeted with loud applause. Neatly avoiding mentioning his country`s recent war with China, the Japanese Minister showed how well he had learned the words and sentiments Europeans had long employed to cloak their real meanings: "His Excellency said that he hoped the vessel might be peacefully employed, but in order to secure peace it was necessary to be prepared for war."(Applause) (2) Eight years later Yashima was sunk by mines off Port Arthur, in the course of the first war in which a major European power was defeated by an Asian nation.

A few weeks after the launch of the Yashima, Noble set out for Japan. He consulted Armstrong before deciding to make the voyage, and received in reply a letter of advice that showed how much the latter retained both his affectionate concern for their chief executive and his good sense: "the most important consideration for yourself, your family, and the Elswick Firm, is the establishment of your health, and in my opinion a sea voyage to Japan and back coupled with most

Andrew Noble and William Armstrong in the 1890s
(Courtesy BAE Systems)

interesting novel experiences while there would be the most effective step for this purpose that could possibly be taken, besides being most important in a business point of view. I feel sure that all your co directors now in England [this may have excluded Stuart Rendel] will hold this opinion except one [probably Hamilton Rendel] whose dissent only dates from my suggestion that Vavasseur should assist Saxton [Noble`s son] during your absence. My advice is that you consult your Doctor and abide by his recommendation." While Noble was away letters from Armstrong helped keep him in touch with events at home. On 23 April for instance, he wrote to him from Eccleston Square: "I attended the Committee meeting yesterday and then came on to London. I am glad to hear of your arrival at Hong Kong and trust that you are now safe to reach Japan before the departure of the commission." He reported contacts with Whitworths concerning patents relevant to orders for five battleships, about possible manufacture of cordite and marine engine supply. There was reference to "the Barrow scheme", a possible involvement of Armstrongs in development, along with the Naval Construction and Armaments Company in armour plate manufacture there. (3) In fact, while Noble was away, though now in his 86th year, Armstrong took an active part in negotiations with the Duke of Devonshire, Chairman of the Naval Construction company. This scheme fizzled out, and the Barrow operations passed instead to Vickers.

Meanwhile after general consideration for some time-in mid 1894 Armstrong reminded Noble he had suggested it shortly after the formation of Armstrong Mitchell-negotiations began for an amalgamation with Sir Joseph Whitworth and Company. They took up most of the remainder of 1896, but on Thursday 17 December the draft agreement for the Armstrong and Whitworth merger was carried by the first train of the day from Newcastle to Rothbury and then on to Cragside. When he received it from Noble`s messenger, Armstrong at once telegraphed his approval and authorised the calling of a special meeting in London for the following Tuesday, three days before Christmas. On Saturday 19th, apparently from Jesmond, he let Noble know that he would leave home at 11.30 on Monday to catch the ordinary midday express to London. He would be staying at 65 Eccleston Square, and wanted to see Noble at the Athenaeum at 10 on

Tuesday morning, before the meeting. This meeting duly confirmed the arrangements. (4) There was another special meeting of the directors, and then two weeks later in an extraordinary general meeting of Armstrong Mitchell held at the Elswick Mechanics Institute on Wednesday 24 February 1897 Armstrong moved, and Noble seconded the proposal: "That the name of this company be changed to Sir WG Armstrong, Whitworth and Company Limited"(5)

The creation of Armstrong Whitworth provided another interesting side light into Armstrong`s character. Although Joseph Whitworth and his company had for so long been the enemy, he was now open-minded and conciliatory. There survives a much-amended draft of a letter from him to a new-and unspecified-director. In it, he noted that at the last meeting he had advocated a policy that avoided confrontation. He thought his proposal had been opposed with "unnecessary vehemence". He went on: "Forgive me for speaking a few words of advice at the outset of your career as a Director. I recommend you to cultivate a general conciliatory manner, which I can assure you will in the long run give you more influence over your colleagues than unnecessary argument. Above all bear in mind the words of a great diplomatist who said the world is made for those who keep their temper." Such an approach helped make old rivals into loyal colleagues. A striking confirmation of this was provided by Major General Sir Henry Alderson, a man Armstrong had known from days spent at Shoeburyness thirty years before, and who in late January 1897 presided over the Manchester meeting of Sir Josiah Whitworth and Company, which approved the merger. Alderson now wrote Armstrong a gracious letter. In it, he recalled he had been so long associated with experiments with Armstrong and Whitworth guns, that "...it seems somehow quite natural to be again associated with the two well-known names in my later life." "Now that the amalgamation is recently completed I feel I must send you a line to tell you how very sensible I am of the honour of being a director of the new firm." Next week when he would attend his first board meeting he hoped to meet Armstrong.(6) By this time, there were troubling signs of the rapid advance of Vickers, but after so many years, Armstrongs still seemed to dominate in heavy armaments.

Although still active in company affairs, Armstrong was occasionally ill. Sometimes he was willing to use age and increasing fragility as excuses for evading irksome duties. For example, late in November 1890 he informed Noble: "I almost always get a cold at a ship launch and as I don`t suppose that my presence on Monday will put an extra penny into the Treasury at Elswick I shall not come in until Wednesday on which day I shall attend the Committee meeting." Fourteen months later, as he put it, he "suddenly took the influenza" and had to spend at least 3 days in bed. By the time he had thrown it off, he realised that he could not so easily get over its effects: "It is astonishing how it pulls one down, and I suppose octogenarians don`t recover their strength so readily as younger people. I get very little out as yet but I am fully employed with my electrical apparatus which is now quite a success and I am getting some very remarkable results."(7)

Into the early months of 1897, he was still active in company affairs. One focus of attention was a possible association with the Wallsend Slipway and Engineering Company, as a source for marine engines. Stuart Rendel and his brother Hamilton were fiercely opposed to Henry Swan, a co-director, who was also prominent at Wallsend Slipway. At the same time, Stuart was conducting a campaign to secure the election to the board of his son in law, Henry Gladstone. In an early January letter to Noble, Armstrong took up both issues, and aired another age-old theme: "I enclose a letter from H Rendel and a copy of my answer...Also one from Stuart Rendel received this morning and not yet answered. We have certainly had enough of his nominees, and I shall only say that I see no reason to alter the views that I have already expressed on the subject...Hoping that you continue better and that you will condescend to treat yourself as invalid for some time longer, I am affectionately yours, Armstrong."(8) To beyond the middle of this year he continued to entertain in the interests of Armstrong, Whitworth and Company, but his role in the amalgamation with Whitworth and negotiations over Barrow and Wallsend were in fact his industrial swan song.

From the perspective of posterity, the most attractive material legacies of William Armstrong were Cragside, and Jesmond Dene. Nevertheless, for contemporaries his great creation was Elswick. At almost the same time as he retired from an active involvement in company affairs, a Newcastle paper celebrated what he had built up there over fifty years. The account was written in the excessive style of the age, even seeing beauty where a later generation found horror: "We are accustomed to associate the poetry of the world with quiet hamlets, meandering streams, and pastoral landscapes, garnished with many coloured flowers. To a mere bucolic mind, nothing seems more fatal to poetic feeling than the bellowing of blast furnaces and the roar of machinery. But there is poetry of the highest order in the wonders imaged forth in all the pageantry of mills and workshops, forges and fires that give life to the western reaches of the Tyne. A man of genius has there flung his thoughts into iron and invested them with all the romance of a high historical and prophetical imagination. It is a vast incarnation of intellectual ingenuity hallowed by the presence of human beings and the sorrows and triumphs of human hearts. Grim demons have been transformed into beneficent angels. Through the din of countless hammers may be heard the songs of happy children and the rejoicings of parents to whom Lord Armstrong`s scientific wizardry has supplied the means of material well-being." Sixty years on, but looking back to the late 1890s, another commentator on the human aspects of this same scene saw all this through very much less rosy spectacles: "for many the "Factory", as they called it, was their whole life. They were born within the sound of the "Big Hammer", they attended the Factory School, and, later, if so inclined, the Works Institute, they were married in St Stephen`s Church (itself a by product of the works), their wives needed no clock but the Factory hooter, and, at the end, they were buried in Elswick cemetery."(9) By the time which these accounts described, Armstrong very rarely came to the works, but spent almost all his time in the bucolic setting of mid Northumberland.

ARMSTRONG AND THE EARLY YEARS OF A NATIONAL MILITARY-SCIENTIFIC-INDUSTRIAL COMPLEX: ASPECTS OF VICTORIAN PREPARATIONS FOR WAR.

The mid-nineteenth century application of contemporary technologies and industrial finance to the development and refinement of weapons of war was accompanied by the emergence of a prototype of the military-industrial complex that became so prominent a focus of discussion and controversy a century later. Sometimes the various connections of these early complexes were purposely forged; sometimes they emerged quite innocently because of personal contacts ripening into friendships. Whatever their particular nature, Armstrong and his new country home of Cragside played important parts in the process.

The close involvement of government as exemplified in committees of enquiry and the protracted trials of gun systems that accompanied them were inevitable in view of the high costs of the new weapons. Colonel John Henry Lefroy, who became secretary of the Royal Artillery Institute, was involved in a number of these enquiries. By 1868, by which time he had become director-general of ordnance, he was quoted in a debate involving the House of Commons Ways and Means Committee: "Most of the expense incurred by the Ordnance Select Committee is inherent in the costly nature of the material now employed. Down to 1858, we had no gun in use that cost much more than £100; we have this year paid about £7,000 for two guns. A charge of powder and shot rarely cost above 15s; now every shot from a 9-inch gun costs at least £4. 5s and in the 12-inch gun about £7. 12s. Many varieties of projectiles we are obliged to fire cost a great deal more. The ammunition alone required to test a 9-inch gun for strength and endurance, a process that must be gone through, costs over £1,300. Turning back to guns tested as late as 1860, I find it cost about £150."(1) In such circumstances, it was not a sign of conspiracy, but of practical and economical necessity, that there should be close contacts between armament makers and those who commanded the armed services, with the government whose army and navy estimates provided the funds, and with politicians who controlled or challenged government. Firms making weapons of war might try to influence government ministers and senior military officers by correspondence or interview.

Two other groups involved in the new "complexes" were civilian scientists and independent engineers. The scientists might work in military establishments, as did the chemist Frederick Abel who over many years collaborated with Andrew Noble in research into propellants, or RE Freeth, also at Woolwich. They might be military men themselves, as with Charles Wright Younghusband. The arrangements for the whole business of contact between the firms and such men were hazy compared with those operating a century later. Abel for instance was sent both presents of game shot on the Northumbrian moors and invitations, which he usually declined, to join Armstrong`s or Noble`s shooting parties there. Sometimes ideas of obligation or influence were complicated. In 1865 Freeth wrote to Noble on behalf of a brother, who was eager that his 15 year-old son should gain an apprenticeship at Armstrongs.(2) Younghusband, who in the mid 1860s served on the Ordnance Select Committee, was involved later, again with Noble, in the introduction of high muzzle velocity guns. In summer 1868, Armstrong wrote to tell Noble that Younghusband, then "much out of health", had been to Cragside. He had then gone back to Jesmond, but, as he had benefited so much from his first visit, he returned with the Armstrongs to Cragside, where he would stay for the next few days. In their talks about ordnance Younghusband had told him about Belgian successes in making papier mache caps which had completely stopped the escape of gas from breech loading guns - something the Prussians had failed to achieve.(3) Years later, after retiring from the army, Younghusband became an

Armstrong director.

As well as entertaining possible customers, Armstrong held meetings at Cragside with operators of rival systems and those whose expertise might help his own company. An example of the first was a visit from the Swedish inventor, Thorsten Nordenfelt, a man responsible for important advances in machine guns as well as the design and construction of submarines. A more directly productive visit was that of Henry S Dyer, an officer contact from the time of the Armstrong and Whitworth Committee. After leaving the army, Dyer eventually joined Joseph Whitworth`s firm. In October 1882, a month before his agreement with Whitworth expired, Dyer visited Cragside, and Armstrong and Noble decided he should be invited to join them to build and run a steel plant at Elswick.(4) By 1885 Dyer was a director as well as a manager. He became an important figure in their Italian operations and in relations with labour.

Another way in which Armstrong and his company helped build up a military-industrial complex was through developing expertise on which the nation came to rely not only for its supply of war materials, but as a source of abilities to tackle new problems or exploit new possibilities. This was brought out most clearly over the years in relation to the shaping of the navy. George Rendel had received training as a mechanical engineer in the Elswick engine works, before working for a period in his father`s civil engineering business. For years he was Armstrong`s closest collaborator in the elaboration of his ordnance system, and from the mid 1860s began to develop expertise in warship design. At first, these were small vessels, of which Staunch was the prototype, but in the 1870s, he achieved success in designing cruisers, particularly vessels distinguished for their speed. In the early 1880s, he left the firm to become an additional Civil Lord of Admiralty, but in the middle of that decade, shortly after retiring to Italy, he re-entered it as effective head of its important subsidiary operation on the Bay of Naples. William White followed a different course. Born in Devonport and trained at the Royal School of Naval Architecture, he was appointed chief constructor to the navy in 1881. Two years later, he joined Armstrongs in order to build their new Elswick naval shipyard, and then in 1885 returned to the Admiralty as director of naval construction. At Elswick, he was succeeded by another engineer from the Admiralty construction department, the 35-year-old Philip Watts, who remained in charge until he replaced White as DNC in 1901. Together White and Watts, after their close association with Armstrongs, controlled Britain`s greatest ever naval construction programmes until 1912. Although Watts retained a consultancy role with the Admiralty for some years, he also returned to the Armstrong board. His term of service as DNC was immediately followed by 12 years of control by Eustace H Tennyson D`Eyncourt, who had trained in shipbuilding at Elswick during Armstrong`s last years. In this sort of intimate contact between private enterprise and government employment and the two-way moves of key personnel there lay the very essence of a military industrial complex.

As seen elsewhere, over many years Armstrong proved adept at another aspect of the increasingly complex relationship between the armaments industry and the flow of government business - pump priming. The public had to be convinced that large expenditure on weapons of war was the only sure way to avoid war. Society could have the peace it desired, even though this would mean large profits for those who designed and made the guns and warships which if used would shatter that peace. In the modern world, it has frequently been alleged that the existence of private armament firms fosters war. A slightly more refined analysis might conclude that their activities make any warfare that does occur more destructive of life and property. At least there is a good deal of evidence to support the belief that, in pursuit of business, manufacturers of war material are willing to take advantage of the opportunities which international disputes present, to try to convince those who control the destinies and purse strings of those nations directly involved, and onlookers as well, that they must arm in anticipation of the possibility that the disagreements will end in fighting. From that point, it is an easy step into what amounts to fomenting warfare, perhaps by identifying inadequacies in national defences, or by urging governments to make sure they are not found to have put the saving of money before the security of the people whose taxes provide it. Invariably, representatives of armament firms have denied such accusations. Throughout the nineteenth century, it was common for their advocates to quote the simple Latin tag-"Si vis pacem, para bellum". The worldwide scope and extraordinary destructive power of twentieth century war ended such complacency, though the nuclear stalemate of the Cold War depended on much the same principle.

Although time and again, Armstrong urged government to ensure the defences of the realm were well maintained against rising threats from less happy lands, neither in public statements nor in correspondence did he refer much to the implications of technical advance in weapons for destruction or to his own attitude to any moral issues they might involve. Perhaps the most interesting as well as most optimistic review of the situation he provided was in his presidential address to the Newcastle upon Tyne meeting of the Institute of Mechanical Engineers in 1869. In it he first provided a summary or overview of the mechanical progress achieved in the century since Watt`s development of the steam engine. He then referred to the tremendous contemporary undertaking of the Suez Canal, before turning from mechanical engineering "... as applied to purposes of production ...to it as connected with the opposite element of destruction." He also took the opportunity to justify his methods of gun construction as compared with those of Krupp and Whitworth. The most interesting theses of this paper were that modern warfare was less bloody than that of pre-industrial ages, that the nature of the weapons which modern technology had put into the hands of governments of advanced societies discouraged rather than fostered war, and, predictably, that it was essential that the processes of invention and innovation should never be shackled.

His comparison of ancient and modern conflict was a model of cool logic. "When battles were fought hand to hand, war, so far as mechanics are concerned, was an affair of muscular force, and was, in that form, the most sanguinary, because combats were the most close. When other forces were called into play, inventive appliances became necessary, and these, as they have advanced, have more and more widened the distance separating combatants, and have thus operated to prevent that greater sacrifice of life which would have otherwise resulted from the employment of more destructive weapons. It is, therefore, not to be supposed that future wars will be rendered more murderous by the intervention of the engineer. On the contrary, we may fairly anticipate that, the more the element of intelligence supersedes that of animal force in military struggle, the more will the barbarity of war be mitigated. Science naturally sides with civilisation, and tends to establish a supremacy over barbarism; and we find this tendency, as in the case of the late Abyssinian war, not only giving overwhelming superiority to the cause of civilisation, but deciding the issue with the least possible waste of life." [His example was scarcely convincing on the latter point. It all depended on one`s perspective. In April 1868, a British expeditionary force was victorious in the battle and siege of the Abyssinian town of Magdala. A few soldiers in the British force were wounded; none was killed. Abyssinian losses were 500 killed and 1,500 wounded.] The simple argument from "sanguinary" early fighting to life-economising modern war was refuted by the evidence. That he could advance it showed either a remarkable lack of imagination about what rapid, accurate fire from his own guns could really do to human bodies, or it was a grotesque deceit perpetrated on fellow members of the institution.

He went on to claim that devices for national defence, such as coastal batteries, were cheaper than offensive weapons, that "... the most legitimate use of instruments of war is for the purpose of home defence," and concluded: "The tendency therefore of mechanical invention, as applied to war, is to discourage aggression, and thus to maintain peace. We may, consequently, hope that it will hasten the arrival of a period when civilised nations will abandon the arbitrament of arms, and settle their differences by rational and peaceful means." He recognised it was of course the civil branch of mechanical engineering which above all had the honour of promoting peace, and: "It is by the facilities it gives to intercourse and exchange, and by the reciprocal benefits which flow there from, that it teaches men how much they have to gain by peace, and lose by war." But though ending as he began, by praising the arts of peace, he made clear that nothing should restrict the freedom of inventors even if their efforts were devoted to increasing the powers of destruction: "But, whatever our sentiments may be in regard to war, it would be absurd to contend that we ought to withhold from invention when the object sought to be attained is the destruction of life and property. It is our province, as Engineers, to make the forces of matter obedient to the will of man, and those who use the means we supply must be responsible for their legitimate application." In other words, they could invent, make and sell whatever weapons they could; it was for politicians to account for practical outcomes. For all his apparent reasonableness, Armstrong was providing a rationale for a complete lack of restriction on the activities of armament makers. (5)

It was all too disingenuous. No man of his keen intelligence could be ignorant of the fact that rather than moderating the horrors of warfare, the modern weapons of which he was a leading pioneer, made them worse. The whole situation was spelled out a few years later by Captain C Orde-Brown of the Royal Artillery, now working at Woolwich, in an article "Ammunition" written for the 9th edition of the Encyclopaedia Britannica. This made clear both the horrors of modern, mechanised warfare and the matter of fact way in which those associated with it, including Armstrong, could make use of broad statements to help disguise the full implications of the reality-almost, perhaps, from themselves. Rifled guns, Orde-Brown pointed out, had superseded smooth-bored cannon in the armaments of "all civilised nations". He considered the various types of shell fired by this modern artillery. "Common" shell, a projectile filled with powder, could have a devastating impact, which even his measured prose conveyed: "At the battle of Sedan in 1870 the Prussians made such havoc among the crowded French troops that the ground became covered with "heaps of flesh and rags". A similar result was produced by the fire of mortars concentrated on the Russian troops in the Redan at the termination of the siege of Sebastopol: "The slaughter in the two last named instances is ... to be attributed to the concentration of fire on masses of men rather than to the description of shell used, for the showers of bullets ejected by Shrapnel shell would have struck many more men, although the ghastly spectacle of dismembered human bodies would not have been exhibited." Orde-Browne moved on to consider this Shrapnel shell, noting "... the Boxer Shrapnel shell for the 40-pounder breech-loading Armstrong gun...is a good specimen of this class of projectile." His opinion was that: "In skilful hands it is capable of producing results far beyond any that have as yet been achieved." But, "The Armstrong segment shell fulfils the same general purpose,-that is to say, it is designed to sweep down bodies of troops." Its segments of iron were dispersed more widely than the contents of a normal Shrapnel shell, and he thought this held great possibilities: "At Dartmoor in 1869, [the same year in which Armstrong was arguing in front of the Mechanical Engineers that modern warfare was less sanguinary than former methods] the average number of hits for every segment shell fired during the series of experiments, including failures of all kinds, was 17.1. The meaning of this estimate may be appreciated by applying it to some action. For example, at Waterloo the English artillery fired 9,467 rounds. On the Dartmoor scale, this would give 161,885 casualties. This result shows that after making the most liberal deductions for the peculiar circumstances of war, appalling effects might be produced by modern artillery with segment or Shrapnel shells."(6)

Thirteen years after his speech to the Institute of Mechanical Engineers, on 10 January 1882, Armstrong referred to modern armaments in another presidential address, this time for the Institute of Civil Engineers. The defence of armaments he now offered was in some ways simpler. It was geared to stimulate British governments to a lively concern to protect the wealth that the nation-or at least some sections of it-already possessed. Yet again, the contributions made by engineers to everyday life were mentioned, and provision of devices for war was recognised as a regrettable necessity. "It may be fully admitted that the general amelioration of the material conditions of the world is the noblest object of our science; and if men and nations ceased to be bellicose and rapacious, such would naturally be the direction which all engineering practice would take; but we live in a world of contention, where no individual state can ensure its independence, and carry on its industrial occupations safely, without protecting itself against the possible aggression of its neighbours. Thus, it is that the science of the engineer is invoked for the purposes of war as well as for those of peace; and it is probable that the engineering element will in future enter more and more largely into the operations of war, until the issue will be chiefly dependent upon the superiority of mechanical resource displayed by one or other of the contending parties." After stating this general case for the trade in which he was now so largely engaged, he was unwilling to let the opportunity slip to press for the re-arming of the Royal Navy. For, as he told his audience, despite the nation`s pacific inclinations, there was every reason for concern and for appropriate action: "There is no country in the world less disposed to be aggressive than our own, but there is none so likely to invite the greed of an assailant, or so vulnerable in relation to its commerce ... England (sic), being the richest of nations, offers the highest premium for successful attack."(7)

Through most of Armstrong`s lifetime it seemed possible to claim that the intelligent contemplation of the possibility of bringing about mutual destruction by the use of modern weapons might help preserve peace between the "civilized" nations. The use of artillery or naval guns, or later of the new "machine" guns in "colonial" wars, or in necessary disciplinary expeditions against "barbaric" nations, was another matter, but there was little concern to focus on the morality of this aspect of things. Yet, over the half-century following the Crimean War, there were a number of conflicts, which in retrospect, can be seen to have provided pointers to the way things were going. The awful effectiveness of efficiently organized, mass movement of men and materials over the railway networks of the major powers, and the unending "progress" in mechanising the processes of destruction and slaughter, were vividly displayed in major land campaigns in the early stages of his career in armaments. Notable examples were the American Civil War, and the three conflicts in six years by means of which Prussia forged the political basis of the German Empire. Adopting a purely commercial perspective, Armstrongs opted to supply both sides in the first of these wars. Despite some effort in that direction, it played no part as supplier to the combatants as Prussia triumphed in turn over Denmark, Austria and France. But, in the aftermath, it attempted to gain work repairing the armouries of some of the participants.

Armstrongs also supplied the armies of other nations, but these were mostly small, and often far away, as in Egypt or in aspiring, quarrelsome and usually unstable South American republics. Above all, it was distinguished for its contributions to sea power. Here too there were some demonstrations of the destructiveness of modern weapons, as in the Adriatic fighting between the new Italy and Austria, which culminated in the battle of Lissa, or between the Peruvian and Chilean navies in the War of the Pacific. Generally, naval battles were not as sanguinary as major land battles. In this period, the fleets of the two leading naval powers of the world, Britain and France, were engaged in no major actions. However, as with armies, technical advances changed the potential effects of fighting at sea. Only in the last few years of Armstrong`s life was an inkling gained of the full horrors caused by this progress. Elswick equipment was of major importance, and both the company and Armstrong himself revealed their attitude to the monster they had created. This demonstration was provided by modern warships in the first clash of newly emerging major powers in the Far East.

In spring 1894, China and Japan each sent troops to a disturbed Korea. By early July, there were over 10,000 Japanese in Seoul. At this time, the Chinese decided to reinforce their forces at Asan 40 miles to the south. Among the transports employed was a British steamer, the Kowshing, which set out from Taku carrying about 1,200 men. As it approached the Korean coast on 25 July, it was accosted by the Japanese warship, Naniwa, a cruiser built nine years before at Low Walker. Naniwa was commanded by Captain Togo, who in the 1870s had trained and served in the Royal Navy. He called on Kowshing to surrender and to follow his own vessel, but the Chinese soldiers refused to let the British officer in charge of their ship comply. He proposed instead that he should take the troops back to China. This time the Japanese refused, and after a warning, the Naniwa-whose main armaments had been made by Krupp and not at Elswick-opened fire. A western account summarised what followed: "A scene of indescribable confusion followed. The vessel sank with her living freight, a few escaped by swimming to a neighbouring island, three of the British officers were picked up by Japanese boats, and all the rest perished." (8) In less than half an hour more than 1,000 Chinese soldiers were drowned. In a world of telegraphic communication, the sinking of this merchant ship in peacetime was reported in the western press. Not for another seven days was war formally declared. Recalling Emmerson`s painting of him, one can imagine the 83 year-old Armstrong, slippered and sitting comfortably in his chair in the Dining Room inglenook at Cragside, learning about the episode as he read The Times. Above him was the comforting inscription "East or West, Hame`s Best". Did he recall the reassuring remarks he had made so many years before to the Civil Engineers or the Mechanical Engineers about the effect of armaments in preventing war? Unfortunately, we have no means of knowing. The next few months brought more conclusive evidence of the effectiveness of Elswick-built-ships, the destructive power of their guns, and some inkling of his attitude to the realities rather than theories about warfare.

On 17 September 1894 there took place what was probably the most significant naval engagement since Trafalgar. Off the Yalu River, near the boundary between China and Korea, 12 Japanese warships engaged the Pei-yang squadron of the Chinese fleet, which consisted of 16 warships, of which six played little or no part in the battle. Four of the actively involved Chinese vessels and three ships of the Japanese fleet had been built at Elswick. Both sides had Armstrong and Krupp guns. The Chinese vessels were generally older than those of the Japanese squadron, but more important to the outcome, they were handled less well. Four Chinese ships were sunk, three of them being the Armstrong-built cruisers, Chih-Yuen, Chao-Yung and Yang-Wei. Japanese casualties were 115 killed and 103 wounded. 600 Chinese sailors died in the vessels that were sunk, and in their surviving warships 300 to 400 men were either killed or wounded.

Half a world away, there was a welcome upturn in business. Two months after the battle of the Yalu, the board minutes of Armstrong, Mitchell and Company contained the sentence: "Sir Andrew Noble reported that owing to the War in the East, and a generally unsettled outlook, we are being severely taxed for the provision of all sorts of guns." On 13 September employment in the warship yard at Elswick was 1,046; six months later 1,592 and a year after the Yalu it reached 2,650.(9) Naturally Armstrong could no longer argue, as he had done in his Mechanical Engineers address, more than a quarter century earlier, that modern armaments of the kind his company made helped preserve the peace. Instead, taking up the generalisations of his 1882 Civil Engineers speech, he used events in the Far East to justify more expenditure on improved weapons nearer home. Soon after the Yalu, he spoke with characteristic caution and clarity about its implications, to the Armstrong, Mitchell annual general meeting: "The great sea fight which has taken place in the East will probably have an important influence upon future naval programmes ... The views that I have expressed at former meetings upon this and other subjects of a similar nature I leave to be strengthened or weakened by the light of experience, when the facts of this remarkable engagement become accurately known." The Treaty of Shimonoseki, which ended the Sino-Japanese war was signed on 17th April 1895, and before his next AGM Armstrong could be more positive. As preparations for this meeting went ahead, he wrote on 1 September 1895 to Noble: "As to the balance sheet, the only remark I have to make is this-people will naturally look upon the past year as exceptional owing to the Chinese and Japanese war and will therefore naturally expect an exceptional dividend." In October, he told shareholders that the war material they had supplied had proved "thoroughly efficient." "They have received very flattering recognition of services rendered, together with important orders for further supplies unvaried in pattern."(10) Naturally, he did not add that, though these orders would contribute to a strong upward movement in their profits, they would do little or nothing to pacify the Far East. In fact, they would increase the stakes in any future contest there.

Just before the outbreak of its war with China, Japan ordered the battleship Yashima from Elswick. It was laid down in December 1894, in the middle of the fighting, and was launched 14 months later. The Japanese "Ten Year Naval Expansion Programme", announced in 1896, was largely financed by the indemnity of £30 millions imposed on China under the terms of the Treaty of Shimonoseki. One of the battleships of this new programme was the Hatsuse, laid down at Elswick in January 1898. But for a major armament firm such as Armstrong, Mitchell, it was desirable that China too should be kept in play. On Sunday 13 June 1897, writing to Armstrong from Jesmond Dene House, Andrew Noble indicated how complicated such a balancing act could be: "I was kept in London for an extra day by the Chinese Ambassador. I had an interview with him yesterday. He expressed great pleasure at the prospect of seeing you. I told him you would be away till after the Jubilee. When he said my visit will be after the Jubilee. I suppose Li Hung has told him of his visit to Cragside. I have to see him again. Are you going to London, and for how long?" He added a P.S. "I was chiefly in London arranging contracts with the Japanese Government."(11) His reference to the visit from Li Hung must have revived memories of an occasion almost a year before. It had exposed the scandal of the readiness of western armament firms to supply both sides in cases of implacable antagonisms.

Li Hung Chang was China`s leading representative in the negotiations which resulted in the Treaty of Shimonoseki. In 1896, this distinguished 73-year-old statesman acted as ambassador extraordinary for the Chinese Emperor, visiting leading European countries and the United States in order to obtain help from western industry in restoring some of the power his country had lost because of its war with Japan. In the course of his travels in Europe, he stayed with both Friedrich Krupp and William Armstrong. On Thursday 20 August 1896, after visiting Cragside, he journeyed by train to Newcastle and from there to Elswick. He was shown around the Ordnance Works, and afterwards passed along the quay at which a battleship was being completed. He asked for details of its tonnage, speed, armour, armament and cost, and answers to these questions were provided by Andrew Noble. However no one seems to have told him explicitly that the warship was Japan`s Yashima. At the beginning of his day in Newcastle, and in response to a civic welcome, Li`s spokesman had made generous reference to his host: "Although this is the first time the Viceroy has met with Lord Armstrong, the friendship formed between them dates from a long time-since the exchange of his portrait with that of Lord Armstrong, whose portrait he has always kept hanging in the parlour, so that the physiognomy of Lord Armstrong is always familiar to him. He is a great advocate of peace between China and the rest of the world, and he finds that the ultimate object of Lord Armstrong, in manufacturing quick-firing guns and immense tonnage of men-of-war, is also to guarantee peace. So that there could not be better sympathy between Lord Armstrong and himself. " (12) Lo Feng Luh, the viceroy`s spokesman, was widely credited with an excellent grasp of English; in his remarks on this occasion at least, it is perhaps kinder to assume that he suffered a considerable degree of incomprehension of reality.

CRAGSIDE AND THE WIDER LIFE OF THE 1890S

By autumn 1890, Armstrong was a generally healthy, mentally alert and busy eighty-year-old. The fact that Margaret was six years older now became more significant than in their younger days. Until this time, she too had remained active. Although childless, she was keenly interested in child welfare and indeed, in the public sphere this was known as her leading concern. In 1887, she laid the foundation stone for the new Fleming Memorial Hospital for Sick Children in Newcastle. Two years later, she acquired the old hospital in Hanover Square, Newcastle, which she restored as a place of call for medical and surgical treatment of sick children. In June 1888 she laid the foundation stone of the church to be built for the recently formed new parish of St Aidan`s in South Benwell. In spring 1889 after writing to George Rendel, Armstrong added a brief but revealing PS: "Lady Armstrong is at Jesmond and in her usual health."

In July 1892, he went on a tour of Ireland; as seems to have consistently been the case throughout their married life, Margaret stayed at home. On 14 July, he wrote from Glengariff on Bantry Bay. The weather was very hot, but even so, he had been out on the water in a rowing boat for two hours. His letter was a newsy one, but showed clearly that they still arranged their own very separate lives: "My Dear Margaret, I don`t know for certain where you are but shall address this to Cragside, from whence it will be forwarded to you if not there." Shortly after he got home, Margaret was ill, but he still seemed hopeful, in mid August reporting from Cragside to Noble: "Dr Jebb came here yesterday and expressed himself much satisfied with Lady Armstrong`s progress. She is now very anxious to get back to Jesmond and I think she will make the attempt in a week or ten days. It is very kind of you to propose to come to see her, but she does not like to see her friends in her present invalid condition and she has seen no gentleman as yet." Even now, he ended: "Her general health holds up wonderfully."(1)

After being in "failing health" for most of the next year, Margaret died in their Jesmond Dene home on Saturday 2 September 1893. As well as her husband, their chosen heirs William and Winnefreda Watson-Armstrong were with her. Two days later, Margaret Armstrong`s life and virtues were recorded by the Newcastle daily press. The words of one notice were generous, but not effusive: "In all the honours that have fallen upon Lord Armstrong, his wife ever took a position of kindly considerateness and graceful dignity; and in the many social and philanthropic undertakings with which he has been conspicuously identified, she proved a true help-meet to him." She had a warm love for young people, and "...the story of a suffering child never came to her ears in vain."(2)

Armstrong retained his clear, sharp mind to the end of his life, and his health and vigour into the late `90s. He now received more recognition for his achievements and tackled new tasks. In spring 1891, he was awarded the Bessemer Gold Medal by the Iron and Steel Institute. In an exchange of letters about this honour with the ISI president, Sir James Kitson, he expressed some reservations about the award, though he nowhere recalled his early disagreements with Henry Bessemer. From 1894, he devoted time and much money to the restoration of much of the "once royal pile" of Bamburgh Castle, then largely in ruins. The buildings he erected were regarded by some experts as detrimental, but unquestionably, they produced an unforgettable image of the splendour of the Northumbrian coast. (3) He kept a full diary of local and county commitments.

Yet, though extremely intelligent, and now with ample leisure, he never seems to have taken a wide interest in matters far removed from his everyday preoccupations. He was not in any sense an intellectual, although at Cragside he had provided himself with a perfect setting for such a way of life if he had chosen it. An appreciative modern writer has suggested, "The library, next door to the dining room is one of the most sympathetic Victorian rooms in England ... the windows look west down to the ravine [of the Debdon Burn], the bridge and the enormous stillness of the conifers; the evening sun streams into the room and lights up the warm brown of the oak panelling and woodwork, and the soft brown of the capacious leather chairs and sofas ... " By the mid 1880s we know that the breast high book shelves round the library walls already contained "... volume after volume of the highest class literature". (4) Yet neither Armstrong`s correspondence nor the recollections of his friends provide any evidence that he ever spent long, appreciative and thought-provoking hours reading or browsing in that most congenial of settings.

On the other hand, he had always made a conspicuous virtue of application and perseverance in practical matters, and he now had a long lifetime of experience and achievement to justify those claims. In a letter to a journalist at the very end of his life, he wrote, "I attribute my success to always keeping a definite aim before me and devoting my whole energies towards its attainment." He supported this statement by quoting the scriptures: "Whatsoever thy hand findeth to do, do it with all thy might"-apparently not recognising that a good deal depended on what that was. He rather lamely added, "And there is little doubt that if more people followed this advice more people would be successful."(5)

In the early 1890s, he again took up research in lines of experimental science that were independent of his business interests. He devoted to this work both the greater resources he could now command, and his apparently undiminished powers of concentration and perseverance. John Worsnop, a local man who assisted him in these experiments, recorded that during the winters of 1894, 1895 and 1896 their usual working day was from 9 am to 7.30 pm. If there were no guests at Cragside, Armstrong "frequently" allowed no more than 10 minutes for dinner and then worked on until 9.30 pm. He showed "patience, perseverance and dogged determination...He never seemed to tire, and often regretted his inability to accomplish more work." Worsnop provided one illustration of his extraordinary powers of concentration, which enabled him to be completely oblivious to what happened around him: "I remember him coming into the laboratory one morning at nine o`clock, and after passing the compliments of the day, he sat on a chair which stood close to a large gas-stove with his legs crossed, and, one hand in his pocket and his chin resting on the other, he commenced to work out an abstruse problem. My colleague and I saw that he did not wish to be disturbed, and we moved into the adjoining room: but in case our services should be required, we returned to the laboratory every ten or fifteen minutes. On several occasions, we purposely made a noise, but he apparently neither saw nor heard us, and was quite unaware of our presence. At last he became cognisant of his surroundings, and, looking at his watch, he said "it is now one o`clock, come back at quarter past two and I`ll have something for you to do." During the whole of the time, so far as we observed, he never once changed his position, and though he was as motionless as a statue, I question very much whether any man in the county of Northumberland worked so hard that morning as he."(6)

By 1897, the electrical researches were coming to fruition. He was clearly excited, when early in May he wrote to Noble-who had long before used the same type of instrument in his own "chronoscope", a device to measure the velocity of projectiles in a gun. Armstrong claimed he had brought his "Ruhmkorff machine" (an induction coil) "to great perfection", and had "got some really extraordinary results which I can`t help thinking will excite great interest when known." He had been in correspondence about this work with Lord Kelvin. The results of his electrical researches were published that year by Smith, Elder and Company in what a contemporary account called "a beautifully got-up work" entitled Electrical Movement in Air and Water. Worsnop was responsible for the fine photographs of various types of electrical discharge. On Sunday 13 June Andrew Noble, having just returned home from London, wrote with his thanks for a copy of "... your magnificent monograph".(7) Two years later, along with Henry Stroud, Professor of Physics and Civil Engineering in Durham College of Science, in Barras Bridge, Newcastle, Armstrong published a supplement to the 1897 book.

Unfortunately, whereas into the second half of the nineties, Armstrong was young enough in body and mind to enjoy everyday life, recreations and research, the sciences had moved on so much that he could not now make the same impact as he had done almost half a century before. Then, his electrical experiments had culminated in his election to a Fellowship of the Royal Society, with the additional honour of knowing that Faraday had been one of his sponsors. Now, as peer assessment quickly showed, instead of pioneering, Armstrong`s experiments, and the conclusions he drew from them, represented an almost obsolescent approach to the subject. The 1897 book was provided with a sub title: "with Theoretical Inferences". This inclusion proved to have been a mistake, for any attempt by Armstrong to develop theory about electrical discharges was completely upstaged by the publication within a year of "The Discharge of Electricity through Gases" by the Cavendish Professor of Experimental Physics, JJ Thomson. Thomson`s work, as McKenzie has pointed out, raised discussion of the nature of electricity to a new plane. In fact, among other implications, it would eventually lead on to the atomic physics of the next century. When they published their respective works on electrical discharges, Armstrong was 87, a gifted amateur: Thomson was a 42-year-old professional, and a product of exemplary scientific training. A decade later, in long articles in the Encyclopaedia Britannica on "Electricity" by JA Fleming, and "Electric Conduction" by JJ Thomson himself, the researches of Lord Armstrong were not even mentioned. (8)

Year after year, Armstrong seemed to retain his physical as well as his mental vigour. His health must be attributed in part to a sound constitution-notwithstanding the illnesses of childhood and youth. Through the last forty years, it had been well supported by wealth and a sensible life style. In the mid-1880s, Alfred Cochrane, had been impressed by what he saw of their chairman: "His life is as simple as nature, and now at the age of 74 he retains the freshness and powers of youth." That may have been true, but the comment of a modern writer is apposite: "But then Sir William didn`t have to live along Scotswood Road."(9) Healthy rural Northumberland seemed in many respects not, as it was, less than 30 miles, but a world away from the smoky, dirty setting of Benwell, Elswick or Scotswood, thousands of whose inhabitants laboured to provide the flow of profits on which life at Cragside depended. Almost a decade after Cochrane, Armstrong`s physical condition could still impress a visitor. Though there may have been exaggeration, an assessment made in his 83rd year, conveys this favourable impression: "In the resolute-looking eyes and the firm yet kindly face, there is the bright light and glow of good health, and the tall, well-proportioned figure rises from a chair with something of the elasticity of youth."(10)

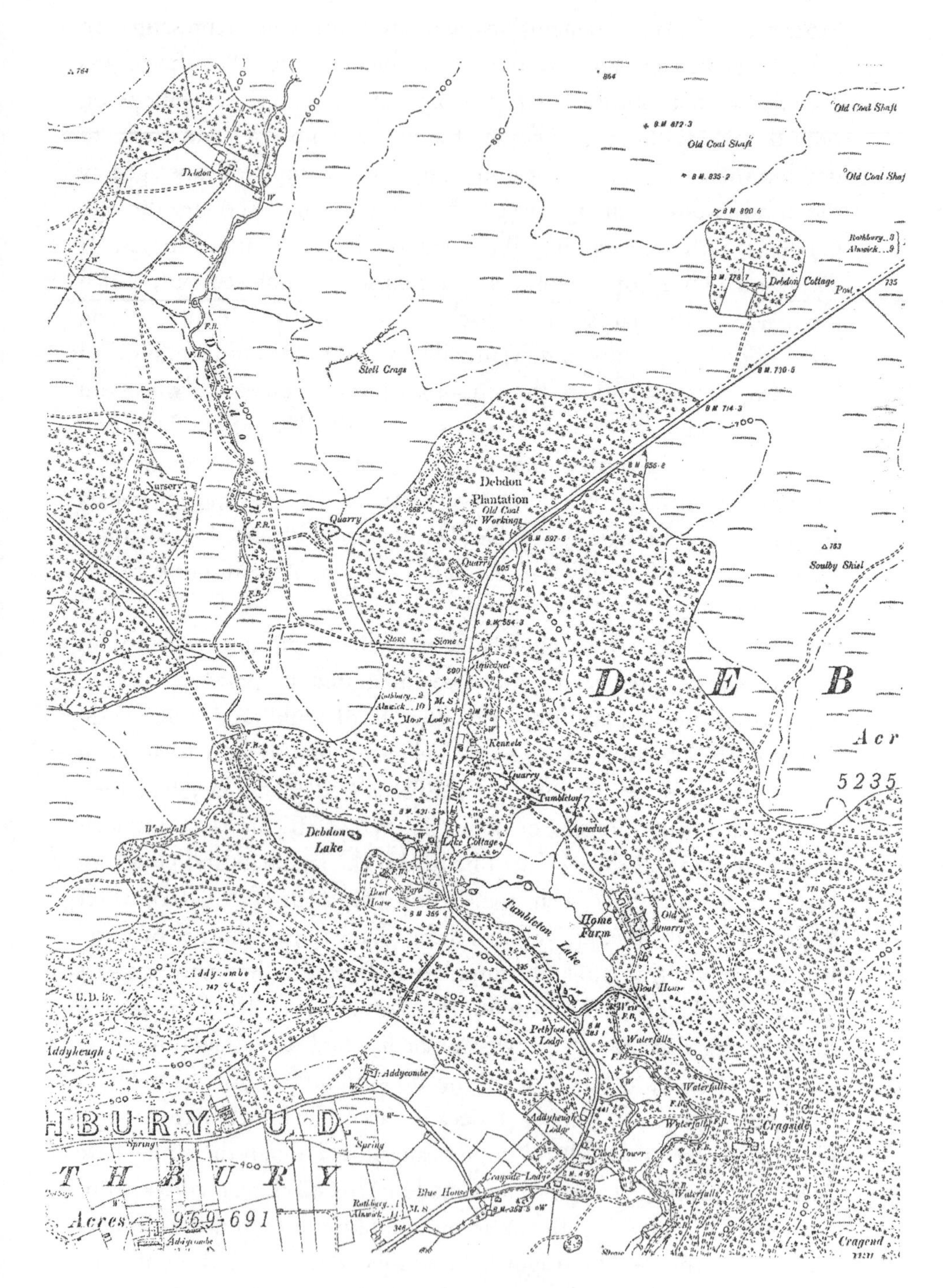

Cragside area 1896.
(Ordnance Survey Six inches to the Mile map. 1896 revision)

From the late 1880s the routines of life at Cragside were eased by the arrival of Armstrong`s great nephew, William Watson, eventually renamed Watson-Armstrong. As Armstrong told George Rendel early in 1889, after he left Downton agricultural college-"where he greatly distinguished himself"-Watson had come to Cragside in spring 1888, as Armstrong`s secretary and land manager. He had given satisfaction in both roles, and "has attached himself to me very much in the way that you did: "in the days when we were young"." He admitted he had done some match making: John Adye`s elder daughter Winny was "a sweet, intelligent and pretty girl" and he had tried to bring her and his great nephew into contact "in the hope that they might fall in love and make a match of it.....This result has taken place". They were to marry that summer and he looked forward to them taking up permanent residence at Cragside, giving it a cheerfulness "it can hardly be said at present to possess except when young people are there."

After Margaret Armstrong died, the Watson-Armstrongs looked after him, apparently very lovingly. One example of the comprehensiveness of their care was provided in late November 1895, in a letter from Winnefreda Watson Armstrong to Andrew Noble concerning business entertainment at Cragside. Before that event, she and Watson-Armstrong would be visiting London for a few days: "Lord Armstrong is going to see "Trilby" with us on Friday and is quite looking forward to it. I am so glad to think that he has such a capacity for enjoyment at his age, it seems to keep him quite young ; he really doesn`t look a bit like 85 today, much more like 65 and seems so happy."(11)

As 1897 began Armstrong, characteristically, was more concerned about the health of senior colleagues than about his own. On Monday 4 January, "most cordially" reciprocating Noble`s New Year good wishes, he added words which he might have written as much as 30 years earlier. It was his earnest hope "....that you will have better health in the new year we are entering, but this I am convinced will not be realised unless you moderate your labours and your incessant flittings from place to place." A few weeks later another younger director was his focus of concern: "Your telegram this morning as to Cruddas gives me great concern. I fear the worst."(12) In fact, WD Cruddas, son of his early business partner, remained a director for another 14 years.

Concern for old friends extended beyond the business. In spring 1897, both George and Stuart Rendel, each writing from a refuge in a kindlier climate-the former in Capri, the latter from his Riviera chateau-thanked him for visiting their sister Fanny who was unwell. She had reported warmly to Stuart after his visit, and now it was Stuart, not far short of a quarter of a century younger than Armstrong, who felt the need to apologise for the quality of his writing, affected as it was by neuritis. (13)

Through into summer 1897, Cragside life continued its normal course. On 11 May Armstrong welcomed Noble back home in improved health, and was eager to tell him what he had been doing: "I have been very busy lately with electricity ... " But a few weeks later there came a sharp break in the routine. On Thursday 12 August 1897, the King of Siam stayed with Armstrong at Bamburgh Castle, before journeying back to London next day. It was during the King`s brief trip to the North, and apparently as a result of visiting Elswick works in hot weather, that Armstrong suffered a sudden collapse in health. One account suggests it was a case of sunstroke. Whatever the cause, the effects were crippling and proved permanent. After this, for more than three years, though his mind remained clear, his body, until now so miraculously full of energy, would be that of a sick, old man.

Even now, some things at least seemed for a time to follow their accustomed course. In mid September, writing to Gladstone, Stuart Rendel mentioned Armstrong`s illness, but during the shooting season gifts of game were as usual sent out from the estate. There were some formal responses. James Forrest, secretary of the Institute of Civil Engineers, wrote that the present was "... fully appreciated as evidence of continued friendly feeling." Although his card of acknowledgement was addressed to "My Dear Sir William", Vernon Harcourt was sufficiently aware of his benefactor`s current state to add: "I was glad to get a good account of you from your niece the other day."(14) Other correspondents realised that Watson-Armstrong now exercised day-to-day control of Cragside. CP Chan had been invited to visit the house but on 27 December wrote to tell Watson-Armstrong that other engagements ruled this out: "I am deeply grieved that I am a unable to avail myself of your kind hospitality but hope to have the pleasure of seeing your (!) beautiful residence before returning to China."(15) As the months passed, it became clearer that Armstrong would not recover his physical health. Outspoken as ever, Hamilton Rendel, writing to his brother in March, alluded to the changes this might cause. Younghusband "ought to be pensioned off." Noble had mentioned that Lord Armstrong had already been saying that he ought to resign the chairmanship "... but I doubt him doing so yet a while at any rate."(16) By July, Armstrong himself registered how far he had slipped, though there were still signs of his old resilience. In a letter to Noble-written by an amanuensis and only signed "Armstrong" in his own hand-he referred to a conversation they had the previous evening: "I was very sorry to cut short our interview last night, but I am much more available for conversations in the mornings than in the evenings. And I hope that the next time that you come, which I trust will be soon, you will be able to give me a morning sitting as the artists say, which will give room for talk on family matters as well as on business affairs. Last night I began to feel a little fagged and had medical reasons for terminating our interesting interview. Yours affectionately, Armstrong."(17)

Even now, he retained contact with company affairs. Generally Noble seems to have kept him well informed, even about relatively minor matters, as for instance in June 1899 when he reported a fire at Elswick which "has done much mischief."(18) More important, as late as spring 1900 his opinion was taken into account in company decision taking about their works at Pozzuoli, which since its completion in 1892 had not been a great success. The Italian government was trying to persuade them to join a consortium of armament firms. A vital meeting at Elswick in February decided to make terms for their involvement so unacceptable to the Italians that they would be sure to decide that they could not be included in the scheme. Armstrong was reported as "most enthusiastic" for this approach. On 16 April, Noble sent him a telegram he had just received from the company secretary, John Meade Falkner, who was in Rome, and a copy of a letter he himself had written to Admiral Albini, now their senior Italian director. Referring to the way things seemed to be going, he added, "This is just what you wished."(19) By November, the Italian government had rejected their proposed purchase of the Naples Arsenal.

Armstrong c.1900 (Courtesy The National Trust)

Notwithstanding his physical disabilities, Armstrong commented on a number of occasions on speeches or addresses by Andrew Noble, in each instance conveying his opinions in letters dictated to others. After one speech had been read to him in September 1898, he responded warmly: "I think it could not have been better and I feel sure you would have a very sympathetic audience." Ten months later, "Winny" read him another paper by Noble "...which I think is admirably adapted for the purpose intended and very clearly expressed, but my defective sight has not enabled me to scrutinize the details of the illustrations. This however is of little importance, as I could not under any conditions of sight have been able to suggest alterations in what you and your assistants have so thoroughly considered. I feel sure the paper will be highly appreciated and we may hope that it may operate in some degree as an advertisement leading to business. Wishing you well through your labours without aggravations of gout." Shortly afterwards Noble gave the inaugural lecture at the autumn session of the Central Technical College of the City and Guilds London Institute. Notwithstanding his own position in scientific research and business, he made clear he did not favour replacing study of the classics with that of modern languages. On this occasion, Armstrong was sufficiently aroused as to assert his own slightly different view. Winny again wrote his response, but proved unable to resist the opportunity to insert her own reactions: "I have read your inaugural address on Technical Education and I think it full of common sense ("so do I" W W-A). It is closely in accord with my own views and in fact I may say that the only difference between us is that the training of the mind either in school or in so-called secondary education could be quite as well effected by the teaching of living instead of dead languages, while the utility of the acquisition of the former would be immeasurably greater than in the case of the latter. I would make an exception in favour of Latin, but only to a very limited extent. Translations exist by most competent authors of every classical work that is worth reading."(20)

Now and then, despite Noble`s efforts, Armstrong clearly felt himself cut off from events. There was a plaintive note in a letter he dictated in April 1899 at a time when Winny was away: "Your note on your return from Rome gave me much pleasure, the more so as you write so seldom that it is a treat to hear from you." He went directly on to the theme he had returned to so often before: "But there is one matter of great interest to me which you have not mentioned and in fact you never do, and that is the state of your health?" Any holiday Noble took "... always seems to slide off in business. Whether you went in this case with a set purpose of pleasure or business I do not yet know." "I hope it will not be too long before we see you here, but I will not call you to come before Winny has returned." His letter ended "Always yours affectionately" and was signed in his own hand "Armstrong". He also wrote a PS. in the same very shaky hand "You must be growing into a mighty man of copper"-a reference to Noble`s membership of the board of the Mountain Copper Company which had operations in Shasta County, California. (21) A year later he was clearly exasperated that he had to learn from the newspapers "... that we`ve taken out a patent for a new shrapnel. Also that experiments have been made at Silloth in the presence of experts with smooth bore guns fired with nitro-glycerine, which to me seems extremely paradoxical." He went on, plaintively: "Is there no one at Elswick that can spare a few minutes of his time to write to me a short note that would give me some slight intelligible idea what all this is about, that is to say as to the patents and the Silloth experiments. Very affectionately yours, Armstrong."(22)

As months lengthened out into years, his mind remained clear, but his physical state was fragile. Now, he even had to be sheltered from some less happy items of news. When, at the beginning of 1899 his almost exact contemporary, the sixth Duke of Northumberland, died, his grandson, Earl Percy, wrote to ask Watson-Armstrong to inform Armstrong. He had not wanted to trouble him by writing to him directly "... in his present state of health."(23) That summer he took great interest in the preparations for the summer meeting in Newcastle of the Institute of Naval Architects, and even entertained them at Cragside, though there is no evidence that he felt able to make an appearance. (24) Now and again there were echoes from the past, sometimes seeming out of step with the mundane narrowness of his present daily routine. At the end of 1899, he received a letter from a friend of almost 40 years. This proved that not all of his correspondents were fully aware of the state of things. Admiral Count Albini, the first agent of their Italian business, wrote almost jauntily from Rome: "Dear Lord Armstrong, Desirous to express to you my best and most sincere wishes for a Merry Christmas and a happy new year, I have taken the liberty to send you a small box of Italian candy sweets in the hope that you will accept it as a demonstration of the constant feelings and sincere remembrances of a distant old friend."(25) A few weeks later, there was an even more vivid reminder of his past powers and responsibilities-as well as a sign of a woeful lack of awareness of his present situation. It came in an apparently standardised letter from the Prime Minister, summoning him to attend the House of Lords: "My Lord, Her Majesty`s Proclamation has fixed the thirtieth of the present month for the opening of Parliament. I hope it will be consistent with your Lordship`s arrangements to attend in your place upon that day, as subjects of grave importance are likely to be brought before the House at the beginning of the session. I have the honour to be your Lordship`s obedient servant, Salisbury."(26) Rather than being active with new business, the year just beginning would bring bereavement, and further limitation and decline.

In summer 1900, and apparently unexpected, Armstrong received a letter from Henrietta Huxley, widowed five years before. It revived memories of earlier friendships and times of vigour: "All the shrubs and trees about this house [North House, Eton Avenue, London NW] which Hal and I saw planted have grown up into great beauty. I thought how yours at Cragside must have grown and I longed to see the dear old place again, but that I know can never be." She ended: "Goodbye my dear old friend and believe me ever very affectionately Henrietta Huxley."(27) During the same summer Armstrong and the Watson- Armstrongs entertained retired General Sir John Adye, Winnefreda`s father. Adye was an accomplished artist, who on earlier occasions had painted some fine watercolours of the estate, which are still on display in the house. Nine years Armstrong`s junior, he died on 26 August during his visit.

In October 1900, Armstrong was taken over to Bamburgh to see the progress of his work of reconstruction. On his return, he went down with a "chill". A few days later, he passed his ninetieth birthday, an occasion for an effusion from a local poet who wrote in the spirit and very much the vein-and quality-of the Scot, William McGonagall. (28)

Armstrong failed to throw off the effects of this illness. In mid December, in the presence of his valet, Adam Crozier, he signed a Power of Attorney to Watson-Armstrong; it was lodged with the Bank of England on 21 December. By then his condition had worsened, and before Christmas, reports from Rothbury raised grave fears about his state. He was much weaker on the morning of Boxing Day and by evening was sinking rapidly. He died at 1.10 on the morning of Thursday 27 December. The telegraph office in Rothbury had been kept open especially so that news of his passing could at once be wired all over. At 7.30 am, the bell of Rothbury parish church tolled and the town was plunged into mourning. The day`s newspapers spread the news of his death and contained the first assessments of his life`s work. On Sunday 30th December 1900, it was the turn of the preachers - and soon of another local poet. (29)

Monday 31st December 1900, the last day of the extraordinary century to which he had made such substantial contributions both for peace and for war, was chosen for William George Armstrong`s funeral. As under the regular schedule, ordinary trains reached Rothbury only at 10.35 am and 5.35 pm-and for the former it was necessary to leave Newcastle as early as 8.20-three special trains were provided. (30) From Cragside the coffin, covered by a purple cloth, was carried on a farm trolley drawn by two farm horses. The first carriage of the funeral cortege contained Watson-Armstrong and his wife, Andrew Noble and the company secretary, John Meade Falkner. H. Westmacott represented Percy Westmacott and with John Noble occupied the second carriage. The new Duke of Northumberland rode in the third. Stuart Rendel, Josiah Vavasseur, Alfred Cochrane, GJ Carter, HS Carrington and AG Hadcock represented the Elswick and Openshaw works. The manager and foremen of the Elswick Engine Works sent a wreath. The presence of J Thompson, who had worked in the Elswick Works offices when they were in Hood Street in 1847 was an eloquent witness of the place the business which Armstrong had created had for so long played in the life of Tyneside. Charles William Mitchell, the only surviving son of Armstrong`s former shipbuilding partner, and Henry Swan, head of Walker yard, were there. Noteworthy for their absence from the funeral procession, as well as from the list of those who sent wreaths, were George and Hamilton

Rendel.

At the service in Rothbury Parish Church, the 90th Psalm was followed by the hymn "Now the labourer`s task is o`er", which was said to be "very feelingly and meaningly" sung. (31) Afterwards, as he had requested, the body of William George Armstrong was buried in what contemporaries described as an "unostentatious manner" by the side of Margaret Armstrong in a grave that lay a few feet from the bank of the River Coquet.

AFTERMATH, ASSESSMENT AND LEGACIES

On Sunday 30 December 1900, the curate in charge of Rothbury parish church, Rev. William George Pringle, preached from the text "Know ye not that there is a prince and a great man fallen this day in Israel."(2 Samuel 3 v38) In his sermon he claimed that "... if the qualities of intellect, refinement, and Christian kindliness are the true index of a great and princely nature, then the words of his text were applicable to Lord Armstrong." He spoke of his personal character and influence, especially among those around him, who knew him as "a simple hearted Christian gentleman." "Few men in the century had led a more truly Christian life, based he believed on a faith broadly and deeply founded, than the venerable man whose loss they mourned today, but for whose life and example and intellectual greatness they returned humble and heartfelt thanks to Almighty God."(1) He seems to have made no reference to the business in which Armstrong`s wealth had been made.

When eventually a stone was erected over the grave, it was inscribed in a simple but thought-provoking manner. "His scientific attainments gained him a world-wide celebrity and his great philanthropy the gratitude of the poor." The front of the monument bore the words of what was said to be his favourite precept, the words he had not so long before quoted as holding the key to his success: "Whatever thy hand findeth to do, do it with all thy might."(Ecclesiastes 9 v 10) In 1902, a cross was raised in his memory in the centre of Rothbury at a simple ceremony led by the Newcastle-born ironmaster, Lowthian Bell.

On Tyneside there was a greater impact, for, as the Mayor of Newcastle pointed out to the Council when it met on 9 January, "the hive of industry" which Armstrong had initiated now provided "daily bread and all the worldly comforts they enjoy" for something like one third of the population of the city. By his "scientific attainments, creative genius and industrial enterprise" he had helped make Newcastle upon Tyne "one of the foremost cities of the Empire, and by his high personal character, noble benefactions and practical interest in the welfare of the city he endeared himself to the entire community and will live long in their grateful memory." Even in distant retrospect, these seem reasonable claims, but in the immediate aftermath of a long and distinguished life, it was difficult to avoid hyperbole. The Mayor even had to restrain himself: "He was undoubtedly the greatest Novocastrian that has existed-at all events during the latter half of the nineteenth century." The Sheriff, seconding a motion recording the Council`s deep sense of loss, fell into the trap of hyperbole. For him, the engineering skills and scientific attainments of Armstrong were not greater than "... the beauty, the simplicity and the nobility of his life." Like others who had been at the funeral, he had come away with the feeling that the region had lost a personality "whose influence for good will be felt for generations yet to come."(2) In stark contrast with the emotion and eloquence of the Council, when the Directors of Armstrong Whitworth met on 23 January, their record of the event was simple. Queen Victoria had died on the previous day and their resolution of sorrow at her passing surpassed in length that to their former head. Their minutes read: "Lord Armstrong`s Death It was agreed that the Secretary should draw up a letter expressing the condolence of the Company with Lord Armstrong`s family." Andrew Noble was unanimously elected chairman. Individual colleagues had no doubts about Armstrong`s standing. Cochrane, then in middle management, wrote that his age gave "…to acknowledged greatness an added dignity….it would have been hardly an exaggeration to describe Lord Armstrong at the time of his death as the most illustrious of Englishmen."(3).

The death was followed by a flood of tributes, obituaries and reflections on Armstrong`s life and work. All recognised a great man had passed on; most were positive about the achievements that had gained him that status. Of all the appreciations, what seemed to have a ring of real authenticity came from another Northumberland landowner, the 4th Earl Grey of Howick, a man with wide experience as an African traveller and administrator, and who would soon be

Governor General of Canada. He apologised to Watson-Armstrong for his inability to be present at the funeral and expressed simple appreciation of an outstanding man: "Among my pleasant recollections are some talk with him in past years. I remember now with the feeling of gratitude I experienced at the time my delight at his conversation in which he beamed forth kindness, eagerness, tolerance for my stupidity and the power, which belongs only to few of making the obscure, and complex appear simple and intelligible to the dullest ignoramus. It has never been my lot to meet anyone in whom these delightful qualities were more conspicuously marked...I like to think of him going down with his beautiful, lucid intellect still undimmed at the close of the century to whose triumphal progress he has contributed so much."(4) The thoughts of a number of other, fuller and heavier appreciations were also shaped by the fact that the end of his life coincided with that of a century of unrivalled industrial advance, by pride in the place which economic power had given Britain in the world, and the realisation that further major shifts were underway or lay ahead.

The Engineer began its tribute with the words: "In the long list of eminent names in our profession there have been few as widely known as that of Lord Armstrong." The writer of the memoir for the Institute of Civil Engineers was more positive about his place in the Victorian age: "Nobody during that century had been more closely identified with the practical and material progress of mankind."(5) Another writer was carried away in his eloquence about Elswick: "A man of genius has there flung his thoughts into iron and invested them with all the romance of a high historical and prophetical imagination. It is a vast incarnation of intellectual ingenuity hallowed by the presence of human beings and the sorrows and triumphs of human hearts." In a long obituary and leader, the Newcastle Daily Chronicle recognised the greatness of the man, but took up and explored those intermixed themes of triumph and sorrow. Because it was published on the day of his death, it saw some things out of balance or perspective, but in many respects the Chronicle`s insight was exceptional in its quality: "It is hard to realise that the vital connection between Lord Armstrong and Newcastle can be renewed no more, that the wonderful marriage of mind and matter of which Elswick was the giant birth is dissolved at last, and the life which has meant more than any other to no mean city for the better part of a century has drawn its last breath and belongs now to the irrevocable things of yesterday. Lord Armstrong was more than a great citizen of Tyneside; he was one of the great citizens of the world. He was more than the maker of Elswick, for he was one of the makers of modern civilisation with its portentous contrast of industrialism and militarism, with its machinery of production on one hand and its engines of destruction on the other." The leader writer returned to this "portentous" contrast later in his article, tracing out dangers but concluding that even they might have a beneficial outcome: "Lord Armstrong may be best remembered in the end, by the world at large, as a strangely representative figure of the latest phase of nineteenth century civilisation.....We subject the rudest powers of nature to the service of peace, and we employ the most refined powers of the intellect to devise methods of destruction more awful than flood or earthquake. ....Lord Armstrong was equally typical of the vital and mortal activities of modern civilisation. The inventor of hydraulic machinery, the inventor of the hydro-electric machine, and life-long student of electrical phenomena... was no less a pioneer of the modern armaments which seem to threaten a decimation of mankind in the battle of Armageddon. There is something that appals the imagination in the cool application of a clear and temperate mind like Lord Armstrong`s to the science of destruction. We do not know whether all this is such a monstrous paradox as it seems. Nothing could have been more unexpected by the earlier prophets of democracy than the apparent return of militarism with a vengeance at the end of the liberal and humanitarian century ... And yet there may have been a miscalculation of methods only and not of results. The world if never so equipped for war was never so reluctant to make it. The sight of means to do ill-deeds all round keeps the ill-deeds undone. In the nature of things the militarism of the time must bring its own abatement, and Elswick in the end may prove a more effective advocate of peace than Exeter Hall."(6) It was a pious hope, appropriate for the day on which a great man passed. It is more difficult to anticipate the future than to look back, and it is well to remember that, whereas Armstrong had been born five years after Trafalgar and five before Waterloo, when he died no one could know that Jutland and the Somme were little more than fifteen years ahead.

A few of those who celebrated his life looked at it in a wider social setting. Was it perhaps not only war or preparation for war that was evil, but also the lavishing of national wealth on the immensely costly paraphernalia of armaments, when this meant that tackling the poverty that blighted so many millions of lives was delayed? Some of those who preached end of century sermons in Newcastle on Monday 31 December 1900 chose to focus their remarks simply on the passing of a great Northumbrian. In St Ann`s Church the Rev W B East was full of praise: "He raised up a wonderful institution of industry. He built himself a lovely home, making "wilderness to bloom as the rose", and changing "a bleak Northumbrian moor into a region of varied beauty." In contrast, Canon Gough chose a less sunny, indeed a starkly realistic interpretation. Preaching to the text "The times of this ignorance", he did not specifically mention Armstrong, but he painted a picture of turn of the century British society for which such words as Rev. East`s "bloom", and "varied beauty" were shown as woefully short of the mark. Much of what Gough said might have been applied directly to Elswick. He referred to "terrible overcrowding in unhealthy localities", "conditions of life which a more enlightened age may well indeed ascribe to "times of ignorance", days rendered sunless through an atmosphere vitiated by poisonous chemicals and darkened by palls of smoke; in which half the struggle of existence is the struggle to keep clean, in not a few cases despairingly abandoned." There had been failure to solve the social problems of the time: "Take only the relation between capital and labour ... We have tried combinations, we have tried arbitration; we have suggested or tried all manner of things; and where are we? Living on the edge of a volcano, that may at any time burst forth and paralyse our commerce, hinder our industries, even if it does not someday wreck our social system."(7)

An obvious and objective, if woefully inadequate, measure of Armstrong`s achievement was his wealth, some £1.4 million, roughly equivalent in purchasing power to £104 million today. His title lapsed, but the houses and estate passed to his chosen heir, his 37-year-old nephew, William Watson-Armstrong, who in 1903 was made a Baron as the second Lord Armstrong. Watson-Armstrong was generous in commemorating his benefactor, in for instance, a generous endowment to the Royal Victoria Infirmary, Newcastle. But he proved much less able and reliable than his predecessor, was forced to give up his directorship of Armstrong-Whitworth, and, following heavy financial losses, had to sell off many of the paintings Armstrong had accumulated. During June 1910 Christies held two sales of "The Armstrong Heirlooms", the first of them of 43 items of Chinese Porcelain, the second of 102 "Important Modern Pictures and Drawings."(8) For three quarters of a century, Watson-Armstrong and his successors continued to enjoy Cragside and they retained Bamburgh for even longer. But the position of great houses was changed by the circumstances of the twentieth century. After the Great War, large workforces of poorly paid men were no longer so readily available and gradually many labour-intensive operations had to be given up. At Cragside, the huge glass structures that had enclosed the ferneries, the ingeniously equipped glasshouses, the "Italian gardens" and "Orangery" and the time-consuming practice of carpet bedding all fell into decay. For decades, they were almost forgotten.

The great industrial operation Armstrong had built was at its peak around the time of his death. With it was associated the great mass of dull streets and humble homes, which had been built over the slopes between the West Road and the Tyne, where fields had extended when he began. It had become one of the most monotonous, drab districts called into being and shaped by Victorian industrial development. A few of these crowded streets witnessed to their origins in the names they bore, those of partners, or others involved in the progress the company had achieved - Noble Street, Brunel Terrace, Sopwith Street, Lefroy Terrace. From St John`s Cemetery through Benwell and on to Scotswood ran Armstrong Road. (Strangely, Armstrong Street, and Rendel Street lay across the Tyne in the isolated settlement of Dunston). Deprived of many life chances in these blighted environments there were born, lived and died many thousands of workers and their dependents whose subsistence was drawn from one or other of the departments of Elswick operations. These depressing residential landscapes and their associated adverse social indices persisted until the great house clearances of the 1960s. They were then replaced by more convenient, comfortable if less spectacular residential development. The numerous pubs, with names eloquent of the working places of their clientele, survived a little longer, but they too are gone.

It is now over a century since Armstrong died. To almost the eve of the Great War, the great company he had created continued to be led by a now rapidly aging Andrew Noble, who was then succeeded by the highly talented, but scarcely similarly practically endowed John Meade Falkner. Less than ten years after the Armistice the largest part of WG Armstrong Whitworth and Company, those departments concerned with armaments and naval construction, was merged with Vickers of Sheffield and Barrow to produce Vickers-Armstrong. Most traces of the Armstrong connection gradually disappeared, though until the 1970s the name of the old company could still be made out in gradually fading paintwork on the buildings seen from across the river near Scotswood Bridge. In the mid 1980s the whole, huge block of the Elswick works, little altered in external appearance since the end of Armstrong`s life, was demolished. Its site was cleared for a new business park, laid out between Scotswood Road and a new "Armstrong Way." Vickers Defence Systems had already built a large tank factory at Scotswood and, recognising the importance of history-and the strength of local pride-named it the Armstrong Works. Here one could still be reminded of the expansive days of the Victorian and Edwardian arms trade as one scanned the names and nationalities recorded in the visitors` book of yet another industrial operation devoted to supplying the world with the powers of destruction.

Elsewhere Armstrong`s legacy is largely anonymous, but generally happier. In Jesmond Dene, the Banqueting Hall, built by John Dobson to entertain his visitors, was derelict well before the end of the twentieth century, but the Dene itself remains a source of great pleasure to the citizens of Newcastle to whom he presented it in 1883. Out in the county of Northumberland, the observant driver on the A68 may note in passing that in Ridsdale, not far from the old ore workings and ordnance range, even now, there is a Gun Inn, though quite rightly most of his or her attention will focus on Rothbury. The centre of that attractive little town contains the memorial to Armstrong, the parish church has the rood screen given in memory of Margaret and the graves of the Armstrong family lie in the overflow section of the churchyard. On the way out of town, along the Alnwick road, are the almshouses that Armstrong gave for the old and poor in thanks for his own mother. A mile further on, where Walter White found a desolate landscape in the late 1850s, the road runs alongside the Cragside estate, owned by the National Trust since 1977. Walking or driving through mile after mile of beautiful rhododendrons and azaleas, or sitting on the terrace by the huge and recently restored glasshouses, looking out to the Simonside Hills, one may, for a time at least, forget some of the less happy outcomes of Armstrong`s renowned perseverance. Instead, one can simply give thanks for his energy and imagination.

On the day of Lord Armstrong`s death, the Newcastle Chronicle ended on a note which turned from his long involvement with the ultimate forces of physical power among nations, back to simple, local concerns: "... even were the last ship launched from Elswick to be shattered shard on shard, Jesmond Dene would still be quick with beauty to keep the name of William Armstrong as green as every spring."(9) Unfortunately, such a happy thought could not be the last word. Along with Krupp, Armstrong had been the leading inventor and producer of the "improved" heavy weapons involved in the industrialisation of warfare in the Victorian age. For a fuller measure of his achievements, it is necessary to revisit a part of central Newcastle, which lies scarcely more than half a mile from where he was born in 1810. A little way north of the modern central shopping area, beyond where a soaring figure of "Winged Victory" celebrates the Boer War, is Barras Bridge. There, in front of the Natural History Museum, where Claremont Road runs out into the old Great North Road, a fine statue of Lord Armstrong was dedicated in July 1906. (10) Although its bronze is now often defaced by the attentions of local birds, he still looks out across the main road, roughly in the direction of another, bigger monument, a few score yards away in the little park alongside the church of St Thomas the Martyr. This second sculpture depicts not one, but many figures, a diverse group of men of much humbler situation. They commemorate a vastly larger number, for this is the memorial to the dead of Tyneside in the Great War. There is no simple, causal connection between the two memorials, but to see them together may provide food for thought.

One more thing remains to be remembered, and pondered. In an

"The Response 1914". The Memorial to the Dead of Tyneside, Newcastle upon Tyne. (Courtesy Newcastle City Libraries)

even wider sense than any considered so far, the preoccupations of Armstrong`s last 45 years can be seen to have been related-adversely-to the interests and well being of ordinary men and women. Expenditure by governments on armaments made by his company undoubtedly helped provide the livelihoods of many thousands of men and their dependents, but the opportunity cost for their employment was high. In other words, when taxes or other government funds were spent on guns, warships or other munitions of war, products whose end even in the happiest of outcomes lay in obsolescence and eventual scrapping, and sometimes in destruction, injury and death, another and inevitable result was that more socially useful investments-schools, improvements in public services etc-had to be foregone. The "common" people themselves were all too often aroused to jingoistic enthusiasm for spending on the preparations for war that denied to them these more beneficial ways of using limited national resources. In responding in this nationalistic way, they were in fact helping to protect and perpetuate the wealth of the middle and upper classes. Moreover, if-as in fact soon happened-the deterrent of an armed peace eventually failed to prevent war, not only would there be even bigger profits for those who owned the means to make weapons, but the working class millions would be enlisted to defend the same society, one in which their interests had for so long been neglected. There is of course no indication that a man as hard working, generally mild-mannered and even "kindly" as William George Armstrong ever thought in this way about his relationship with the thousands of ordinary men who worked at Elswick. Even so, any quiet consideration of the situation points to the fact that the very mechanisms of economy, society and state structures in Victorian Britain seemed almost to have been designed to produce outcomes so favourable for those in his position and lines of business, and so dangerous for others.

NOTES

Abreviations used in notes
WGA. William George Armstrong
MA Margaret Armstrong
AN Andrew Noble
GWR George Wightwick Rendel
SR Stuart Rendel
CG Colliery Guardian
MJ Mining Journal

Preface

1. A Noble in Royal Society memoir of Armstrong.1901 pp9,11

Ancestry, childhood and youth

1. St Fond 1784
2. Royal Society memoir 1901 p 1; P McKenzie pp16,17
3. Lewis 1833; Oliver 1835 pp77,78
4. Worsnop 1901
5. Ibid
6. WGA to SR 30 May 1857

Law, experiments and scientific recognition 1830 to 1846

1. WGA quoted F Dolman October 1900 p 575
2. A Cochrane 1909 p 19; A Noble quoted Dougan p 26
3. F Dolman quoted McKenzie p 19; WGA "The Application of water as a motive power for driving machinery" Mechanics Magazine 29 December 1838
4. Cochrane 1909 p 23
5. G Chrystal "Electricity" in Encyclopedia Britannica 9th ed. 1879 p 101

6. J Wigham Richardson. Memoirs 1911 p 32, quoted Dougan p 29
7. WGA to A Donkin 3 October 1843
8. W Cobbett. Rural Rides Everymans ed. Vol 2 p 286 Rural Rides GDH and M Cole ed; 1930; DF Dibden 1838. A Bibliographical, Antiquarian and Picturesque Tour of the Northern Counties of England and in Scotland. London p 402.
9. Middlebrook p 205; Rennison p 5
10. AG Greenhill and WC Unwin. "Hydromechanics"in Encyclopedia Britannica 9th edition 1881 p 522
11. Newcastle Chronicle report of Literary and Philosophical Society lecture of 13 December 1845 in Addresses by Sir William Armstrong. Newcastle City Libraries
12. L.F. Vernon-Harcourt. "River Engineering" in Encyclopaedia Britannica 9th edition 1886 vol 20 p 578;Middlebrook p 194
13. Lane p 49.
14. WGA to Times 14 March 1872 p 7
15. Hamer 1931 p 268

Early Elswick: mechanical and civil engineering 1847 to 1855

1. Cochrane 1900 p 7; Cochrane 1909 p 32
2. WG Armstrong cash book
3. Cochrane 1909 pp 47,48
4. Cochrane 1900 p 11; Cochrane 1909 pp 56,57; A Short History of Sir W G Armstrong Whitworth and Company. (c. 1910)
5. WG Armstrong cash book
6. GWR to SR 5 February 1857; WGA to MA 3 February 1857
7. WGA et al. Industrial Resources of the Tyne, Wear and Tees 1864 pp 300-305: CG 31 October 1863 pp 346,47
8. Dolman 1893 p 574; Cash book
9. Cochrane 1909 p 90
10. Cochrane 1900; Fairbairn 1948 passim

The art and science of mass destruction: the early history of the Armstrong gun

1. WGA to MA 9 April 1851

2. B Poole 1852 pp 238, 251, 255
3. E Maitland "Gunnery"in Encylopedia Britannica 9th ed. 1880 vol 11 p 305
4. AG Hadcock "Ordnance"in Encyclopedia Britannica 11th ed. 1911; H Bessemer Autobiography 1905 pp 329, 330
5. R Mallet 1862. On the artillery displayed at the London Industrial Exhibition 1862, The Practical Mechanics Journal pp 476, 489
6. Procs. Institute of Civil Engineers 1896-97 Part I pp 372-9; E Maitland op cit, present writer`s emphasis
7. McKenzie pp 52-4; "The Elswick Ordnance Company: Its Origin and Expansion into the Present Firm of Sir WG Armstrong Whitworth and Company." Newcastle 1912 p 12; record of TINA Meetings at Newcastle and in Scotland 26 to 29 July 1887
8. "Cartridge" in Encyclopedia Britannica 10th ed. 1902
9. WGA to MA 15 January 1855, 22 July 1856
10. "Sir William George Armstrong" in Chambers Encyclopedia 1868 p 421
11. H. Bessemer. Autobiography chapters 13-16 and pp 210-212. There are excellent summaries of the designs and competition between guns in this period in the obituaries of WGA in The Engineer 4 January 1901 pp 7,8 and Engineering 4 January 1901 pp 19 - 22
12. Obituary of Joseph Whitworth in Bulletin of American Iron and Steel Association
13. The Times 6 June 1859 p 10d; Engineer 6 June 1859 p 401
14. "The Armstrong Gun" in The Times 24 January 1860 p 10
15. WGA in Industrial Resources of the Tyne, Wear and Tees pp 309 - 316; AN in RS memoir; Hamer 1931 pp 269 - 71; ob. of AN in RS proceedings XCIV A 1917 -18 pp i -vii; SC on Ordnance 1861 in BPP 1862 p 226; H of Commons debate quoted Dougan p 63
16. WGA to MA 24 November 1858
17. T Sopwith . Published Diaries p 264
18. P Westmacott in obituary of AN Procs. RS 1917-18 p iii
19. Gen. Tulloch to SC on Ordnance BPP 1862 vi p 120
20. Historical Register of Remarkable Events 1859 p 352; Engineer 4 March 1859
21. Quoted Dougan p 65

22. Memorial of Law Society of Newcastle upon Tyne and Gateshead (is at Cragside);Engineer 4 March 1859
23. W.Fordyce. Local Records, Newcastle 1867; Memoir of T Sopwith p 265; Dougan pp 65,66
24. Chambers Encyclopedia 1868 vol X p 151.(the account was written in 1862); Reid. Handbook to Newcastle upon Tyne. 1863 pp 235-37

The course of a marriage

1. A Noble (1901) in Royal Society memoir p 2
2. F Rendel to Catherine Rendel n.d. but probably March 1857
3. WGA to MA n.d but in late 1850s
4. WGA to MA 7 May 1843, quoted McKenzie pp 25,26
5. WGA to MA 23 January 1852; WGA to unknown correspondent 8 Feb 1852
6. WGA to MA 12 January 1853
7. WGA to MA 23 July 1853
8. WGA to MA 7 Feb 1854
9. WGA to MA 9 Feb 1856, 24 November 1858
10. WGA to MA 23 and 24 Feb 1859
11. WGA to MA 3 September 1854 (?), 9 Feb 1856
12. WGA to MA 15 Jan 1853, 23 July 1853, 24 Jan 1854, 7 Feb 1854
13. WGA to MA 30 Aug 1857
14. G Cruddas to MA 24 Feb 1859
15. J Tyndall to MA 17 Feb 1864
16. WGA to MA 20 Jan 1857
17. WGA to MA 23 May 1855, 17 Feb 1856, 11 June 1868
18. E de Riano to WGA 7 July 1884, 2 Sept 1884, 14 Oct 1884
19. WGA to GWR 10 June 1889; WGA to AN 4 Aug 1891

An unstable relationship: Elswick and Woolwich 1859 to1863

1. Chambers Encylopedia 1868 Vol X p 151
2. SC on Military Organisation BPP 1860 vii pp 575, 576
3. WGA to AN. 31 December 1860
4. CG 23 February 1861 p 121

5. CG 24 August 1861 p 118
6. AN to SC on Ordnance 1861 in BPP 1862 vi p 226
7. The Times 24 January 1860 p 10
8. Engineer 17 August 1860 p 108
9. CG 9 April 1861 p 215
10. BPP evidence p 212; J McCarthy pp 233-237
11. Engineer 22 April 1864 p 250, 29 April 1864 p 259; The Times 18 April 1864 p 5d; J McCarthy p 254; F Brinkley "Foreign Intercourse" in "Japan" in Encyclopedia Britannica 11th ed. 1911 p 239
12. Cochrane 1909 p 88; Ev of Capt. JC Coffin of the War Dept. to SC on Ordnance 25 July 1862
13. CG 23 Feb. 1861 p 121, 18 May 1861 p 313, 15 June 1861 p371, 21 Dec. 1861 p 147
14. J McCarthy p 251
15. The Handbook to the Industrial Department of the Exhibition 1862 p 339; ibid vol 3 p 13
16. SC on Ordnance 1861 in BPP 1862 pp 123, 124, 164, 188, 198, 270. See also appendices to this report for a fuller outline of the history and costs of the Armstrong gun and of the Elswick Ordnance Works.
17. Report of SC on Ordnance July 1863
18. Hamer 1931 p 273
19. Engineer 6 Feb. 1863
20. WGA to Earl de Grey 5 Feb.1863; de Grey to WGA quoted in BPP 1863 XXXII p 221
21. The Times 13 Feb. 1862 p 9b
22. Dougan p 91

Armstrong and Noble

1.WGA to AN 22 Feb 1860; Trans NE Coast Institute of Engineers and Shipbuilders XXXII 1915-16 pp 314-320
2. WGA to AN 21 July 1865, 28 January 1865
3. WGA to AN 11 May 1861, 20 Feb. 1865.
4. WGA TO AN 22 Feb. 1860, 20 Jan. 1865, 7 March 1870, 10 March 1870; J Tyndall to WGA 5 March 1870

5. WGA to AN 15 April 1862, 11 Feb. 1867
6. WGA to AN 7 Aug. 1863
7. WGA to AN 11 and 22 Jan 1871
8. WGA to AN 10 Jan. 1869
9. WGA to AN 30 June 1869
10. WGA to AN 20 Nov. 1869
11. WGA to AN 8 Dec. 1869
12. WGA to AN 23 July 1876, 22 Jan.1882, 19 Aug. 1883
13. WGA to AN 27 October 1882; WGA to SR 27 Oct. 1882
14. WGA to AN 28 Oct. 1882
15. WGA to AN 23 Feb. 1883, 17 July 1885

New competitors and new gun trials

1.WGA to MA 9 Dec 1859; JH Lefroy to SC in BPP 1862 vi; Bessemer, Autobiography pp 203,207
2. WGA to MA 8 October 1861
3. WGA to The Times 25 November 1861, (published 27 Nov. 1861)
4. EP Halsted 1861/62
5. SC on Ordnance BPP 1862 vi p 135
6. WGA to MA 1 March 1860
7. WGA to MA 21 March 1860
8. CG 15 June 1861 p 371
9. WGA to The Times 6 Nov. 1862 p 4c; J Whitworth to The Times 10 Nov. 1862 p 5b
10. WGA to The Times 6 Nov 1862 p 4a

Health, pressure of work and new ventures: early Cragside and the Ridsdale operations

1. F Dolman 1893 p 573
2. WGA to MA 16 Feb 1856, 24 Jan. 1854
3. WGA to Mrs Ramshaw 28 March 1859
4. WGA to MA 9 December 1858, 4 Feb 1860
5. WGA to MA 14 June 1865
6. WGA, draft account of the death of JM Rendel 23 Nov. 1856
7. WGA to R Stephenson 23 Nov 1856

8. WGA to MA 24 September 1859
9. WGA to MA 18 Oct. 1859
10. Diary of T Sopwith entry of 18 September 1859
11. D Boyd 1974
12. WGA to MA 7 May 1843 quoted McKenzie p 25
13. Slater 1855
14. WWhite1859 pp 198, 199
15. Parson and White 1828 p482; W White 1859 p 198
16. DD Dixon 1903
17. J Worsnop 1897
18. MD Noble 1925 p 68
19. WGA to MA 11 March 1864
20. WGA to MA 17 March 1865
21. WGA to MA 14 June 1865
22. WGA to MA 3 June 1866
23. WGA to MA 6 Sept.1867
24. CRWarn 1975; Investors Guardian 5 Nov 1870 p 299
25. WGA to AN 23 August 1868, 16 September 1868
26. MJ 12 July 1862 p 472
27. WGA to AN 21,22,24 and 26 July 1865
28. WGA to AN 21 March 1867
29. WGA to AN 24 March 1867

The Armstrong and Whitworth Committee: Westminster and Shoeburyness

1. WGA to MA 16 July 1863; BPP 1866, Report and Minutes of Evidence of the Special Armstrong and Whitworth Committee; Evidence of 6,8 and 12 January 1863, 30 January and 7 February 1865
2. Engineer 27 Nov. 1863 p 310; 18 Dec 1863 p 356
3. WGA to AN 10 Feb.1865
4. Hamer 1931 pp 275,76
5. JH Lefroy to AN 9 Feb. 1865
6. WGA to AN n.d but mid June 1864; see also WGA to AN 16 June 1864
7. F Eardley-Wilmot to WGA 24 Oct. 1864

8. WGA to AN 11 Jan (or 11 June) 1864
9. WGA to AN 11Feb 1865
10. WGA to AN 20 Feb. 1865
11. WGA to AN 17 and 19 June and 31 July 1865
12. WGA to AN 27 June 1865
13. Report of the Special Armstrong and Whitworth Committee pp 51-54; Hamer 1931 p 276
14. Engineer 15 June 1866 p 439; JH Lefroy to AN 21 Oct 1868
15. J Whitworth quoted Engineering 22 June 1866 p 424; "The Whitworth and Armstrong Guns" in Engineering 15 Feb. 1867 p 161; Engineering 14 June 1867 p 621; Engineer 19 Aug. 1864 p 115, 3 Dec. 1869 pp 365,366
16. Cochrane 1909 p 88

Wider thinking and conservation

1. OJR Howarth 1931 p 226
2. WG Armstrong "On the Employment of a Column of Water as a Motive Power For Propelling Machinery" paper for Newcastle Literary and Philosophical Society 1845
3. WGA Presidential Address to the Institute of Mechanical Engineers 1869 p 185
4. WGA quoted MJ 29 Aug 1863 p 619
5. Dougan pp 126,27
6. Chambers Encyclopedia 1868, article "Tyne"
7. Comment in Monthly Chronicle (Newcastle) Nov 1889 p 515
8. WS Jevons. The Coal Question 1865, and quoted in Cassells` Illustrated History of England vol 8 c 1896 p 216
9. J Tyndall quoted Cassells` opcit
10. Mitchell, 1962 Abstract of British Historical Statistics p 483; The Times 9 Nov 1872 p 6

Guns for the world: Elswick ordnance after 1863

1. SC on Military Organisation 1860 p 577
2. AT Blakeley to SC on Ordnance 1863 in BPP 1863 XI p 269
3. Engineer 20 May 1859 p 358; J Whitworth to The Times 14

December 1875 p 8
4. SC on Ordnance 1863
5. SR to an agent 15 June 1864; SR to M Carvallo 9 Aug 1864
6. Hamer 1931 pp 278,279
7. AN to SR 23 Aug 1864
8. WGA to AN 29 October 1864, 10, 16 and 20 Feb 1865
9. WGA to AN 6 April 1865, 1 and 21 July 1865, 1 Oct 1865
10. WGA to AN concerning a letter from Freshfields. n.d but c 1865
11. WGA to AN 30 Aug 1866
12. WGA to AN 31 Aug 1866
13. The Times 13 Jan 1864; SR account of expenses, commissions etc c.1910
14. AN to SR 28 March 1864; Hamer 1931 p 278
15. WGA to AN 27 Dec 1867, 20 Sept 1868

Armstrong ordnance and the British armed forces 1863 to 1880

1. WGA to JH Lefroy 20 Nov 1863
2. Engineer 9 Dec. 1864 p 356, 24 Feb 1865 p 117, 24 Aug. 1865 p 114; WGA to R S Fraser 2 Oct 1868
3. SR pamphlet on relations between Armstrongs and the government arsenal.published Sept 1886, but written well before then. (Vickers, File 64)
4. WGA to AN 17 Dec 1865
5. Engineer 3 Dec 1869 pp 365,66
6. WGA to E Childers 19 Feb 1870; E Childers to WGA 21 Feb 1870; WGA to SR 27 Feb 1870
7. AN to SR 21 May 1881
8. Evidence of J Whitworth and AN to Armstrong and Whitworth Committee 1865 in BPP 1866 XLII pp 269,270,285,; BPP 1867-68 XLII p 2; WGA evidence 13 Dec 1867 in Report of SC on Coiled Wrought-Iron Inner Tubes for Ordnance, ibid XVI p 380; H Bessemer to The Times, quoted Bulletin of American Iron and Steel Association 9 April 1879; Rep and Mins of Ev of the Ordnance Committee on the Proposed 35 ton gun competition. BPP 1870 XLIII pp 558,605
9. WGA to AN 29 October 1874

10. AG Hadcock "Ordnance"in Encyclopedia Britannica 11th ed. 1911
11. McKenzie pp 84, 85
12. SR on Armstrongs and the government arsenal opcit 1886
13. SR to AN 1 April 1879
14. McKenzie p 85; WGA to AN 17 October 1879
15. Brassey "The Navy"p 265 and Wolseley "The Army"p 203, both in EH Ward (ed) The Reign of Queen Victoria: A Survey of Fifty Years of Progress. London, Smith Elder 1887
16. BPP 1888/89 L Report of the Committee on the Late Naval Manoeuvres. dated 21 Nov 1888

Labour relations and the strike of 1871

1. Dougan p 93
2. Newcastle Daily Chronicle, quoted CG 24 Aug 1861 p 118
3. B Samuelson quoted The Times 31 Dec. 1867 p 4f
4. J Burnett 1872 p 3
5. The Times. Leader 11 Sept 1871
6. Dougan pp 94-96
7. Historical Register of Remarkable Events p 400
8. MJ 6 Sept 1862 p 611, 26 Sept 1863 p 687, 3 Oct. 1863 p 707
9. Chambers Encyclopedia 1868 "Social Science"
10. WGA to Social Science Congress 1870 pp 1 - 9
11. WGA. Evidence to RC on Scientific Instruction and the Advancement of Science. I 1872
12. Mitchell. Abstract of British Historical Statistics pp 60, 64, 271
13. Burnett 1872; Dougan pp114-117; Allen et al; Pelling 1963
14. WGA to Crawshay 4 June 1871
15. WGA to AN 7 July 1871
16. WGA to AN 20 Aug 1871
17. The Times 18 Aug 1871 p 3a
18. The Times 14 Aug 1871 p 7
19. Allen et al p 144
20. Quoted Jeffrey 1946 pp 87, 88; WGA to SR 7 Sept 1871, 12 Sept 1871; WGA to The Times 14 Sept 1871
21. AN to SR 9 Oct 1871

22. Engineering 6 Feb 1914 quoted Allen et al p 188
23. Cochrane 1900 pp 73, 74

Armstrong -traveller

1. RJC (1887) in Monthly Chronicle October, quoted Cragside 1985
2. SA and HO Barnett (1902) "Holidays"in "Social Progress in Britain" in Encylopedia Britannica 10th ed. pp 687,88
3. Hamer (1931) p 38
4. WGA. (1872) Account of Egyptian travels, pp 4, 5, 7-9
5. Ibid pp 31,32,165
6. Ibid p 87
7. Ibid pp 140, 137, 138
8. Ibid pp 60,61,105,42,43, 134
9. Ibid pp 7, 99, 45, 174
10. Ibid pp 11, 85, 142
11. Ibid pp 54, 55, 9, 141
12. Ibid pp 7, 80, 84, 158, 159, 174, 34
13. Ibid p 176
14. Hamer (1931) p 38
15. The Times 5 December 1882 p 5

Cragside - making and beautifying a great house

1. "Architecture" in Landmarks of Western Art. Newnes 1985 pp 826, 27
2. A Saint. Richard Norman Shaw pp 67, 69; M Girouard, Victorian Country Houses pp 143,44; Building News 10 May 1872 p 376
3. North Country Life and Lore. Oct 1887 pp 359-362; Girouard p 143
4. WGA to AN 20 Aug 1871
5. N Shaw to WGA 13 Oct 1884, 30 October 1884, 4 Nov 1884
6. N Shaw to WGA 13,15 and 22 October 1884
7. RJC in North Country Lore and Legend Oct 1887 p 362
8. TF Bulmer 1886 pp 788- 91
9. TH Ward (ed) 1887 p 514
10. W Roberts "Art Sales" in Encyclopedia Britannica 10th ed. 1902

pp 683,684

11. M Girouard in Country Life 18 and 25 Dec, 1969 p 1696
12. WGA to MA 23 April 1873
13. WGA to MA 18 March 1874
14. WGA to MA 24 April 1875
15. WGA to MA 26 April 1875 and ibid n.d but soon afterwards
16. N Horsley to WGA 21 Dec. 1878, 23 Dec. 1878
17. It is possible to build up what is probably a fairly full list of the Cragside pictures from RJC 1887, Bulmer 1886, Tomlinson 1888 and recent National Trust accounts.
18. Tomlinson 1888 p 332
19. RF Mackay 1973 p 175
20. Monthly Chronicle 1889
21. WGA to AN 23 Dec 1869
22. WGA to AN 11 Sept 1874
23. WGA to AN 23 July 1876
24. W Irvine 1955 p 225
25. H Huxley to WGA 20 Dec 1884
26. WGA to AN 30 Aug 1885

Shaping the Cragside estate

1. McKenzie p; 106; Dixon 1903 p 431
2. Building News 10 May 1872 p 376 ff
3. "Cragside, Northumberland, the seat of Lord Armstrong"in Country Life 14 April 1900 pp 464-69; I am also indebted to a talk on Cragside given by the head gardener, Andrew Sawyer, to Stocksfield Horticultural and Plant Society on 21 September 1893
4. Wallington inscription, from the Pincian Hill, Rome
5. Dixon 1903 p 435; National Trust "Cragside"1985 p 19
6. Allsop and Clark 1969 p 72
7. RJC in Monthly Chronicle Oct 1887 p 362
8. WGA to AN 20 Aug 1871
9. L Snowball to WGA 4 March 1884; Dixon 1903 pp 323, 350; Bulmer pp 794, 795; Kelly`s Directory 1890 p 1027
10. Monthly Chronicle 29 September 1887; WGA to AN 29 Nov. 1865

11. T Allan to WGA 9 and 28 June 1884, 8 Nov 1884; WGA to AN 11 Nov 1884
12. WGA to AN nd but March 1878, 22 April 1878, 7 Dec 1878
13. Imperial Gazetteer 1872; Snowball to WGA 2 September 1884
14. CW Siemens to WGA 19 June 1878
15. MJ 23 Nov 1878 p 1296
16. JH Fleming "Electric Lighting" in Encyclopedia Britannica 10th edition 1902
17. WGA to the Engineer 17 January 1881 quoted McKenzie pp 107-09
18. P Dickson "Water Power at Cragside" in National Trust Magazine, Summer 1987 pp14,15; Kelly`s Directory 1897 "Rothbury"
19. S Middlebrook pp 251-52

New men, a new company and shipbuilding

1. S.Rendel memorandum c 1910
2. SR to AN 7 May 1881
3. SR to AN 21 June 1869
4. WGA to AN 22 Feb. 1882
5. WGA to AN 22 May 1882, 11 Nov 1882
6. Engineer 1 May 1863 p 256
7. GWR to SR 11 July 1869; Engineering 8 Jan 1875 p 35
8. Pall Mall Gazette 25 March 1868
9 .P Brook 1999 pp 24, 30; JS Jeans 1877 pp 131,132
10. P Brook 1999 p 45
11. TINA XLV 1903, pp 332,333 obituary of GWR; N Barnaby quoted Brook p53
12. Cassells` History vol 8 p 26
13. N Barnaby "Navy"in Encyclopedia Britannica 9th ed. 1884 vol XVII p 291; Cassells` opcit p 26
14. quoted Rennison pp 258,59
15. calculated from P Brook
16. Iron and Coal Trades Review 28 April 1893 p 536
17. The Graphic 14 May 1887 pp 518, 519, 522
18. Engineer 30 Aug 1895 p 213: Shipbuilder, spring 1908 pp 238,39
19. HF Swan to SR 24 March 1898; J Vavasseur to SR 8 April 1898

Priming the pump: business hospitality and advocacy

1. WGA to MA 14 and 29 Oct 1858, 8 October 1861
2. WGA to AN 24 March 1867
3. WGA to AN 12 September 1866
4. WGA to AN 22 Nov 1867, 27 Aug 1868, 16 and 19 Sept 1868, 20 Oct 1869; GWR to SR18 Jan 1869
5. WGA to AN n.d but Aug 1884
6. WGA to GWR 10 June 1889; WGA to AN 10 March 1894; Johnson 1895 p 261
7. WGA to AN n.d
8. WGA to H Childers 19 Feb 1870; H Childers to WGA 21 Feb 1870; WGA to SR 27 Feb 1870
9. J Fisher to Lord Spencer 23 May 1895, quoted Marder I p 125
10. Sir WG Armstrong and Co to French Ministry of Marine 15 March 1878 and reply 19 March 1878
11. WGA to AN 12 July 1868; letter of F Krupp to C Meyer 8 June 1868 quoted Berdrow pp 241-43
12. The Times 22 May 1869 p9
13. The Times 11 Jan 1882 p10; for critical reactions see "Ships of War" in Engineering 20 Jan 1882 p 61
14. Armstrong Mitchell AGM 1 October 1884
15. J Wilson to WGA 1 October 1884; A Milner to WGA 17 Dec. 1884

The rounded man

1. WGA to North of England Institute of Mining and Mechanical Engineers "The Coal Supply"1873 p 15; WGA 1887 quoted Haywood 1896 II p 87
2. On the controversy over the Economic Society see minutes and correspondence of the Newcastle Literary and Philosophical Society.
3. WGA to MA 1 October 1860
4. WGA to GWR 29 Nov 1888
5. CG 13 July 1861 p26
6. WGA to MA 3 September 1854, 22 Aug. 1861
7. WGA British Association Address 1863 in Industrial Resources of

the Tyne, Wear and Tees. 1864 ppxii, xiii
8. WGA to MA n.d but c 1881, 1882; Tomlinson p 10
9. Account of stone laying at Rothbury Congregational Church in cutting from local newspaper 18 May 1895
10. WGA Egyptian visit pp 10,21,25,26, 65, 152-54
11. WGA to Inst of Mech Engs 1869 p 6
12. AN in RS memoir 1901 p 11; Cochrane 1900/1901 p 328

An octogenarian in business

1. Cassells` History of Britain vol 8 pp345, 346, 535
2. Launch of Yashima 8 Feb 1896
3. WGA to AN 29 Feb 1896, 23 April 1896
4. WGA to AN 15 July 1894, 17 and 19 Dec 1896
5. The Times 25 Feb 1897
6. Draft in WGA hand of letter to a new director; HJ Alderson to WGA 20 March 1897
7. WGA to AN 24 Oct 1890, 2 Feb 1892, 15 Feb 1892
8. WGA to AN 6 Jan 1897
9. "The Elswick Works 1852-1896"in Daily Chronicle 27 Aug 1896; Fairbairn 1958 p 107

Armstrong and the early years of a national military-scientific-industrial complex: aspects of Victorian preparations for war.

1. JH Lefroy, quoted Engineering 8 May 1868 p 445
2. RE Freeth to AN 5 and 13 May 1865
3. WGA to AN 23 Aug 1868
4. WGA to SR 10 Oct 1882
5. Institute of Mechanical Engineers, 1869 presidential address
6. C Orde-Brown "Ammunition" in Encyclopedia Britannica 9th ed. 1875 pp 744,745
7. Procs Inst of Civil Engineers LXVIII part 2 1881-82
8. G Jamieson and V Chirol "China" in Encyclopedia Britannica 11th ed. 1910
9. Armstrong Mitchell minutes 13 Sept, 27 Nov 1894, 23 March and

12 September 1895
10. Arms and Explosives Oct 1894 p 9, Oct 1895 p 6
11. AN to WGA 13 June 1897
12. Newcastle Daily Chronicle 21 Aug 1896

Cragside and the wider life of the 1890s

1. Monthly Chronicle, various dates; WGA to AN 16 Aug 1892
2. Newcastle Daily Chronicle 4 Sept 1893
3. On Bamburgh see: L Creighton Life and Letters of Thomas Hodgkin. London, Longmans, Green. 1917 pp 178-199
4. M Girouard p 144; Bulmer 1886 p 789
5. WGA "The Secret of My Success" The New Penny Magazine IX 1900 p 114
6. J Worsnop, "Recreations of a Scientist"
7. WGA to AN 11 May 1897; AN to WGA 13 June 1897
8. JA Fleming and JJ Thomson in Encyclopedia Britannica 11th ed. 1910/1911
9. Bean p 36
10. F Dolman in Ludgate Monthly 1893 p 574
11. WGA to GWR 22 Feb 1889; Winnefreda Watson-Armstrong to AN 26 Nov 1895
12. WGA to AN 4 Jan 1897, 5 Feb 1897
13. SR to WGA 18 April 1897
14. SR to WGA 16 Sept 1897; J Forrest to WGA 14 Dec 1897; V Harcourt to WGA 11Dec 1897
15. CP Chan to W Watson-Armstrong 27 Dec 1897
16. H Rendel to SR 21 March 1898
17. WGA to AN 21 July 1898
18. AN to WGA 11 June 1899
19. Armstrong Whitworth minutes 21 Feb 1900; AN to WGA 16 April 1900
20. WGA to AN 29 September 1898, 18 July 1899, 4 Oct 1899
21. WGA to AN 26 April 1899
22. WGA to AN 30 March 1900
23. Earl Percy to W Watson-Armstrong 3 Jan 1899
24. TINA XLI 1899 p 233; ibid XLIII 1901 p 220

25. Albini to WGA 14 Dec 1899
26. Salisbury to WGA 14 Dec 1899
27. Henrietta Huxley to WGA 13 May 1900
28. Birthday ode by John Gordon (?) 26 Nov 1900
29. Lament "William George, Baron Armstrong" by R Ellis Gerrard n.d, Newcastle
30. Newcastle Journal 28 and 31 Dec 1900
31. Ibid 1 Jan 1901

Aftermath, assessment and legacy

1. Newcastle Chronicle report 1 January 1901
2. Procs of Newcastle City Council 9 January 1901
3. Cochrane 1900/01 p 324
4. AG Grey to W Watson-Armstrong 30 Dec 1900
5. The Engineer 4 Jan 1901 p 7; Procs Inst of Civil Engs CXLVII 1901/02 Pt 1 p 411
6. "Lord Armstrong" in Newcastle Chronicle 27 Dec 1900
7. Newcastle Journal 1 Jan 1900, reports of "End of Century Sermons"preached in Newcastle upon Tyne on Monday 31 Dec 1900
8. Christie sales 20 and 24 June 1910
9. Newcastle Daily Chronicle 27 Dec 1900
10. The Times 25 July 1906

BIBLIOGRAPHY

Allen, E et al (1971) The North-East Engineers Strike of 1871: Newcastle: Frank Graham

Allsopp, B and Clark, U (1969) Historic Architecture of Northumberland: Newcastle: Oriel Press

Anon. (1900) "The Secret of My Success: Lord Armstrong`s Remarkable Career" in The New Penny Magazine 114. Vol IX December

By Armstrong:

(1845) "On the Employment of a Column of Water as a Motive Power for Propelling Machinery" a paper to the Newcastle Literary and Philosophical Society 3 Dec 1845. Newcastle: T and J Hodgson

(1863) Presidential Address to the British Association, Newcastle

(1864) (ed) The Industrial Resources of the Tyne, Wear and Tees. Newcastle: British Association

(1869) Presidential Address to the Newcastle meeting of the Institute of Mechanical Engineers

(1870) "Economy and Trade", address to the Social Science Congress. Newcastle. September

(1872) A Visit to Egypt. Newcastle

(1873) "The Coal Supply"Presidential Address to the North of England Institute of Mining and Mechanical Engineers

(1881) Presidential Address to Mechanical Sciences Section, British Association, York

(1882) Presidential Address to the Institute of Civil Engineers, 10 January

(1897) Electric Movement in Air and Water, with Theoretical Inferences.

Various Addresses. Newcastle: City Library

On WG Armstrong:

The World 29 January 1879

Newcastle Journal (1900) Obituary 28 Dec
Newcastle Chronicle (1900) Obituary and Leader 27 December
Newcastle Daily Chronicle (1901) Account of Funeral 1 January
The Engineer (1901) Obituary, 4 January pp 7 - 8
Engineering (1901) Obituary, 4 January pp 19 - 22
Noble, A (1901) in Proceedings of the Royal Society
Linsley, S.M in Dictionary of Business Biography
Armstrong Whitworth (1910) A Short History of Sir WG Armstrong Whitworth and Company Ltd. Newcastle

Barry, P (1863) Dockyard Economy and Naval Power. London
Bean, D (1867) Armstrong`s Men. Newcastle:
Berdrow, W (ed) (1930) The Letters of Alfred Krupp 1826 - 1887. London: Victor Gollancz
Bessemer, H (1905) Autobiography. London: Engineering
Boyd, D (1974) A Victorian Engineer: The Life of Percy Westmacott 1830 - 1917. Privately published
Brodie, B (1943) Sea Power in the Machine Age. Princeton: University Press
Brook, P (1999) Warships for Export: Armstrong Warships 1867 - 1927. Gravesend: World Ship Society
Bulmer, T F. (1886) History, Topography and Directory of Northumberland. Manchester: Newcastle: Beavis, Stewart and Co.
Burnett, J (1872) A History of the Engineers`Strike in Newcastle and Gateshead.

Cassell (1895/6) History of England. VIII 1884 - 1895
Clarke, JF(1997) Building Ships on the North East Coast. (3 volumes)Whitley Bay: Bewick Press
Coal Commission (1871) Minutes of Evidence
Cochrane, A (1909) The Early History of Elswick. Newcastle. Mawson, Swan and Morgan
Cochrane, A (1900) "Lord Armstrong" in Northern Counties Magazine I pp 324-29
On Cragside:
Anon (1872) in Building News 10 May
Anon (1900) in Country Life Illustrated 14 April pp 464 - 69

Girouard, M (1969) in Country Life 18 and 25 December
National Trust (1980) Cragside, Northumberland. London: National Trust
National Trust (1985) Cragside: An Illustrated Souvenir. London: National Trust
National Trust (nd) The Principal Oil Paintings of the Armstrong Collection and the De Morgan Pictures and Pottery at Cragside
"RJC", (1887) on Cragside in North Country Lore and Legend, October

Dibden, T.F (1838) A Bibliographical, Antiquarian and Picturesque Tour of the Northern Counties of England and in Scotland: London
Dixon, D.D (1903) Upper Coquetdale: Newcastle: R Redpath
Dolman F (1893) "Notable Men and their Work: Lord Armstrong" in Ludgate Monthly V October
Dougan, D (1970) The Great Gun-Maker: The Story of Lord Armstrong. Newcastle: Frank Graham
On Elswick:
Daily Chronicle (1896) The Elswick Works 1852 - 1896 27 August

Fairbairn, A.R (1958) History of Elswick. Newcastle: Vickers-Armstrong
Forbes, A (1898) "The Birthplace of Titans: Elswick Ordnance Department" Naval and Military Magazine pp 428-41
Maitland, E (nd) "Our Great Northern Arsenal" in Naval and Military Magazine
The Graphic (1887) Elswick 14 May, pp 518 - 522
Timins, T (1900) "The National Defence.V. A Visit to a Gun Factory." Cassells` Magazine 31 May
Fordyce, W (1867) Local Records. Newcastle:

Girouard, M (1971) The Victorian Country House. Oxford: Clarendon Press

Hamer (1931) The Personal Papers of Lord Rendel. London:
Hogg, J (ed) (1887). Fortunes Made in Business. London. Sampson,

Low

Irvine, W (1955) Apes, Angels and Victorians: A joint biography of Darwin and Huxley. London: Weidenfeld and Nicolson

Jeans, J.S (1877) Notes on Northern Industries. London: E and FN Spon

Jeans, W.T (1884) Creators of the Age of Steel. London: Chapman Hall

Jefferys, JB (1945) The Story of the Engineers. London: Lawrence and Wishart

Jenkins, S (n.d but c.1990s) The Rothbury Branch. Oakwood Press

Johnson, R.W (1895) The Making of the Tyne. London: Walter Scott

Jones, E.R (1889) on Armstrong in North Country Lore and Legend. January p 6

Keys, D and Smith, K. (1996) Down Elswick Slipways. Newcastle: City Libraries

Kingford, P.W (1964) Engineers, Inventors and Workers. London: Edward Arnold

Lane, M.R (1989) The Rendel Connection: A Dynasty of Engineers. London: Quiller Press

Lewis, S (1833) A Topographical Dictionary of England. London: S Lewis

McCarthy, J (1897) A Short History of Our Own Times. London. Chatto and Windus

McCord, N (1979) North East England: The Region`s Development 1760 - 1960. London: Batsford

McGuire, D.F (1988) Charles Mitchell 1820 - 1895: Victorian Shipbuilder. Newcastle: City Libraries

McKenzie, P (1983) W G Armstrong. Newcastle. Longhirst Press

Marder, A. J. (c. 1954) Fear God and Dread Nought. I. The Correspondence of Admiral of the Fleet Lord Fisher, 1859 - 1904. London: Jonathan Cape

Middlebrook, S. (1950) Newcastle upon Tyne: Its Growth and

Achievement. Newcastle: Newcastle Chronicle and Journal

Noble, M.D. (1925) A Long Life. Newcastle: A Reid

Oliver, S. (1835) Rambles in Northumberland and on the Scottish Border. London: Chapman Hall

Parson and White (1828) History, Gazetteer and Directory of Northumberland and Durham. Newcastle: W White and Co.

Pelling, H. (1963) A History of British Trade Unionism; Harmondsworth: Penquin

Pollard, S and Robertson, P (1979) The British Shipbuilding Industry 1870 - 1914. Cambridge, Mass: Harvard

Poole, B (1852) Statistics of British Commerce. London: Smith and Simpkin, Marshall

Reid, A(1863) Handbook to Newcastle upon Tyne. Newcastle: Reid

Reid, A(1880) Past Events. Newcastle: A Reid

Rendel, S (1875) The Question of the Guns as Now Debated. London: Spottiswoode and Co.

Rennison, R.W (1979) Water to Tyneside: A History of the Newcastle and Gateshead Water Company. Gateshead: Newcastle and Gateshead Water Company

Richardson, J.W (1911) Memoirs: Glasgow

Rowe, D.J (1971) "The Economy of the North- East in the Nineteenth Century: A Survey." Northern History VI pp 117-147

Saint, A (2010) Richard Norman Shaw: New Haven. Yale

St-Fond, BF de (1799) A Journey through England and Scotland and to the Hebrides I

Scott, J.D (1962) Vickers: A History. London: Weidenfeld and Nicolson

Slater (1855) Directory of the Northern Counties

Sopwith, R(2001) Thomas Sopwith: The Allenheads Years 1845 - 1871. Nenthead: North Pennines Heritage Trust

Sopwith, T (1891) The Diary and Life of T Sopwith

Tennent, E (1864) The Story of the Guns
Tomlinson, W.W.(1888) Comprehensive Guide to the County of Northumberland. London: Walter Scott

Walton, A.D (1964) Some Notes on Elswick. Newcastle: City Libraries
Warn, C.R (1978) Rural Branch Lines of Northumberland. Newcastle, Frank Graham
Warren, K. (1989) Armstrongs of Elswick: Growth in Engineering and Armaments to the Merger with Vickers. London: Macmillan
Westmacott, P.(1863) "The Engineering Manufactures of the Tyne, Wear and Tees"in C.G 31 October pp346,47 and 7 November 1863 p 367
White, W. (1859) Northumberland and the Border. London: Chapman and Hall
Worsnop, J. (1900) "Reminiscences of the late Lord Armstrong"in Newcastle Journal 28 December

INDEX